Martin Levy

Roundhouse
Joe Berke and the 1967 Congress on the Dialectics of Liberation

Martin Levy

ROUNDHOUSE
Joe Berke and the 1967 Congress on the
Dialectics of Liberation

Bibliografische Information der Deutschen Nationalbibliothek
Die Deutsche Nationalbibliothek verzeichnet diese Publikation in der Deutschen Nationalbibliografie; detaillierte bibliografische Daten sind im Internet über http://dnb.d-nb.de abrufbar.

Bibliographic information published by the Deutsche Nationalbibliothek
Die Deutsche Nationalbibliothek lists this publication in the Deutsche Nationalbibliografie; detailed bibliographic data are available in the Internet at http://dnb.d-nb.de.

ISBN-13: 978-3-8382-1659-1
© *ibidem*-Verlag, Hannover • Stuttgart 2024
Alle Rechte vorbehalten

Das Werk einschließlich aller seiner Teile ist urheberrechtlich geschützt. Jede Verwertung außerhalb der engen Grenzen des Urheberrechtsgesetzes ist ohne Zustimmung des Verlages unzulässig und strafbar. Dies gilt insbesondere für Vervielfältigungen, Übersetzungen, Mikroverfilmungen und elektronische Speicherformen sowie die Einspeicherung und Verarbeitung in elektronischen Systemen.

All rights reserved. No part of this publication may be reproduced, stored in or introduced into a retrieval system, or transmitted, in any form, or by any means (electronic, mechanical, photocopying, recording or otherwise) without the prior written permission of the publisher. Any person who does any unauthorized act in relation to this publication may be liable to criminal prosecution and civil claims for damages.

Printed in the EU

To Julian and Alex, in the hope that they will be 'true professionals.'

Contents

Introduction 9

1. The Joe Berke Experience 17
2. Kingsley Hall 43
3. Pulling the Congress Together 55
4. Welcome to the Roundhouse 77
5. 'Call me Mr Carmichael.' 107
6. A 'Self-Governing' Congress 121
7. Stokely! Stokely! 165
8. Doctor Dog 199
9. And then there was Marcuse 235
10. Too Much 253
11. The Infernal Nexus 267

Appendix 271
Notes 273
Bibliography 297
Index 313

Introduction

> 'We were eaten up by repressed violence and we were soured by the constant terror of inconceivable violence being visited on ourselves and the rest of man.'
> — Jeff Nuttall.[1]

Where did it come from this Congress on the Dialectics of Liberation, this anti-congress, this be-in, this being-there, which stuck two fingers up at capitalism and the West and denounced the educational, military and industrial elites as shams, time-servers and liars? It certainly didn't come from the universities. If one can say anything definitive about the origin of the Congress, it is that its motivation was firmly, resolutely, unapologetically non-academic. The organisers of the Congress knew only too well — had they not been through higher education themselves? — that the universities were a part of the problem that they convened the congress to do something about: violence in all its forms, which is to say, the 'violence called love' *and* the boot on the solar plexus.[2] They hated higher education, hated what it had become: a bureaucratised system of mass lectures and ignorant status-seeking. If the Congress was to succeed in its aim of 'demystifying violence and the social systems from which it emanates and to explore new forms of social action',[3] then higher education would have to be 'liberated' from administrative and intellectual bondage, so that new forms of education could be born: educations as they could be.

Paul Goodman got there first, as he often did during the early '60s, building on previous writers to be sure, but turning the rising criticism of higher education into a philosophy of startling common sense and integrity. *The Community of Scholars* of 1962 spread the bad news of bureaucracy-driven disempowerment: passive and contract-grubbing faculties, programmed ignorance and sclerosis, 'company men and time-servers among the teachers, grade-seekers and time-servers among the students'.[4]

The universities had been taken over by administrators, he stated. 'How did they get in?'[5] What did they want, these apparatchiks, these interlopers, with their statistics, their endless committee meetings, their pecking orders, their notions of good order and efficiency? They had no educational value. They had burdened the universities with a pomp and a size that were irrelevant to their needs and standardised much that was naturally youthful and spontaneous. 'Like the American economy itself, the system of universities is really a machine for its own sake, to run and produce brand goods for selling and buying. Utility is incidental. More revolutionary products like free spirit, individual identity, vocation, community, the advancement of humanity are rather disapproved. But frictionless and rapid running is esteemed; and by clever co-ordination of the moving parts, and lots of money as lubrication, it can be maximized.'[6]

Goodman counselled secession. Bands of scholars should abandon the colossi, rid themselves entirely of the *'external control, administration, bureaucratic machinery, and other excrescences that have swamped our communities of scholars.'*[7] Such a course was difficult, he conceded. But it had been done many times before, most famously with the founding of Black Mountain College in North Carolina in 1933, which was 'really the first Beat school'.[8] It should be done again, with renewed perseverance.

But the main point he wanted to get across was that young people were not flourishing in the universities. They were not growing up. For that to happen, education would have to function on its own terms, the students would have to associate with teachers in 'traditional', non-managerial ways and 'according to their existing interest.'[9] In other words, the young people had to understand that education was *'about* something', that it had joys, meanings, commitments that transcended the merely utilitarian—rather than being 'a step on the ladder when there isn't much at the top,'[10] except for useless corporate-type jobs (even when they're available) and a dishonourable retirement.

The organisers of the Congress anchored their revolutionary politics to Goodman's reasonable enthusiasm, adding a chunk of anti-psychiatry here, a pinch of Hermann Hesse there—a brotherhood, an illuminati—and a slice of Alexander Trocchi, his notion of the 'spontaneous university' a particular influence.

The main organiser of the Congress on the Dialectics of Liberation was not R.D. Laing, as many people think, but Joe Berke, a psychiatrist and poet from Newark, New Jersey, and one of Laing's first American supporters. Laing had other fish to fry, though his contribution was, of course, essential.

During 1965, while Berke was helping to set up the Goodman-Marx- and Veblen-inspired Free University of New York (FUNY), Laing helped create the small anti-psychiatric community of Kingsley Hall, one of the first and certainly the most influential of a string of similar asylums. And it was only during the spring of 1966, following Berke's settlement at the Hall in the autumn of 1965, that Laing finally agreed to put his considerable influence behind the ambitious project.

As for the understanding of violence that underpinned both the congress and the asylum, that differed markedly from traditional psychiatric thinking, being deeper and far broader in its implications. In one sense, it looked back to Nietzsche's 'transvaluation of all values', though it wasn't Christianity it had in its sights (Laing himself was profoundly influenced by Christianity) so much as the 'technological' society, which it stigmatised as barbarous, not only in its treatment of the so-called mentally ill (through practices like involuntary confinement and lobotomy), but in its instrumentalisation of all human relationships.

According to Laing, violence wasn't 'out there'; it was 'in us', though often disguised as its opposite. As he put it in a lecture, he first gave in 1964, and republished afterwards in *The Politics of Experience and the Bird of Paradise*:

> From the moment of birth, when the stone-age baby confronts the twentieth-century mother, the baby is subjected to forces of outrageous violence, called love, as its mother and father have been, and their parents and their parents before them. These forces are mainly concerned with destroying most of its potentialities. This enterprise is on the whole successful. By the time the new human being is fifteen or so, we are left with a being like ourselves. A half-crazed creature, more or less adjusted to a mad world.[11]

This, Laing said, was what society considered 'normality'.

The Congress opened at the Roundhouse, on north London's Chalk Farm Road, on the morning of July 15 with a lecture by Laing and closed on the 29th with a happening by Carolee Schneemann and a performance by the British pop group, The Social Deviants.

Gregory Bateson spoke apocalyptically about humanity's overweening 'purposive consciousness'; Stokely Carmichael grew furious about racism and imperialism; Thich Nhat Hahn opined softly about Vietnam; Paul Goodman chatted about decentralising the 'technical-managerial' society; Herbert Marcuse talked ponderously about liberation from affluence; and Allen Ginsberg chanted and clattered finger cymbals. 'The Provos were there from Amsterdam. There were students from West Berlin, political activists from Norway and Sweden as well as a large contingent from the New Experimental College, Thy, Denmark. There were representatives from the West Indies, Africa, France, Canada, America, Holland, India, Nigeria and Cuba', remarks the poet Susan Sherman, one of Berke's American friends, who covered the congress for *Ikon* magazine.[2]

There were question-and-answer sessions, numerous seminars, and films and poetry readings in the evenings. Thus, formal presentations were only one feature of the Congress. Also important were the activities and responses of the 'ordinary' participants, including the two-hundred-and-fifty or so registrants or 'gammas' in the organisers' slightly patronising parlance. For many of these mostly young people, the Congress was a turning point, not a gig on the radical consciousness-raising circuit, but a point zero from which a new kind of politics was able to emerge. For some it was Black Power, for others it was the women's or gay liberation movements. It was also amongst the best fun they had ever had. The Congress changed them and they changed the culture around them.

Academic conferences were two-a-penny in 1967, as they still are today, often trivial diversions for the educationally moribund: the single-issue squad, those 'in the know', postgraduates with a dissertation or a thesis to punt, mid-season professionals in need of a career-lift, jargon demons, technological scrap metal merchants — one eye on a job in IT, the other on a career in the 'helping professions'. But the congress transcended these trivial denotations. It joined students with autodidacts, workers by hand with workers by brain, the young with the middle-aged and the occasionally old, dropouts with activists, and Gandhian proponents of non-violence with the apostles of the Molotov cocktail. To a large extent, it was self-governing. Entrance was by ticket or subscription.

One of the Congress's most provocative outgrowths was the Antiuniversity, of Rivington Street, Shoreditch. Opened in February 1968 in rooms rented from the Bertrand Russell Peace Foundation, it too countered the 'intellectual bankruptcy and spiritual emptiness' of the modern university, with the aim of promoting a 'position of social integrity and commitment'.[13] It offered classes by, amongst others, Barry Flanagan (Sculpture), Roy Battersby (Documentary Films), Juliet Mitchell (Women and Revolution), Cornelius Cardew (Experimental Music), David Cooper (Psychology and Politics), R.D. Laing (Psychology and Religion), David Mercer (Drama), Obi Egbuna (Black Power) and Francis Huxley (Dragons). Berke himself led a course on 'anti-institutions'. 'How can we discuss how we can discuss what we want to discuss?'[14] ('Maybe we don't need to discuss it', was one wag's timely response, thus reminding us that humour was also a part of the Antiuniversity experience.)

Admittedly, this book is a hybrid. It is neither a biography nor a history but a combination of the two, as that seemed the best way of bringing Joe Berke's contribution to the planning of the Congress into focus, while at the same time describing what went on there in the detail that the reader will expect. Inevitably this gives the book a now-you-see-Berke now-you don't quality, but it is justified on the grounds that the speeches (and the ancillary events, including the Q&As) are by and large what the Congress was about. Berke's contribution to the congress as it unfolded in July, like that of his fellow organiser Leon Redler, was interesting. But it was not *that* interesting.

Although Berke wrote about the early part of his life in the United States and his first years in England,[15] he never wrote an autobiography proper — even though he would have been more than justified to have done so. Not only was he a pioneer in the non-medical treatment of severe mental illness, but rather like other American ex-pats, people like Joe Boyd, Susan Zeiger, aka 'Suzy Creamcheese', Bill Levy, Jack Henry Moore, Jim Haynes and Steve

Abrams, he was an outsize figure in his adopted country's counter-culture more generally.[16]

Of course, the Congress has already been written about — ad nauseum some would say in books and popular and academic articles. But I think I'm right in saying that this is one of the first books to make use of the extraordinary Joseph Berke Archive at the Mulberry Bush, in Gloucestershire, and certainly *the first* to make use of the Joseph Berke Papers now in the Wellcome Collection, in London. The Mulberry Bush contains what might be described as the official (or anti-official) side of Berke's professional (or anti-professional) interests. It includes, for instance, his Research Committee on Cannabis and his Arbours Association papers, his correspondence related to *Fire* magazine, large parts of his magazine collection, and drafts of his various books. But most importantly, for my purposes, it contains his correspondence with the people who attended the Congress and the audio recordings of all the major speeches that were delivered there. It was a shock and a pleasure to discover who far these differ from the collection printed in Penguin's *The Dialectics of Liberation*, of 1968. Yet this slim book is the source of almost all of the academic commentary on the subject.

When I accessed the Joseph Berke Papers, they were still in Joe Berke's possession. He kept them in a garage close to his house in Highgate. Most were damp and some were covered in mould. It was a delicate operation removing what I judged to be the most important into his house for safer keeping. I remember my excitement opening one file and then another and finding personal letters from Allen Ginsberg, Alex Trocchi, Michael Hollingshead, Simon Vinkenoog, Carolee Schneemann and Julian Beck as well as, of course, R.D. Laing, Leon Redler and David Cooper. It was also a joy. Hopefully one day, the Wellcome Collection will publish the complete collection online so that they are accessible to scholars everywhere.

I didn't write this book as an analytical account of the planning and execution of the Congress. I wrote it, or rather I wrote chapters 4-9, as a narrative account of what happened there. To a large extent, it unfolds in chronological order. I was interested, as I'm sure most of the book's reader will be, in what was said at the

Congress rather than in what I happen to think about what was said. However, the book does contain some commentary and some corrections of fact in the notes at the back of the book where warranted.

Acknowledgements

Lots of people contributed to this book. Some helped with research, some with advice, while others simply told me their stories. I am grateful to all of them. But two figures stand out: the late Joe Berke and Peter Davis. Without Joe, the book would not have been written. Not only did he put up with my endless emails, but he allowed me to rummage through his extensive archive. I am pleased that Joe's wishes were followed and that the part not in the wonderful Planned Environment Therapy Trust (PETT) Archives at The Mulberry Bush in Toddington, Gloucestershire, is in the Wellcome Collection, London, where it awaits cataloguing.

Peter, thank goodness, filmed part of the Congress. He is thus an actor *and* an accomplice, without whom I would have had neither the *Anatomy of Violence* documentary nor his extensive collection of outtakes to work with. His friendship during the writing of this book has been a pleasure. Peter is a fount of knowledge on all sorts of things. But his knowledge of the Congress is exceptional.

My co-conspirators Jackie Ivimy and Jakob Jakobsen were a source of inspiration in numerous ways. When my enthusiasm flagged, as it often did in the early days, they were invariably there to provide conversation, support, and enlightenment. Craig Fees at PETT proved himself a prince of archivists. At how many other archives are you invited to sit down for a drink and a chat before starting your research? Thanks to Craig, I was able to work from digital copies of the Congress recordings at home. I hope that the book doesn't disappoint him.

As for the other people who helped, in big ways and small, they are listed here in no particular order.

Morton Schatzman, Geoffrey Bamford, Marshall Coleman, David Gale, Roger Gottlieb, Vickie Moller, Jeremy Holmes, Neil Hornick, Ros Kane, Jackie Warner, Trevor Pateman, Shree Berke, the late Myrtle Berman, Anthony Chaney, the late Clancy Sigal, Howard Senzel, Robert Priddy, Adam Saltiel, Phillip Guddemi, Adrian Laing (in particular for material owned by the R.D. Laing estate), Martin Paddio, Stephen Ticktin, Jutta Laing, John Haynes, Christoph Ohlwärther, John Saville, David Triesman, Dag Kolderup, Juliet Mitchell, the late Murray Korngold, John Foot, Joseph Rosenstein, Leon Redler, Adrian Chapman, Vickie Hamilton, Christine Downes-Grainger, Paul Zeal, Marjaleena Repo, Alex Wilson, Jonny Burnip and Hans Kundnani. My thanks and gratitude to them all.

1. The Joe Berke Experience

The back-story to the Congress begins with one man. Not the Scotsman R.D. Laing nor his close associate, the South African-born David Cooper, but Joe Berke, one of their American colleagues. Everyone who knows about the Congress knows about R.D. Laing and David Cooper; how they challenged the medical model of schizophrenia and developed their own liberationist or existential psychiatries or anti-psychiatries. But without Joe Berke, there probably wouldn't have been a Congress.

Berke was born on January 17, 1939, in Newark, New Jersey, so like Laing and Cooper, he came to England as an outsider. On both sides of his family, he descended from European Jews, Ukrainian on his father's side, Romanian on his mother's.

Fig 1. A day at the seaside. Baby Berke with his mother and grandmother. Photographer unknown. Courtesy of Shree Berke.

Apparently, Berke's maternal grandmother was sent to London for an arranged marriage due to the lack of an eligible young man in her Romanian village. She married a tailor named Robert Friedland in Liverpool. A few decades later, their daughter, Rose, met Berke's future father, Joseph, in New York, and the couple married in 1929 at a wealthy uncle's apartment in Manhattan.

Unfortunately, Berke never met his father, for he died in Rose's arms from a pulmonary embolus a few months before he was born, leaving her a small teacher's pension, but with little chance of finding another husband. 'Mother sees me as the messiah,' he told me during one of a number of interviews I did with him before his death in 2021. 'She sees me as a wonder child, a replacement for my father.'[1]

During Berke's first years, the family — Joe, Rose and his maternal grandparents, Robert and Susan — lived in a rented house on Farley Avenue, in Newark's Upper Clinton Hill, a mostly lower middle-class district in the inner suburbs, with movie theatres, delicatessens, record stores and all the other conveniences of American ingenuity and affluence. Their house was one of a row of colonial-style buildings with large, unfenced gardens at the back where Joe and his pals ran riot over the neighbours' plants, playing soft ball and climbing the trees and doing all the other things that children do when they're left to their own devices.

Rose worked as a bookkeeper in a bank. Berke described her later as a 'sensitive, creative, but frustrated' person, whose great ambition in life was to be a concert pianist, but who was held back by her father, who did not approve of women studying at an advanced level.[2] Robert died of a cancer-like syndrome when Berke was five, in the midst of a polio epidemic, throwing the youngster into a deep depression, for he loved his grandfather deeply. 'In those days, they didn't take children to funerals, didn't even tell them that people were sick. One day he was there, and the next day he wasn't.'[3] Consequently, he had had no time to prepare himself.

Owing to malformations in his fingers and toes — the side effect of a fertility treatment given to his mother — Berke was never an athletic boy. He was intellectual, with a passion for science, reading, chess, carnivorous plants, and stamp-collecting. He went to Bragaw Avenue School first, then, when the family moved to nearby Osborne Terrace, onto McGuire High and then to Weequahic High school, which was one of the 'best' academic schools of its time. (It is known today as the school that gave Philip Roth his education).

Fig 2. Joe Berke, carnivorous plant collector and voracious reader. Photographer unknown. Courtesy of Shree Berke.

One older boy, whose name Berke long remembered, used to ambush him after school. He defended himself by feigning asthma attacks until, eventually, he tackled the bully at a Jewish summer camp. 'To my absolute horror, I discovered that [the bully] was in the same bunk as me. The first opportunity I had, I knocked him to the ground and bit a chunk out of his leg, whereupon he was thrown out of the camp for being unkind to me.'[4] This trial of strength taught him an important lesson: if someone is going to attack you, attack them first. It was a triumph that he always remembered with pleasure.

Although Rose kept a kosher household, the family was conservative rather than orthodox, which meant that while Berke attended Hebrew school after classes, he didn't learn to read or speak the language competently. Yet, he loved the synagogue. The sound of the singing filled him with joy and, on several occasions, he even forged tickets so that he could get a good seat on the high holy days, when a favourite cantor was in attendance.

Berke left Weequahic High School joint-top of his class. He was a rather earnest boy by this stage and an established prize-winner; intellectually sharp, energetic, a little unscrupulous perhaps, but very sociable, having devoted much of his free time to the school clubs, to helping to bring on the younger folk, and to the school newspaper, *Calumet*.

One of his teachers, Hannah Litzky was Allen Ginsberg's aunt. 'Your seriousness of purpose, your determination [and] your intelligence are truly admirable', she wrote in his yearbook.[5] Like the other teachers, she expected him to do well in life, perhaps becoming an important academic or an eminent scientist.

*

Following three years of pre-meds at Columbia, in 1960 Berke enrolled at the prestigious Albert Einstein College of Medicine, Yeshiva University, in the Bronx, and so began his connection with Laing—not through his most famous book, *The Divided Self*, but through a book called *Psychoanalysis and Existential Philosophy,* edited by Hendrick M. Ruitenbeck, which excerpted one of the chapters.[6] This was during the late autumn or early winter of 1962, when Berke was in his third year of general medicine and second year of psychiatry, having chosen that speciality because, like many aspirant doctors at the time, he felt that most medics 'weren't really interested in people so much as in diseases,' and he wanted to study the 'whole' man, which is to say, in Laing's and others' terms, the 'person' rather than the 'organism'.[7]

Fig 3. Joe Berke at the Albert Einstein College of Medicine. Note the beard, not yet a 1960s convention. Photographer unknown. Courtesy Shree Berke.

At this time, he was working with so-called psychotic children at the nearby Jacobi Hospital, and Laing's theoretical formulations, namely engulfment and implosion anxieties, false self and true self and ontological insecurity, seemed to speak to some of his own concerns as well as his patients'. For there were days when he too felt desperately out of sorts, his spiritual, political, and ethical anxieties finding little sustenance in the daily round at the hospital or in his studies back at the college.

Most students apparently enjoyed their studies at Einstein, but Berke, generally, did not. He found the teachers for the most part arrogant and the textbooks uninspiring. Like most students, he had come to Einstein full of ideals. But the reality, even in the psychiatry department, was often extremely prosaic, the 'official' talk amongst the doctors being mostly about the latest drugs or the latest psychoanalytical therapies, couched in jargon that left him feeling alienated.

One incident discouraged him particularly deeply. During a case conference led by faculty member Jose Barchilon, he was abruptly taken to task for not applying Freud's Oedipus complex to the situation of a young man, even though he was convinced that it did not provide the appropriate context. Then there were other parts of the course that bothered him: dark days spent measuring the concentration of anti-diuretic hormones in the renal blood flows of dogs. Sometimes he wondered if he had been right to study medicine after all. Perhaps he would have been better off training as an academic, or following in the footsteps of his mother's brother, Jules, who was running a thriving engineering business.

Fortunately, one of his teachers did command his respect. This was Dr John Thompson, one of the newer members of the faculty. Berke describes Thompson in one of his books as a 'handsome, silver haired Scotsman, a friend of poets, writers, artists, philosophers, men of thought and action all over the world, and himself a poet as well as psychiatrist,'[8] but this only hints at his eminence.

In fact, Thompson was one of the century's key innovators in medical ethics, having made major contributions to the prosecution of Nazi doctors at Nuremberg. Sent into Germany as a scientific intelligence officer during the final months of the war, Thompson had concluded that up to ninety per cent of top German doctors had engaged in lethal or disabling experiments on humans. Yet, the lesson he had drawn from this experience was not that German doctors were uniquely flawed, but that all doctors, wherever they practiced, had the potential to become destructive, given the right encouragement and the appropriate circumstances.

Thompson, Berke adds, did not 'talk down to patients or students', like the other faculty members. 'Nor did he categorize people, or what they said or did, according to what was nosologically fashionable.'[9] Instead, rather like the Laing of *The Divided Self* and of Laing's other books and practices, he always tried to observe whoever he was speaking to from their point of view so as not to prejudge them from his own frame of reference.

After all, as Berke himself would later remark, behaviour that is odd or upsetting in one context may make sense in another. Just because a person 'kicks off' whenever their father arrives, it doesn't necessarily follow that they are 'mad.' From their point of view, they may well be acting in a way that is reasonable.

Indeed, it is for this reason that mental illness, he also says, is very different to physical diseases, like diabetes or cancer.

> Now a disease is a disease. You don't have a disease in the presence of one person and not in the presence of another. No cancer that I have ever heard of disappears when Dr X arrives and reappears when he leaves or someone else arrives. ... That the signs and symptoms of severe "mental illness" changed according to whom the patient was with made me suspect that "illness" was not a sufficient explanation for the personal states and interpersonal situations with which I was becoming increasingly familiar.[10]

Yet, that was how psychiatry was generally taught at the college, even if it was rarely acknowledged as such.

During Berke's time at Einstein, Thompson became his mentor, providing not just the phenomenological understanding of mental illness that was missing from the other parts of his studies, but a continuing master class in the practicalities of the doctor-patient relationship. Again, like Laing, Thompson wasn't frightened by people in conditions of severe and often chronic mental distress. If they seemed beyond hope by some, then that was because the doctor or other carer had not found the right way to communicate with them.

Thompson also supported Berke in his political interests, for these were the days of the peace and the civil rights movements, of anti-nuclear protesters in the north and 'freedom riders' in the south, and Berke too was swept up in the fervour, becoming increasingly radical. During his pre-college years his favourite author had been Hermann Hesse, the German-Swiss writer of cult fiction like *Magister Ludi* and *Steppenwolf*, to whose deep and abiding influence he now added *The Communist Manifesto*, magazines like *Liberation* and *Monthly Review*, and Ginsberg's *Howl*, and other left-wing and/or Beat publications.

During 1962, he embarked on his first major political activity: a general strike for peace. This was organised by Julian Beck and Judith Malina, two maverick theatre people, with whom he would subsequently become well acquainted. Beginning with a march down Fifth Avenue—Berke carried his stethoscope—'there were torchlight processions, speeches, picketing in front of the New York office of the Atomic Energy Commission, and a rally in front of the United Nations. ... The folksinger Pete Seeger sang "We Shall Overcome," and the then-unknown Bob Dylan sang "Blowing in the Wind" for the first time at a strike benefit.'[11]

At Einstein, he set up a discussion group, to which he and close friends Morton Schatzman, Leon Redler and Jerome Liss invited Thompson and other intellectuals, nonconformists for the most part, like the anarchist Paul Goodman, the Syracuse University professor Thomas Szasz, and Timothy Leary, of Harvard University. On one occasion, with Thompson's encouragement, Berke and the other members of the group left their studies and took off to Washington for the weekend to protest the testing of nuclear weapons in the atmosphere.

It was therefore a tragedy, not just for Thompson's family, but for Berke too when Thompson died at the relatively early age of fifty-nine in 1965, during a snorkelling holiday off the coast of the Virgin Islands. He had lost a friend as well as a mentor.

*

During November 1962, Berke wrote to Laing to ask if he could work with him in London. His first enthusiastic reading of Laing was no flash in the pan therefore, but the beginning of a deep and lasting commitment. 'At the Albert Einstein College I have received an excellent theoretical and practical training in psychiatry', Berke writes. 'Also I have had the opportunity in the past few years to work with psychotic children in various capacities and have read extensively.'[12] But Laing did not reply. So, he wrote again the following January, this time telling him that he planned to continue his studies with Dr Maxwell Jones, one of the pioneers of the 'therapeutic communities' approach to mental illness, at the Dingleton Hospital in Scotland, and then down at the Henderson Hospital in South London. Perhaps the two could meet up and exchange a thought or two?

Fortunately, Laing did reply this time. And, during the following autumn, after another exchange of letters, the two met up at last, at Laing and his close colleague Aaron Esterson's Hallam Street, Marylebone, offices. This meeting with Laing fixed Berke's future for they immediately hit it off, both on a personal and on a professional level. Laing at that time hadn't met many Jewish Americans, let alone such an effusive and utterly devoted one as Berke. Yet, listening to his compliments about *The Divided Self* and his newer book, *Self and Others,* he decided there and then: if working with him was what Berke really wanted to do, then yes, he could indeed come and do so.

During the autumn of 1963, R.D. Laing was already well on the way up in his career, in some psychiatric circles at least his name a byword for original and disruptive behaviour and a somewhat forceful individualism. Most psychiatrists, now as well as then, are conformists by nature; people who turn up, do a job, and then go home to their families, leaving the larger questions of meaning and philosophical method untouched, whereas Laing was intensely interested in both of those questions.

Like Berke, he was a natural student who had steamed through grammar school and most of university, until Icarus-like he had failed his final examinations. Such a comprehensive failure was surprising to say the least. But Laing had upset too many people to be allowed to graduate without some mark of displeasure; and failing him first time round was probably the professors' best way of signalling their disapproval of what they perceived as his habits of arrogance and hurtful plain-speaking, characteristics which did occasionally overbalance his charm, his irreverence, his scrupulous intellect, and his seemingly boundless energy.

By the autumn of 1963, Laing had moved beyond *The Divided Self* into a zone that was palpably more troubling. In contrast to his early days, he no longer saw himself as part of the 'straight' medical community at all, finding most of his colleagues if not sinister and downright sadistic, then intellectually vacuous and timeserving. Like Thompson, he had long had nothing but contempt for the conventional psychiatrist's armamentarium of electrical, surgical, and chemical therapies. Now he saw the psychiatrists themselves as little better than policemen.

As for schizophrenia, perhaps the most lamentable of all the mental disorders, he was now beginning to emphasise its potentially life-enhancing qualities: a breakdown could also be a breakthrough if the person experiencing the breakdown was supported rather than 'treated.'

This idea was grist to the Berkeian mill, for though Berke was considerably younger than Laing, his own understanding of schizophrenia had long been travelling along a similar path — as indeed had a number of other American psychiatrists, notably Don Jackson and the expatriate British anthropologist and psychiatrist Gregory Bateson. He was therefore extremely gratified to be taken on by Laing and asked to share in the older man's intellectual and spiritual adventure.

Much of Laing's considerable energies during the previous five years had gone into a project elucidating the relationship between the patterns of communication within families and the genesis of schizophrenia, and it was this research that Berke now spent hours and hours poring over. Hallam Street, he soon discovered, was not merely Drs Laing and Esterson, but a small and argumentative community of psychiatrists, psychologists, nurses, and social workers, most of them left wing and all of them committed to a phenomenological as opposed to a biochemical understanding of mental illness.

There was Sid Briskin, a calm and very competent social worker — Laing's' 'right hand man' —, the clinical psychologist Herbert 'Phil' Phillipson, and Joan Cunnold, a nurse 'refugee' from William Sargant's unit at St. Thomas' Hospital on the south bank of the Thames, where lobotomy was practiced, and electrical shock treatment really was used as a way of punishing difficult patients. Then other close colleagues or friends of Laing and Esterson would often stop by: another psychiatrist named David Cooper, who was running a unit at Shenley Hospital called Villa 21 on Laingian lines, and writing a book with Laing about Jean-Paul Sartre; a sculptor and former naval officer named Jesse Watkins; and another young Jewish American called Clancy Sigal, who had written a highly regarded novel about an aspirant painter from the Yorkshire coalfields, and who, like many in the Laing circle, also had mental health problems himself, in his case depression, anxiety and insomnia.

The Hallam Street group's research, compiled mostly on tape, confirmed Berke's earlier observation that schizophrenia wasn't like a physical illness, but that, in Laing's terms, it had a 'politics', a congeries of family pressures, bizarre communication and victimisation. If he needed further confirmation in the English context, he found it when Laing took him on visits to the homes of his 'patients'. It was clear to him then that the so-called psychotic member of the family was not always the most disturbed; that the behaviour of other family members was often more bizarre.

> People did not talk to each other, but at each other, and tangentially, not directly. There was a continual shifting of position. It was difficult to follow who was talking about what, because the issue always seemed to be shifting, ... Parents seemed impervious to the point of view of their children, and vice versa, but to a lesser extent. And most infuriatingly, what people said was often contradicted by the way they said it (tone of voice and/or facial and bodily movements).'[13]

Laing and Esterson (and Berke himself), again like Gregory Bateson, interpreted these contradictory behaviours as 'double binds', which is to say as modes of communication that could almost have been designed to provoke troubling if not 'mad' behaviour. But they also employed a vocabulary that Berke didn't then use. It included words like 'process' and 'praxis', 'series' and 'nexus', and 'mystification' and 'intelligibility', words that the pair had borrowed from the post-war philosophy of Jean-Paul Sartre, and which Berke found as alienating as the psychoanalytic jargon which he had to listen to at Einstein, but which nonetheless he soon discovered that he would have to learn if he wanted to become a fully-fledged member of Laing's extraordinary circle.

During this period Berke lived in a flat that Laing had found for him on Fitzroy Road in Primrose Hill, thus admitting him to a subsidiary role in the on-going drama of Ted Hughes, the philandering and sometimes brutal Yorkshire poet. On February 11, earlier that year, Hughes' wife, Sylvia Plath, had gassed herself in the kitchen there. Then, during the spring, Hughes' mistress, Assia Wevill, had moved into the flat, occupying the same rooms where

Plath had mulled over the possibility of divorcing Hughes and beginning a new life. And it was Assia who had sublet part of the flat to the American.

Laing also pitched Berke into his family and social life. And Berke met all the Laings: The Scotsman's hard-pressed nurse wife, Anne, the couple's daughters, Fiona, Susan and Karen and their sons, Paul and Adrian. On one occasion, they all went to the pictures together to see the latest James Bond film, *From Russia with Love*. Then he also spent time with Aaron Esterson and his wife, Naomi — on one occasion discussing the educational prospects of their young son, Julian (Berke thought that he should go to the fashionably progressive Summerhill, in Suffolk. But the Estersons sent him elsewhere).[14]

It was also during this period that Berke first experimented with LSD, a wholly positive experience for him. This was in a quiet room, also in the company of Esterson. 'Afterwards, I remember we went out to a restaurant and, for the first time in my life, I ordered rabbit. And I hated it. First, because it wasn't kosher. Second, because I didn't like the taste of it.'[15]

That fall, Berke began to realise that his future lay among the little group in England and, with the thought of returning to England very much on his mind, he helped Laing with the search for the 'place', the 'asylum' or the 'Schizophrenia Centre', which would eventually supplant Cooper's Villa 21 as the testing ground for Laing's theories, traipsing off with him or Briskin or one of the other Hallam Street workers to meet estate agents, home owners or indeed anyone else for that matter, who could conceivably help them with money or a property. This, Laing made clear to Berke, would be a place of their own, free from state or over-bearing psychiatric influence, where 'patients' would be people again, and the doctors themselves 'liberated' of their professional authority, and therefore freer than ever to undertake their own psychological 'voyages.'

Through Laing, Berke at this point also met Mary Barnes, the future 'queen bee' of Kingsley Hall, with whom his own destiny would later become intimately involved, first as a co-resident of Kingsley Hall, then as a friend and fellow voyager. Berke warmed to Mary instantly. Seeing her enter Laing's office a virtual catatonic, then after a couple of hours leave with her head held high was, he later remembered, quite an experience.[16]

*

Following his placement with Laing and company in London, Berke felt it as 'quite a come-down to have to fit back in the old hospital routine, especially when [he] could see better than ever, that psychiatric treatment', even in our '"most advanced" [American] wards, was essentially oppressive.'[17] He left the UK on November 22, 1963, still drunk following a wild party with some friends up in Glasgow, his head reeling with thoughts of all his new experiences. He was so inebriated that when the pilot passed on the news that President Kennedy had been assassinated, he felt more irritation than shock. 'Just heard that Kennedy was shot', he wrote to Laing, scribbling with a shaky hand somewhere over the Atlantic, 'Ah, Don't bug me man, I'm with it.'[18]

Yet what at first seemed a backward step turned out to be just as productive and positive as his London experience, for during the following two years, Berke, unknowingly and tentatively at first, put together the experiences and the ideas that would ultimately lead to the Congress. That winter, he found an apartment in Manhattan at 307 East 27th Street and threw himself heart and soul into the Lower East Side's exhilarating bohemia. This was not a transatlantic version of the London Soho bohemia of the 1940s and 50s, say, focused on a few pubs and involving a bunch of shabby-genteel, mostly privately educated middle-aged men, but a youthful 'cultural rebellion', centred on poetry for the most part — performed live and then reproduced in cheap and swiftly printed mimeographed magazines — but involving all of the arts, which the poets/performers mixed in bracing and often startling combinations.

Most of the young people involved in this experiment were young people like Berke himself: educated and lower or middle-class for the most part, very left wing and disaffiliated. They all said they hated capitalism and materialism. Many used drugs to expand their consciousnesses, and some embraced the sexual revolution by either living with their partners or by embracing gay or other non-normative lifestyles.

For the most part, their culture heroes were the Beats: Allen Ginsberg, Gregory Corso, Jack Kerouac, William Burroughs, Neal Cassady, Herbert Huncke, non-academic, very individualistic characters, who lived on the margins of society, and who also valued unlimited personal freedom and spontaneity. Indeed, it wasn't long before Berke met and befriended Allen Ginsberg himself at a poetry reading at one of the area's thriving coffee houses. Ginsberg's beard, he wrote Laing, was '10x better and bushier' than his own. With his hair down to his shoulders, he looked like a bear, though a 'very nice and interesting one.'[19]

Back at Einstein, Berke enthused about Laing to Thompson and to all his other friends. He told Morty Schatzman and Leon Redler that Laing was going to turn the psychiatric profession on its head, that he was the new Freud, a genius. As soon as they could, they should all get over to London to meet him, he insisted. He lent copies of Laing's books to anyone who would read them and argued heatedly about their contents with some of the more conventional professors. Then he also thought a lot about how Laing's ambition to set up an asylum outside the psychiatric system related to his own experiences at college. Perhaps education too needed to take place outside the academic system, with its absurdly powerful administrations, and all the other impediments to joyful and spontaneous learning.

In any case, like many young people with radical affiliations he was already aware that something was happening outside conventional university education. In California, for instance, little colleges were springing up, while at Berkeley a New School had been formed, offering classes in 'Dream Politics and the Cold War' and 'Problems of the City in Contemporary America'.

Then, of course, he had read Paul Goodman's *The Community of Scholars*, which argued the case for academics to start up their own universities. (Indeed, while in England, he had written a letter to one of the radical papers on just such an undertaking, Emerson College, in Pacific Grove, California. 'For further radical analysis and superb suggestions for improving the situation of "higher" education, get hold of Paul Goodman's *Community of Scholars'*, he suggested.)[20]

Over the next year or so, Berke sent Laing many gossipy letters about love, work and all the other extraordinary and humdrum matters that concerned him. Having seen Laing work wonders with Mary Barnes, he often pondered what it would be like to go into therapy with him himself. Laing had no objection, so that was something else that he now began to look forward to, alongside some sort of role at the 'Schizophrenia Centre', when at last an appropriate building was found for it.

Some of his letters passed on compliments for Laing from fellow critics of psychiatry, like Thomas Szasz, a 'nice fellow',[21] who had read *The Divided Self,* and from Leon Redler, who had by now been bowled over by Laing's published writings in much the same way as he had. Like Berke, Redler was involved in the peace movement. He was also drawn to civil rights. During the summer, while Berke interned as a mixed medical intern at Long Island College Hospital, Redler headed south for Mississippi to take part in the famous 'Mississippi Summer Project', a fraught and violently resisted attempt to increase black voter registration.

In his letters, Berke encouraged Laing to read the same authors as he was reading, recommending, for example, a new book called *Culture against Man* by the St. Louis professor of anthropology and sociology Jules Henry, and an article by Hermann Hesse in the fall '63 issue of *Psychoanalytical Review*: 'much of what Hesse says is relevant to your ideas on creativity,' he informed him.[22] Having also begun to write and perform poetry himself, he also sent him copies of a couple of his best poems, including, *The Delivery, Or Oh to be Young and Gay*, about a ghastly experience he'd had delivering a baby in one of the city's poorer hospitals. Then he also wrote an introduction to one of Laing's best lectures called 'Violence and Love', both of which were broadcast on New York's WBAI, a noncommercial radio station with a reputation for challenging conventional opinion.[23]

Berke also told Laing about his hospital experiences, about the time he had smoked pot all night: 'Wild, these city hospitals.'[24] And about his meeting with an 'extremely interesting 32 year old negro fellow,' who had been admitted to a psychiatric hospital by his wife, following what looked like a breakdown and whose name was Jose Quinonis. Quinones, he told Laing, had a 'superb knowledge of far eastern religions' and of a certain 'afro-Cuban religious cult'. 'From the standpoint of the middle class Jewish registrar who admitted him, he was quite mad. From his standpoint, I don't know if he is mad at all. Anyway, he's soon to be discharged and has promised to introduce me to LUCUME [sic] thought and practices.'[25]

That said, there were many days when he still found the college part of his medical education 'a fantastic drag',[26] despite frequent experiments with LSD, which seemed to offer extraordinary therapeutic possibilities. 'Was quite depressed for a good bit of time after returning [from London],' he told Laing at the beginning of February, 'but things are looking up a bit now, as I'm enjoying the beginning of an affair with a rather pretty dancing student.'[27]

In addition to reading his poetry at Le Metro, he also became the cafe's resident medic, giving advice on sexually transmitted diseases and 'dispensing' marijuana and other drugs to the poets and to the many other younger people who by mid-1964 were flooding into the area. One of his first 'patients' was the future Warhol script writer, Ronnie Tavel, who was then working with filmmaker Jack Smith. Tavel brought along a whole bunch of problems. One day he was up, the next day he was suicidal. Berke counselled him to concentrate on his work, and for a while the two became friends, part of the same sometimes wild circle that included poets Ed Sanders (founder of *Fuck You* magazine and future Fug), Will Inman, Diane Wakoski and John Keys and another poet simply known as Szabo.

If Berke did return to London to work with Laing, it was this circle that he would leave behind. But the passage of time and his growing experience of conventional psychiatry only made him more determined.

*

Before Berke could get back to London, however, he began to devote himself to a new enthusiasm, which also brought him intellectually and emotionally closer to Laing, nothing less than an ambitious supranational scheme to revolutionise contemporary existence. During the summer of 1964, a small collection of mimeographed articles had started to do the rounds of America's more louche addresses. Entitled the *Sigma Folio* and tagged as an 'entirely new dimension in publishing'[28], it was put together by its subscribers and posted out by a thirty-eight-year-old, part-Italian, part-Scottish, writer named Alexander Trocchi.

Almost everyone in Berke's poetry circle knew something about Trocchi. He was a drug addict, a poet, a novelist, an editor and a publisher, a sometime pornographer and Hudson River longshoreman, who like a host of other British ex-patriots had also contributed to the Lower East Side poetry movement. If Ginsberg was Beat, then Trocchi to some extent was Beatier. While the American poet was wowing the West Coast with *Howl*, Trocchi was knocking round Paris with the Lettrists Guy Debord and Ivan Chtcheglo. Yet he lacked the business savvy and the plain common sense of Ginsberg and would often find himself unable to follow through on his literary and other commitments.

Laing and the Hallam Street group of social workers and anti-psychiatrists had fallen into Trocchi's orbit during the previous spring, swept up in the enthusiasm accompanying Trocchi's initial Sigma prospectus. Brought closer together during a weekend event at an intentional community in Oxfordshire, Laing had found himself entranced. Trocchi seemed to be everything in a friend and a collaborator that he had dreamed about, and he looked forward to a 'long future of being together.'[29] Then, at about the same, time Berke jumped aboard as well as others like William Burroughs, Michael McClure, Colin Wilson, Rosemary Tonks, Timothy Leary and an intriguing young woman named Beba Lavrin. The idea that emerged out of the weekend meeting was that the Hallam Street people would unite their enthusiasm for anti-psychiatry to the revolutionary enthusiasms of all these other people. They would join together to foment a cultural revolt, with the Laing group's planned 'Schizophrenia Centre' doubling up as a Sigma centre for Europe.

Or, as Clancy Sigal put it in a letter to Trocchi written during the previous April, the conjoined group would take on the 'Puritan harems of the jammy conscience.'[30]

Like everyone else, Berke was particularly impressed by the manifesto accompanying Trocchi's prospectus, 'Invisible Insurrection of a Million Minds.' It attacked all that the conventional mindset apparently held dear: from the fashion industry and advertising to the nation state and mechanisation. 'Cultural revolt must seize the grids of expression and the powerhouses of the mind', Trocchi wrote. 'Intelligence must become self-conscious, realise its own power, and, on a global scale, transcending functions that are no longer appropriate, dare to exercise it. ... The cultural revolt is the necessary underpinning, the passionate substructure of a new order of things.'[31]

The news media, the art establishment, the purveyors of most popular music—all, in Trocchi's opinion, had substituted the merely spectacular for the real, the living, the human. The artists'/insurrectionists' job would therefore be to seize back the means of their own artistic production, in other words, to '*eliminate the brokers*', so that new art forms could emerge untrammelled.[32]

'How to begin?', Trocchi asked himself—and here, from Berke's point of view, was probably the key feature of the article—'At a chosen moment in a vacant country house (mill, abbey, church or castle) not too far from the City of London, we shall foment a kind of cultural "jam session": out of this will evolve the prototype of our *spontaneous university*'.[33]

This would be nothing like a conventional university, Trocchi insisted, nothing like a newer version of an Oxford or a Columbia, but something like the defunct Black Mountain College in North Carolina, where no one had left with a degree, but everyone had participated fully in the life of the community.

Very much in the style of the period, Trocchi ended the article on an apocalyptic note.

> The cultural possibilities of this movement are immense and the time is ripe for it. The world is awfully near the brink of disaster. Scientists, artists, teachers, creative men of goodwill everywhere are in suspense. Waiting. Remembering that it is our kind even now who operate, if they don't control, the

grids of expression, we should have no difficulty in recognising the spontaneous university as the possible detonator of the invisible insurrection.'³⁴

Soon, Berke devoted heart and soul to Trocchi's project, marshalling his poet friends and hooking up with other movers and shakers in New York's underground communities, such as the young Englishman, Michael Hollingshead, whose own dubious plans for world revolution encompassed the dosing of the world's water supplies with LSD, and who had the ambivalent reputation of having first 'turned on' Timothy Leary.

'He's a manipulator and probably a rogue, but this notwithstanding, he will probably be an important asset in initiating the Sigma project', Berke told Laing during October. Hollingshead, he added, had discovered a 'rich businessman', who he was turning on with 'women, booze [and] drugs,'³⁵ and who could probably be manipulated into buying them a brownstone, which they could use as a base for the New York end of the project.

Laing, who was then speculating on doing a book with Trocchi and William Burroughs about drugs, counselled discretion about Hollingshead. Trocchi, he said, was not at all keen on him.³⁶

Meanwhile, as always, Berke kept Laing up to date with other news from New York: about Ginsberg, for instance, who had spent an entire weekend in a 'wild scene with Peter [Orlovsky, his partner] and 4 chicks and mescaline turning on and fucking'.³⁷

When Laing flew into New York early that autumn on a lecture tour, inevitably Berke acted as a kind of cicerone to him, introducing him to John Thompson, Leon Redler and to all his other medical friends, not to mention Ginsberg and a bunch of other literary and artistic people. This was a big moment for Berke, who had been looking forward to it for months. 'Some pretty good pot is grown in those parts,' he had told Laing a few weeks before his arrival.³⁸ He encouraged Laing to bring some of his own poetry along—Laing had already written a version of his famous *Bird of Paradise* prose poem. Perhaps, wondered Berke, he would agree to read it at Le Metro?

Laing won over Thompson immediately, whereas most of the other older doctors were cautious. Laing too was impressed by

Thompson. He later told Berke that Thompson was the 'only person who knew more about schizophrenia than he did',[39] which, as Berke later remarked, wasn't just an unarguable statement of fact; 'from such a narcissist as Laing', it was also 'quite a compliment.'[40]

After a day or two of sightseeing, Berke and Laing popped into a cinema and watched the new Hitchcock film, *Marnie*. Then they went to a poetry reading at Le Metro, before topping the day with a party. Not only was Ginsberg present on that occasion, but perhaps the wildest of all of Berke's pals by that point, the anarchist, writer, and tyro musician Tuli Kupferberg, for whom Berke had a particular soft spot.

For Laing's part, his visit to New York was the highlight of his American trip, and on his return to London, he confessed himself bowled over by Berke's passion and energy. One of the many books they'd discussed was Hermann Hesse's cult novel *Steppenwolf*, a copy of which Laing had taken from Berke's apartment 'half by mistake', he said. He had tucked it into his luggage with a copy of the same author's *Magister Ludi*, the idea being that he'd work through them page by page on the plane and back home in London.[41]

In the same letter, Laing also mentioned that after leaving New York he had met Paul Goodman in Washington, and that the meeting had been a success. 'He's a real puritan, all for morality and hope and against exstacy [sic] and drugs of pretty well all kinds'[42] — though in his diary he was rather cutting.[43] Goodman, he added, had told him about a 'new sort of Black Mountain College set up in Copenhagen: Aage Nielsen's new experimental college.'[44] Like Goodman, Nielsen would be an inspiring presence at the Congress. Laing wondered what Berke knew about him.

Meantime, Berke kept up a stream of books and articles, sending Laing a collection of letters and a play by Artaud and a copy of *Evergreen Review*, a magazine that mixed Beat writing with some of the best of the American and European modernists. 'Keep Steppenwolf as a gift. I have an extra copy. Hope you enjoyed it. For many years I and Steppenwolf were one', he told him, a remark that more than hints at a long period of near-unbearable unhappiness.[45]

Following Laing's visit, Berke returned to London during the spring of 1965 for a few short weeks, not to work with Laing, however, but mostly to ensure that there would still be a place for him at the heart of the schizophrenia centre project. He had his degree now — friends had started to call him 'Joe Berke, MD' — plus the firm prospect of being accepted as a conscientious objector, and with Laing having long ago agreed to take him into therapy as well, it seemed like a good time to test the water one more time before finally committing himself to the emotional excitement and intellectual razzamatazz that working with Laing would inevitably offer.

By this time, the search for 'the place' had almost reached its conclusion. Laing and Sid Briskin were negotiating the lease on a large, dilapidated settlement-house in London's East End called Kingsley Hall, to which end they and most of the other Hallam Street habitues had incorporated themselves into a charity named the Philadelphia Association (PA).

Not surprisingly these few weeks for Berke were another roller-coaster experience, with Laing and most of the other people buzzing with excitement, with the occasional exception, however, of David Cooper, who wasn't fully certain that a refuge of their own addressed failures in the conventional treatment of schizophrenia after all, particularly at a time when his own and others' Villa 21 was still, though barely, functioning.

This time Laing found Berke accommodation in a kind of shed in the garden of another one of his contacts. This was a Greek woman called Flora Papastavrou, a close friend of the Hungarian-Jewish writer, Georgy Faludy, and herself a notable eccentric. The house was situated on the corner of Regents Park Road and Berkeley Street, in the Primrose Hill area again. As Berke remembered it, Flora was a lesbian, 'very flamboyant, larger than life, she had a much younger lover. ... She had a salon and all sorts of artists and writers would come there,'[46] including some of the same crowd that he had hooked up with in Glasgow before leaving for New York following his first visit.

With Laing present to stir things up, this visit proved another success. 'I thought, this is big shit. All these things were happening on the artistic side, the political side, the acid side, the smoking drugs side. It was all going on', he remembered.[47]

In other words, 'swinging London' had just kicked off, and the Primrose Hill area, like Chelsea and Notting Hill, was one of its nodal points.

One of Berke's pet projects on this occasion was to discuss the possibility of bringing Jose Quinonis with him to England. With the lessons in Afro-Cuban religion proceeding apace, he didn't want to leave him behind. In any case, Quinonis, by now an in-patient in Pilgrims State Hospital, New York, was being neglected by staff. Fortunately, Laing liked the idea. He would undertake Quinonis' 'treatment and care' in London, as long as Berke undertook to underwrite his passage — not, however, that it turned out that way.[48]

*

In the meantime, while Laing and the PA geared up for the opening of Kingsley Hall, Berke, on returning from London, got ready for another beginning, a rather more substantial one as it turned out, though with ultimately less solidity. 'Am starting university in NY this summer', he wrote to Laing in a letter written sometime during the spring.[49] As simple as that, the significance of the little phrase lying less in the brevity of the words — words on the subject weren't really necessary by this point — than in the fact that it was his own fledgling university that he was 'starting' in.

Much about the beginning of the Free University of New York (FUNY) is obscure, but the names that almost always crop up when the first months are mentioned are Allen and Sharon Krebs, Jim Mellon and Berke; for they are the people who probably did most, in the early days at least, to keep FUNY running.

Yet, according to Berke, the spark was less that of Trocchi's invisible insurrection, or even of Goodman's *Community of Scholars*, than the turbulent spirit of the times, and then a concrete event: the sacking of Allen Krebs from his teaching position at New York's Adelphi University during the summer of 1964, for having travelled to Cuba without State Department authorisation — Cuba being the radical left's poster boy for sturdy independence from Yankee interference.

Nonetheless, while Berke didn't claim that FUNY was inspired by Trocchi, he did link the university to the Sigma project. 'The beginning of the Free University of N.Y. is a key sigma project', he wrote to Trocchi in June. 'It incorporates the concept of [the] University of which you speak in Invisible Insurrection. ... The Sigma Brotherhood will now begin to manifest itself.'[50]

In words which only a '60s social scientist could have cobbled together (Krebs was a sociologist), Berke and the other founders pitched the free university as a response to the 'intellectual bankruptcy and spiritual emptiness of the American educational establishment.'[51] It was, they said, to be contemporary and passionate, non-hierarchical and confrontational, in contrast to the typical American university which had been 'emasculated', its 'exuberance' and 'excitement' destroyed.[52]

One night, several in the group slipped out and posted leaflets all over the city announcing the opening on July 6. Then they handed out leaflets and catalogues at colleges, poetry readings, folk concerts. delicatessens, and bookshops.

That semester, FUNY offered twenty-five courses on all sorts of contemporary subjects: Vietnam, Cuba, sex, drugs, the history of American radicalism as well as some, on the surface anyway, significantly less contemporary, such as 'Revolutionary Egyptology' (tutor: Ed Sanders).

Berke gave a course on the 'Psychotic Experience as an Archetype of Paradise Lost', arguing Laing's case for psychosis as a 'way to personal healing and enlightenment.'[53] On one occasion he invited John Thompson along, who spoke quietly about his own experiences of helping schizophrenics. Like the other lecturers, he held the class in an abandoned photographer's laboratory above a storefront at 20 East 14th street, a block away from Union Square, which the faculty had taken for a peppercorn rent—Krebs himself functioning not only as lecturer and chief ideologue of the project, but also as key holder, cleaner and general dogsbody.

This was all valuable experience for the Congress. Particularly as Trocchi's own moves towards cultural revolt were becoming little short of farcical. The artist and writer, Jeff Nuttall, Trocchi's Sigma lieutenant, put Trocchi's shortcomings this way: 'Each project that [Trocchi's] aspiring sensibility conducted him towards, each ideal, each aim, each plan too huge and too audacious for unstimulated minds, carried with it its sad reverse of negatives. Each gesture of self-realization carried an aspect of snide self-gratification. The funds for [Sigma] poured in. But the funds also poured out.'[54] On heroin, mostly, with the consequence that Laing and most of the other members of the Philadelphia Association lost interest in the project.

Not that Berke was party to most of this. Mulling Sigma over in his Lower East Side apartment, he still saw Trocchi as one of the key fomenters of a cultural revolution. In the same June letter to Trocchi quoted above, Berke wrote of Trocchi, Laing and the other leading Sigmatics as constituting a free university in themselves. 'Now is the time for it to achieve an even more tangible expression. When I get to London in Sept if you have not already done so beforehand, we will find a loft and incorporate ourselves as a University where classes can be initiated as per the enclosed F.U.N.Y catalogue.' 'Free University already exists in hundreds of time-space continuums', he added. 'It is now time for us to initiate Σ as insurrection and build the places of refuge.'[55]

By now, Berke was considered something of an expert on psychosis and psychedelic matters, and with FUNY already set to be a roaring success, he took part in a symposium at the newly opened and fashionable Coda Gallery. He, Timothy Leary's pal Ralph Metzner, Jerome Soll, three or four other MDs and PhDs and a well-known yoga teacher called Rammurti Mishra swapped views about psychosis, LSD and art, in a gallery space decorated with 'psychological and psychedelic' paintings, drawings and assemblages.[56]

Some of the questions asked at the symposium were the same as were asked in other contexts where LSD was mentioned: in what respect was the 'new chemical method' different to older methods of seeking enlightenment? How did it relate to psychotherapy? And most of all, of what use, if any, was LSD to artists? Berke took an entirely sanguine view of all of these questions. Like Hollingshead, Timothy Leary and the other prophets of psychedelic revolution, he was convinced that LSD would change the world for the better. His main concern and the concern of most of the other men on the panel wasn't its efficacy, but its distribution: how to get the drug to as many people in as short a time as possible.

Berke put these and other concerns in another letter to Laing. The exhibition, he told him, had been a huge success. It would now tour Paris and London. Laing, Trocchi, Clancy Sigal and David Cooper should ready themselves for the Paris opening. Exhibited there, the entirely original art works would 'probably tear [the city] apart.'[57]

Bearing in mind Laing's enthusiasm for phenomenology and French existentialist philosophy, he asked him if he could get hold of Sartre. Perhaps he would agree to take part in the French symposium. For his part, he had already asked Trocchi to book a London gallery. Then, with Hollingshead on course to open his own psychedelic 'centre' in London, he also suggested that Laing contact Arthur Eaton, the psychiatrist who had moderated the Coda symposium. 'He might be a very good guy to coordinate and set up our own LSD center in London, as we would be involved with Kingsley Hall', he added.[58]

All in all, he was, he said, having a fantastic time.

2. Kingsley Hall

In early September 1965, Berke wrote to Laing finalising the details of his arrival at Southampton on the 17th and telling him that he would be bringing some friends. One was the poet John Keys, who Berke had introduced to Laing the previous October during the Scotsman's visit to New York. Another was Calvin Hernton, 'probably the best Negro Poet in the US today; you'll dig the guy'.[1]

Berke had first met Hernton at one of the Lower East Side's coffeehouses. 'We're going to Europe, man, you ever heard of R.D. Laing? ... We got this ship and it don't cost but $132 to get over there', Berke said to him.[2] Since then he had become a huge admirer, for Hernton was more than a poet; he was also a sociologist and a Don Juan of distinction, who managed to fuse both enthusiasms in a controversial and plain-speaking study of the United States' sexual and racial hypocrisies called *Sex and Racism in America*. For a short while, he would be the Congress's chief publicist.

Following a raucous party, the little band left Manhattan on September 8 aboard an Italian cruiser called *El Castillo Feliz*, Berke bringing with him hundreds of books and fresh from an LSD session with Timothy Leary at his Millbrook, New York, estate, where he had gone through the whole 'Death—Rebirth sequence.'[3] Not surprisingly, it was a wild voyage, with parties and drug-taking the order of the day. Keys, Hernton and their accompanying 'chicks' fought like cats, while Hernton dubbed Berke 'Dr Yas', on the basis (which Berke later disputed) that he would give LSD to anyone.

Hernton was so impressed by the voyage that he quickly began writing a novel about it. *Scarecrow* includes a fictionalised portrait of Berke: groovy, tactile and endlessly talkative. Curiously, however, he made him sixty-one instead of twenty-six. Otherwise, the portrait was pretty accurate—even down to the straggly beard that gave Berke more than a passing resemblance to Allen Ginsberg.

When the Americans arrived at Kingsley Hall, they confronted a scene that for Berke, at least, was at once utterly familiar and deeply strange, curious, and exceptional. People—doctors and non-doctors—freaking out, held no unusual terrors for him of course, but the Hall was something else entirely.

Fig 4. Kingsley Hall, in the 1990s. By Bill Saville. Courtesy of John Saville.

Most Americans, even today, do not visit the furthest reaches of the East End of London. And the Hall was very East End indeed, being situated a quarter of a mile or so from the Bromley-by-Bow tube station, in Powis Road, just a stone's throw from an unprepossessing modern housing estate. The façade, four-square and stolid looking, had a bleak, municipal quality; and with a plaque memorialising Gandhi, who had stayed there during the early 1930s, fixed ostentatiously to the front of it, it had all the charm of a mausoleum. As for the interior, it was dirty and extremely cold, which did nothing for Berke's respect for English plumbing nor for the bronchitis that he soon developed.

Apparently, Sid Briskin cried that evening. He sensed straight away that with Berke and the other Americans around the Hall would be transformed, as indeed it was, in ways that even Laing had probably not anticipated.[4] Though it had only been open for a few months, much had already been achieved. Already the first group of residents had settled in, and all sorts of creative people had got into the habit of dropping round — madness being not only a grievous affliction (the conventional view) but, thanks in large part to Laing, 'interesting' and even 'trendy'.

Before the opening, Briskin had allowed his own house in Hampstead Garden Suburb to be used as a kind of prototype, taking in several of Cooper's Villa 21 'patients'. Perhaps he had more emotion invested in the Hall than the others. It certainly hurt him to see the way that Berke threw himself into the group, dominating lesser and more diffident personalities. Then there were others who also did not take to the burly American. Clancy Sigal, for one, distrusted him immediately. For his part, Briskin was sexually attracted to Laing; and he was upset that Berke and the other Americans seemed to be engrossing so much of his attention.[5] How long would it be before the whole thing blew apart was probably a question running through many of the wiser heads that evening, as the wine flowed deep and Laing and the Americans locked horns in wit combat until the early hours of the morning.

The first [in]formalities a thing of the past, a few weeks after his arrival in England, Berke sent a long account of Kingsley Hall to the performance artist Carolee Schneemann.

He had first met Schneemann during the previous May. Not only was she 'fantastically wonderful' and a 'beautiful chick'.[6] But she was also a natural focus for his erotic imagination. He was, in other words, completely bowled over. The Hall, Berke said, was 'incredible, incredulous, impossible. ... Wow. ... Wow ... Wow.'[7] The floors creaked, the doors rattled, the heating barely worked, some of the windows were smashed, there were four different types of electrical outlet and some of the residents were living in 'cells' —

little rooms at the top of the hall, which could only be accessed via a terrace that was open to the elements.

Besides himself and the other Americans, the core group in residence, he said, were Joan Cunnold, an elderly anthropologist named John Layard, a woman named Anne, a social therapist from Villa 21 named Mary Garvey, and Mary Barnes, the latter the staff nurse that Berke had first met in Laing's office in 1963: 'catatonic — hugs and kisses me — currently involved in 3-4 levels of regression at once — deepest level a fetus — turns me on when taking a bath,'[8] and Laing himself, who was staying there temporally after one of his regular fallings out with his wife, Anne, and who was then having an affair with a young German woman named Jutta Werner. Then there were ten or twelve other residents, nominal schizophrenics for the most part, a few veterans of Villa 21, but most of them new to the mental health services, and therefore 'uninstitutionalised', that is to say, amateurs rather than 'card-carrying schizophrenics'.[9] This was one of Laing's terms, a nod towards the United States of Senator Joseph McCarthy, where being a card-carrying Communist could land one in serious trouble.

Berke called himself 'chief cook', 'chief shopper', 'chief cleaner' and 'head stomper';[10] for he loved to dance at this point and throwing himself around was a way of ridding himself of the inevitable tensions. If people weren't playing music or screaming their heads off, he said, then they were smashing things up, the anti-rule of the place being that people could do pretty much what they wanted, as long as other people — and this included Berke — could bear to put up with them.

Already, he had had to deal with the police and a 'neighbourhood vigilante committee'.[11] Laing, who hardly slept at all, often woke him up before dawn to practise Yoga positions. Parties erupted night after night, with 'wild dancing to Shango, Flamenco and Indian Music', though 'fucking' he was less sure about. All sorts of 'fantabulous' people had stopped by, he added, including two of Laing's writer pals: Alan Sillitoe and Ruth Fainlight; and then Jeff Nuttall, and Trocchi, of course, and other members of the Sigma crowd.[12]

Amongst other matters, the group, he said, were about to start a school of existential psychiatry and were planning to hold artistic events: readings, films, happenings and music, having already converted a former library in the building into a 'meditation room and LSD turn on center.'[13] And then, of course, he was deep in the planning for the London version of FUNY.

While Laing and the other members of the Hallam Street group had set up the PA as an alternative to conventional psychiatric treatment, that didn't mean they or their associates didn't embody mental or spiritual difficulties themselves, that they were 'well balanced' or in any sense 'normal'. Cooper by this time was alcoholic, so possibly was Laing. Mary Garvey was 'dancing her way out of madness',[14] Layard, in Laing's view, was 'secretly and quietly schizophrenic'.[15] Sometimes Berke's own behaviour was plain nuts. Some of them took a lot of drugs. Yet all were alike in their determination to find some way out of what they saw as 'our present pervasive madness',[16] a world in which the real lunatics were either living outside or actually running the asylums.

One afternoon, very shortly after Berke's arrival at Kingsley Hall, Clancy Sigal broke down, unleashing a wave of paranoia which swept over the small community. For some time, Sigal had been living at Villa 21. Now, with Cooper in the process of cutting his ties with that experiment, he had moved into one of the 'cells' on the roof, convinced that he was about to be reborn as a Siberian shaman. Sigal, according to his own account, was 'high, electrified, charged up, convulsed.'[17] Following his return to his Bayswater flat, some in the group became anxious that he would kill himself. Laing, Berke, Esterson, Cooper and one or two of the other 'brothers' dashed across London, and wrestled him to the ground, and one of them—probably Laing—stuck a syringe full of strong sedative into his thigh, an action, on the surface at least, in contravention of all that the group stood for.[18]

Sigal considered himself betrayed, as indeed he was—though he later got his own back on his former associates by writing a darkly humorous *roman à clef* about them in which Laing appears, very lightly disguised, as Willie Last [Will he Last?], Cooper as Dick Drummond and Berke as the egregious 'Big' Marvin Munshin

[Moonshine], a 'crew-cut, tanklike ex-linebacker from Syracuse University who had large staring eyes that hardly ever blinked and oversize paw-like hands that constantly hugged and patted you when he talked' and an obsession with free universities.[19]

Laing considered the novel 'fairly malicious' (which it is) and tried to get it banned.[20] The irony nowadays is that it is also a mostly accurate account, if in some details exaggerated. As for Berke, he later described the book as a 'very funny, outrageous, biting, venomous and painful satire' of all the group's 'accomplishments and pretensions.' The novel, he says, is a 'shriek, the fictional counterpart' of *Howl*. ... The bitterness of [Sigal's] hurt flows through his words. But then, as Ronnie might say, "Wha' th' fuk."'[21]

*

For Berke the next seven months or so proved to be amongst the most exhilarating period of the first twenty-six years of his life, with both the 'highs' *and* the 'lows', as he put it, experiences of the 'highest order'.[22] His confidence in Laing growing, he spread his wings a little further now. During October, he took part in a poetry reading in Trafalgar Square with Adrian Mitchell, Harry Fainlight, John Keys, Calvin Hernton, and other poets — this being part of a weekend of protests against the war in Vietnam. Then, in November, he treated himself to a brief holiday in Paris, where he wound up at the publisher Maurice Girodias's offices: 'Henry Miller & Becket Lit on the shelf'.[23] Girodias, he remarked, reminded him of photographs of Albert Camus. He bought two books from the publisher, copies of *Helen and Desire*, one of Trocchi's pornographic novels, one copy for himself, the other for an acquaintance.

He loved Paris, the food a particular pleasure, not just the taste, but the smell, one delicatessen, a 'collage of bird and fish and color.' He also thought a lot about Carolee Schneemann during this holiday, imagining himself making love to her in French, feeling her touch, 'intoxicated with the moment.'[24]

She was not his only love interest by this point, however (In any case, she had a regular boyfriend). He was also having tender thoughts about a Borzoi-owning poet and illustrator named

Roberta Elzey, who he had first met in the week before he left New York and who he had dated in a mad dash.

Back at Kingsley Hall, Laing found him yet another job, as a therapist at the Langham Clinic. This was because Kingsley Hall did not provide an income. 'I'm a head shrink and may flip every one out by getting an offer from Harley Street', he wrote to one of his American pals.[25]

Naturally, it was his plan to set up an English version of FUNY that dominated his free time. During October, he wrote a long account of FUNY for *Peace News,* ending the article with a ringing declaration: 'The time has come to formally establish a Free University of London.'[26] With Jeff Nuttall, the photographer Graham Keen and other interested parties, he arranged a meeting to discuss the project at Kingsley Hall. However, after all the talk, all the excitement, the Free University of London (FUL) failed to take off — the English, by and large, still being far too conservative in educational matters, and Laing himself, despite the earlier discussion about using the building for a school of existential psychiatry, being notably diffident about using Kingsley Hall as its premises. Nonetheless, the seed of some sort of free university in London was sown, to be picked up on a later occasion not only by himself, but by others equally disillusioned with conventional higher education.[27]

However, the major focus of his energies at this point was Mary Barnes. This was his central task: to help her on her 'journey through madness.' Mary had moved into the Hall just a few weeks after it had opened during June. It was around her that much of the psychiatric profession's interest in the Hall had quickly gathered. If she deteriorated or died, then the Kingsley Hall experiment would be deemed to have failed. If she survived and made better by the experience, then Laing's notion that psychosis was a potentially healing experience would to some extent be vindicated.

Over the course of that first Autumn, Berke struggled to encourage her to eat, as for several weeks she had refused almost everything that the little group had offered her. She lay then in a small bedroom opposite the kitchen, naked except for a blanket, seemingly inert, almost, in Berke's words, like one of those 'half-alive cadavers' the British army had liberated from Belsen near the end of the second world war, her plan being to go 'far down into herself, return to a period before she was born, when she was a foetus'.[28]

Some of the less committed residents wanted to send her to a mental hospital, but Laing and Berke held firm. After all, there was nothing intrinsically wrong with her intentions, they reasoned; her presence also offered the other residents a number of benefits. For Berke, it meant the opportunity to learn a great deal more about madness.

> Secondary benefits were that I got to meet an unusually charming woman, that I was catapulted straight into the middle of Kingsley Hall politics without having to spend time on the sidelines, and that by identifying with Mary and vicariously participating in her experience, I allowed myself to approach and come to grips with my own tumultuous emotional life, which is in some ways similar, and in other ways quite different, from that of Mary.[29]

During those first months, Berke communicated with Mary by bites and by growls, bringing up to the surface the same 'beastly' qualities that had first emerged in him as a teenager. This was good for him and good for Mary. He felt deeper, richer, more in touch with himself, while Mary learned to better cope with her anger. She liked to paint the walls with shit in those days, smearing, dabbing, and splattering breast-shapes. After a while Berke taught her to paint with more conventional mediums. Ultimately Berke and 'therapy' became the embodiment of everything that was 'good' to her. She followed him around the Hall like a bad-tempered terrier, raged when he left the building, and repeatedly merged her feelings with his.

*

While this drama was unfolding in Berke's anti-professional capacity, Redler joined the community after a stint like Berke at the Dingleton Hospital; and then Roberta Elzey arrived from New York, following a spaced-out telephone invitation from Berke, who unable to cope during a period of fear and depression, had spent an evening on cocaine and heroin.[30]

Roberta arrived at Kingsley Hall on Berke's twenty-seventh birthday, January 17, 1966, carrying a huge Hebrew National salami and a cheesecake from one of his favourite delicatessens. She moved into the hall straightaway, quickly establishing herself as a timid yet, for Berke at least, necessary presence. Whatever Berke's feelings for Carolee at this point, his romantic feelings for Roberta quickly gathered pace, and the pair became one of a small number of Kingsley Hall couples.

It wasn't long before Berke and Roberta rented their own 'turn on pad' across London in a flat on St George's Terrace, facing Primrose Hill. This was partly to safeguard Roberta's mental health. She had already had enough of Kingsley Hall to last her a lifetime.[31] Nonetheless, the couple continued to spend several nights a week. Unfortunately, Roberta's presence was not appreciated by Mary who, consumed with jealousy, peed on their bed, broke into their room while they were sleeping and did everything else she could think of to engage Berke's attention.

Yet, despite these inconveniences, not to mention the tensions of living cheek by jowl with so many other extraordinary individuals, Berke found much at Kingsley Hall to excite him. The evening meals, especially, were one of the highlights of the week, with Berke or whoever else happened to be on hand, preparing an array of gastronomic delicacies.

Usually, Laing sat at the head of the table on these occasions, his handsome face illuminated by candlelight, his conversation either grossly physical or mystical, whatever suited the mood, and almost always delivered via some extraordinary wordplay. He gave the impression that he knew more than other people — he often did. No subject, however abstruse, seemed beyond his powers. Parables, apothegms, fantasies, recollections of family and medical life in Glasgow, tumbled from his lips, often making his listeners feel more like disciples than fellow diners, at a gathering of the elect, the initiated.

'Any incident that could amuse, shock, dismay, edify or provoke the assemblage was fair game. My favourite was "the great appendectomy race". Aaron [Esterson] and I were also experts at the medical horror story and we used to spend hours trading Ronnie tale for tale', Berke recollected.[32]

Other times, Laing sat glumly, casting a cynical or a quizzical eye over the proceedings, allowing others to come to the fore, before suddenly springing with a destabilising word or gesture.

Many of the visitors to Kingsley Hall on these occasions were medical people with hinterlands rather like Laing or Berke themselves, or artists, writers, actors, or dancers. Usually at least one or two had thoughts of joining the community. Others came, says Berke, 'because friends lived there, or because they liked community life, or had heard that Kingsley Hall was a "groovy scene," or to demonstrate their wares at the poetry readings, film shows, music and dance recitals, and art exhibitions which took place in the big hall downstairs.'[33]

By their presence, these people added their own 'extra dimension' to life at Kingsley Hall. 'They emphasized touch and smell as well as sight and sound. They showed how easy (or hard) it is to pass beyond the limits of verbal expression in order to reveal experiences which are remarkably like those which occur in dreams or psychotic reverie.'[34]

In such an environment, it was no wonder then that Berke's and the others' thoughts began to turn again to some other sort of radical educational experiment. How could they bring the radical and lively ideas that they were developing at Kingsley Hall to the awareness of a wider audience?

Was the idea of the Congress Berke's? As far as I can tell it was.[35] At least as a concept it has all the hallmarks of his free university interests and, in any case, from the starters Laing was noticeably ambivalent about the project.[36] But as for the content of the Congress: violence and the dialectics of liberation, that seems to have been either Laing or Cooper's idea in as much as it ties in smartly with their reading of Sartre, not least of the Frenchman's *The Critique of Dialectical Reason,* his philosophical opus of 1960, and a book which, incidentally, the two men were by and large responsible for introducing to anglophone readers.

By the early summer of 1966, concepts from this book had been current in both men's work for some time, not least in their joint publication of 1964 *Reason and Violence* and in their various book reviews and articles.[37] Central to their understanding of Sartre was the idea that violence was only partly about what people consciously did to each other; it was also about what they did to each other unconsciously, often through the simple exertion of their freedom. As Laing put it in the final chapter of *Reason and Violence*: 'Violence is the action of freedom on freedom by the mediation of inorganic matter. Free praxis can directly destroy the freedom of the other ... by mystifications and stratagems.'[38]

As for Berke, if not a Free University of London, a congress then. That would be the next way forward.

3. Pulling the Congress Together

Berke and the other members of what became the organising group began planning the Congress sometime during the late spring or early summer of 1966, yet another critical time for all the Kingsley Hall community. The tensions, which had often run high, exploded. Laing and Esterson fell out in an extraordinary fashion, the little group splintering into two camps: the Laingians and the Estersonians. One of the problems was drugs: too much LSD was making Laing messianic; another was Mary Barnes, whose determination to 'be herself' at any cost continued to unite the rest of the residents against her. One day she scribbled white lines all over the games room. The effect, suggested Berke, was an attempt to envelop the entire community in a 'gigantic spider web.'[1] Such was the stress, Berke sometimes lost his temper; he even slapped her occasionally.

Fig 5. Up on the roof. Kingsley Hall, Spring 1967. Dag Kolderup (with flute), David Bell, Francis Gillett, Noel Cobb and Dorothee 'Dodo' Von Grieff. By Jan Horne. Courtesy Dag Kolderup.

Esterson wanted more order, more forethought, much more 'structure' no less, particularly in the life of Mary Barnes; he was afraid of the little community disintegrating. He suggested the appointment of a 'medical director'. But Laing and Berke wanted to keep things more or less as they were. They acknowledged the need for regular meetings, but only if they were voluntary and arose out of real concerns than rather (as they saw it) from the discredited therapeutic community model, which both associated with Maxwell Jones and his work at Dingleton Hospital.

During May, Berke suffered a personal loss in the death of his mother. Then during the summer, following a trip to Barcelona, he handed the daily management of Kingsley Hall over to two new resident therapists, an American named Noel Cobb and a young Englishman named Paul Zeal, who had studied philosophy at Bristol and recently graduated from London University.

Cobb, a psychologist and poet, had shortly before been kicked out of Norway, for using marijuana and supplying it to others. In fact, his behaviour there had sparked a celebrated court case. Zeal was yet another young person who had fallen under the spell of the Laing of *The Divided Self*. The book 'spoke' both to and for him.[2]

For his part, Cobb found the atmosphere at Kingsley Hall angry, even malevolent — the building itself 'ugly and rigid, like a lugubrious old man'[3] and the residents broken in spirit.

He diagnosed a lack of 'feminine influence',[4] and swiftly set to work. But the labour was slow and not always appreciated. Where were the green spaces in and around the hall that everyone knew to be therapeutic? 'There was nothing much in our local vicinity to remind one of the seasons, except for a few flowers which some of the girls had planted in the tiny roof garden.'[5] 'Psychic swords crossed daily. Laing, for one, seemed obsessed with paring down, whittling away, tearing away any kind of blurriness or unclarity in motivation among the community's members. Confrontation was the order of the day. There were challenges and counter-challenges.'[6]

As for Berke, his departure was another end of an era. Henceforth he had relatively little to do with the day-to-day running of Kingsley Hall, though he continued to stay the occasional night there. He brought Mary's paintings to the attention of some of his new artist friends, people like the sculptor David Annesley and Feliks Topolski, and to the journalist Ruth Abel, who wrote a celebrated piece for the *Guardian,* important for the hall as well as for Mary: 'She paints ... huge vivid canvases with Dubuffet-like figures. Her room is covered with them, floor, walls, and bed, all over the building is some token of her work. The subject matter is mainly religious but the work is highly sexual.'[7]

Berke was so proud of Mary that he sent a copy of the article to Carolee Schneemann in America: 'So bravo except now she's been in bed for three months ... and not laying hand to brush, but that's the art world for you.'[8]

He also continued with his other enthusiasms, for instance, writing a psychological study of the Watts 'negro riots' of 1965 and forming a 'research committee' with Calvin Hernton for investigating the effects of cannabis, and producing a prose poem for the September 1966 Destruction in Art Symposium (DIAS) to which he had been invited in lieu of Laing, who for some reason did not want to contribute to an event with so many artistic oddballs.

Amongst the 'highlights' of DIAS, of which the symposium proper was just a part, and which took place across several venues in London, were nudity and the violation of a dead lamb. The spectacle carried serious consequences for the organisers artist Gustav Metzger and art gallery manager John Sharkey, both of whom were charged with 'causing an exhibition to be shown ... of a lewd, indecent and disgusting nature' and for which they were prosecuted at the Old Bailey.[9] It was a spectacle that also went on to influence the Congress, for it lead Berke and the organisers to take a more circumspect attitude to one of the events than would otherwise have been justified.[10]

Of course, Berke's piece too was about violence and especially the myriad ways that humans go about destroying themselves: by suicide, drink, drugs, self-mutilation, conventional psychiatry, cancer and, to him, an obviously fascinating illness called lupus erythematosus. But the biggest killer was war. He thus ended the piece on a suitably grim note, invoking the racial situation in South Africa, the Vietnam War, and Watts and, finally, the consummation of everything that Western civilisation supposedly stood for, a nuclear apocalypse.

> Let the bombs fall, the biggest bombs, and so a great mandala will unfold, and in the one micro moment all that can be will be; and all that need be stated, will be stated; and western man will have achieved full and everlasting expression of what no longer need be expressed.[11]

Berke was so pleased with the composition that before reading it at DIAS, he showed it to Laing, expecting praise. But the older man looked it over and immediately rewrote parts of it. Berke was incensed. 'It infuriated me because many of the things he wrote were better than the things that I had written,' he told me.[12]

*

From the outset, Berke, Laing, Cooper and Redler billed the Congress as the project of a grandiose-sounding organisation called the Institute of Phenomenological Studies (IPS) — 'phenomenological' not in the philosophical sense, but as a synonym for 'liberationist' and 'existential' and as a 'means [to] a more or less systematic elimination of preconceptions'.[13] The idea, salted with Sartrean terminology, was that the name would appeal to a wide range of people, but particularly to students of the social sciences, fed up with number-crunching and the academic shibboleths of 'disinterestedness' and 'objectivity'.

This was a subject that Laing had turned to before; and would turn to again, not least in a revised version of the 'Violence and Love' lecture, which he had shared with Berke: syntax and vocabulary are 'political acts. ... Human beings relate to each other not simply externally, like two billiard balls, but by the relations of the two worlds of experience that come into play when two people meet. If human beings are not studied as human beings, then this once more is violence and mystification'.[14] Of course, this was also Berke's view as well as other members of the IPS at this point. All of them detested the so-called scientific world view and its corollary of academic neutrality. Not only was it reductive and politically naive; it was, in the terms in which they used the word, violent.

Cooper, in a circular letter sent out to potential participants during the summer, introduced the Congress as part and parcel of other work that the group was pursuing, including his own research into what was really going on in the war in Vietnam and Berke and Redler's multi-generational studies of families, in which one or more of their members had been diagnosed as psychotic.[15]

The situation in Vietnam was entirely understandable, he wrote. For the present world system to function, there had to be winners and losers. Yet, the cost of this conflict was borne by all men.

Everything in Western society was rotten. Not only were we conditioned by the institutions that surrounded us: family, school, universities, and mass communications. But they had even influenced our biochemistry.[16] Alienation had been normalised. Our potentialities as human beings sacrificed to an ideological system wedded to a vision of stasis.[17]

Picking up on Berke's radical educational enthusiasms, the group, he said, were interested in exploring new ways of relating to each other as teachers and students. They would rid themselves of the conventional classroom-type situation of teachers and taught—the first pseudo-authoritative, the second pseudo-abstracted and disengaged, and experiment with new ways of relating to each other which did not involve a bureaucracy.[18]

In effect, this was more or less the same vision that Paul Goodman had expressed in 1962, but without Cooper's Sartrean overlay:

> The credits, grading, 54-minute scheduling, departmentalism, narrow expertise, and bureaucracy constitute an administrative mentality in the faculty that divides teacher from teacher and teacher from student. ... It is not a system calculated to elicit original genius, to help the young find vocations, or to encourage the exploration of nature.[19]

The group's initial plan, Cooper added, was to start off with a series of these seminars during the winter and only then to proceed to the summer conference that would become the 'Dialectics'.

Coupled with the circular letter, the group also sent out invitations to thirty prominent intellectuals, most of them either North American or European, and most of those social scientists. One can only imagine the fun they had constructing this list. Berke says that they all made contributions. 'We threw ideas at each other', he said to me, 'Should we invite this person? Should we invite that person? And so forth.' The only person he then regretted not inviting was the Canadian professor of communications, Marshall McLuhan, author of the hugely influential *'The Medium is the Massage'* (sic). But they didn't consider him 'left-wing enough.'[20]

That said, not all this first list of invitees were that left wing. Mingled with names like Isaac Deutscher, Ernest Bloch, Lucien Goldmann, Ernest Mandel and, unsurprisingly, John-Paul Sartre, all Marxist or Marxian stalwarts, were other names like Erving Goffman and Thomas Szasz, who had helped to form the group's more strictly anti-psychiatric enthusiasms [See Appendix for full list].

Some of the names were obviously Berke's. Who else would have thought of inviting Julian Beck, Paul Goodman and Allen Ginsberg? Laing plumped for the novelist Jacov Lind, Cooper for his friend the theatre and film director Peter Brook. We can only speculate who invited Marjorie Grene, the only woman on the list and an expert on Heidegger and existentialism. Probably it too was Laing. But maybe it was Redler and/or the same person who came up with Carlos Fuentes, the only South American.

The group hoped that these thinkers would then attract a large number of younger thinkers and activists, who would themselves draw in others.

The Congress was now shaping into two parts: a series of public events to be held in a 'various parts of London in halls and in the open air', which would be open to anyone who registered, and a series of 'behind the scenes' events which would be restricted to the speakers.[21]

*

The idea of focusing the Congress on the Roundhouse and making that the venue for all the public events did not emerge until the closing weeks of 1966, long after the idea for the winter seminars had been abandoned, and then following presumably animated discussion about other venues, including the Royal Albert Hall. According to Laing, the Roundhouse was his idea: 'I thought, what about availing ourselves of that excellent structure of the

Roundhouse — I think I had met [the playwright] Arnold Wesker who had acquired it.'[22] And so one of the group got on the phone and asked Wesker for permission to take over the building for the full two weeks. As he had very little else to fill the building with at that point, Wesker agreed, and so the location for the Congress was established.

This was a stroke of genius, as it turned out. The building, a former locomotive-turning house occupying a few acres fronting Chalk Farm Road in Camden Town, was a vast and decrepit shell, but extraordinarily atmospheric. At that point, it didn't even have much in the way of interior walls, let alone a proper floor. There was one narrow entrance, no proper lighting to speak of, and only two toilets. Everything about it was blistered and battered, especially the gallery that ran round the top of it. What it was good for, however, was large scale 'disorganised' events. This had been shown during the previous October when it had hosted London's first 'all night rave', a launch party for *International Times* (later *IT*). The party had attracted over three thousand people to hear The Pink Floyd play 'Interstellar Overdrive' and to dance to Soft Machine, accompanied by Yoko Ono and a miked-up motorbike. 'There were photographers, girls in mini-skirts, men with shoulder-length hair, trendy people, beatniks, beards, dollies, fancy dress, gold lamé, cavemen,' reported Richard Boston for *New Society*, one of a number of publications which covered the launch party, 'and a small object up in the dome, which appeared to be a bat, swinging 'backwards and forwards ... in time to the music.'[23]

Certainly Berke, whose flat was close to the Roundhouse, thought it an excellent idea. He described it in rambling letters (illustrations included) to Julian Beck and Carolee Schneemann as a possible venue for a series of artistic events, which would complement the lectures and other activities. Perhaps Beck could use it for a performance by his avant-garde theatrical troupe, The Living Theatre, Schneemann for a happening? It contained 'one of the most fabulous interior spaces that [he had] ever scene [sic]' he told Schneemann. 'Arnold Wesker tried to develop it for his Center 42, but that didn't work out.'[24]

The venue also appealed because, like Kingsley Hall itself, the Congress was being organised on a shoestring, with all monies to fly in, house and entertain the speakers to be paid for by ticket sales, and the Roundhouse was relatively cheap — just £475 for the entire 16-day period. 'I used to pass by ... and I thought what a wonderful venue. At that time, it was rough. It wasn't all fixed up like it is now. It was a great space. And I thought this was it,' Berke later remembered.[25]

As for the 'behind the scenes' events, the group wanted to provide a forum for quieter, more philosophical, reflection than would be possible at the public sessions. This idea was given particular appeal by one of Berke's friends, a scion of the Pilkington glass family, named Stephen Pilkington, who owned a stately home called Rotherfield Hall, near Crowborough, in the Sussex countryside. Pilkington had bought the house with the idea of setting up a school for disadvantaged children along the lines of A.S. Neill's Summerhill. Eventually, however, he went off the idea and the IPS made the decision to look for an alternative venue.[26]

*

Whilst the men looked after the intellectual side of the Congress, the 'typewriter' side — licking stamps, tracking down invitees' addresses — was mostly the work of the group's secretaries: Diane Dye and Antonia Davy, and then as the arrangements progressed, a very young woman called Jane Haynes, who had fallen in with Laing after a brief apprenticeship as an actress. Haynes too had read *The Divided Self*. A traumatic upbringing had left her with feelings of inauthenticity and reading the book had helped her to recognise that acting had become a way of *not* confronting the issues that troubled her. Married to the photographer, John Haynes, she and her husband became part of the Laing and Kingsley Hall circle. Jane was thrilled to work with Laing. And then Laing's girlfriend, Jutta, helped too, as well as several other people with Kingsley Hall connections.

Indeed, before long, perhaps in large part owing to the Congress, the Hall began to thrive again. 'There was a great expansion of activity—meetings, seminars, yoga, music-making, dancing, happenings and frequent parties', remembered Cobb.[27] The editorial board of *New Left Review* took to meeting there, and an art show was arranged by four graduates of the Chelsea School of Art, which filled the main hall for about a month. Even Laing eased off a little. Instead of barracking the residents, he began to talk repeatedly about his spiritual concerns, discoursing for hours at a time about Jesus, the transmigration of souls and reincarnation. And so, when he and Jutta did move out of the Hall during November 1966 and into a basement flat in Belsize Park Gardens, it was somehow less of a wrench. Two more birds had flown, but the nest itself continued to flourish.

For Berke's part, this was now the time of the organisation he remembered best, with frequent meetings either at Laing's flat or his own in St. George's Terrace, long evenings of wine, pot and conversation. The lounge of the Belsize flat looked onto a small garden, and, as was becoming *de rigueur,* Laing and Jutta kept it extremely simple: a couple of Persian rugs, a record player, a mattress, and some candles—all kept at ground level—being amongst the few possessions in evidence; everything else pushed out of view, so as not to spoil the effect of elegance and spiritual inquiry.

Meanwhile, Berke set the Kingsley Hall community to work on a magazine, *Fire,* so named to symbolise the 'inner explosion of existentialist experience'.[28] This was a labour of love, a thin, folio-sized magazine of great beauty and simplicity containing *inter alia* poems by Cobb and Roberta, essays by Cooper and Gary Snyder, and art work by Paul Zeal's girlfriend Frances Horne and the South African artist Harry Trevor, who had moved into Kingsley Hall following a suicide attempt. To help pay for it, Berke hooked up with an American heiress called Panna Grady (Panna G. or 'Pan of Gravy', as the cynics put it), who lived on one of the Nash terraces facing Regents Park, next door to Feliks Topolski, and who was friendly with many of the original Beat writers. Laing contributed a couple of prose poems, full of the familiar word games:

> I am afraid of myself
> The self one is afraid of
> is
> the self that is afraid of

the self that is afraid of
the self that is afraid.

I am doing it
the it I am doing is
the I that is doing it
the I that is doing it is
the it I am doing
it is doing the I that is doing it
I am being done by the it I am doing
it is doing it [29]

Fig 6. Front cover of the first volume of Fire. Artwork by Frances Horne and Jutta Werner. Private Collection.

*

By the end of the year the organisers had reduced the speakers to ten or eleven, most with either anti-psychiatric and/or Kingsley

Hall connections. The main exception amongst this new, more limited, group was Herbert Marcuse, the German philosopher of 'repressive tolerance' fame and the books *Eros and Civilization* (1955) and *One-Dimensional Man* (1964). The latter was a particular favourite of Laing, who had reviewed it in glowing terms for *New Left Review* during the summer of 1964, pointing out its 'powerful, subtle' and 'compelling impact' and its 'beautiful dying cadence', the 'sad and bitter song of an aging scholar' from the Germany of Brecht and Benjamin.[30]

Erving Goffman was still on this current list as was Ernest Mandel and Mircea Eliade; all dropped out, however — Goffman at a very late stage and ostensibly for personal reasons, though it possibly had more to do with the quartet's radical politics. Amongst the other presumptive speakers at this stage were the philosopher and sociologist, Lucien Goldmann, Paul Goodman, Jules Henry, and a new addition to the original list of twenty-seven, the writer and Latin America specialist, John Gerassi, one of Berke's co-teachers at FUNY and a recent visitor to Kingsley Hall. Gerassi's *The Great Fear in Latin America* (1963) was required reading on the left at this point.

That said, still at the forefront of everyone's minds was the prospect of attracting Sartre himself, then close to the height of his extraordinary and, some would argue, maleficent pre-eminence. Laing and Cooper, of course, had studied Sartre in great depth. One of the first fruits of their collaboration had been the aforementioned study of his post-second world war philosophy, *Reason and Violence* (1964); and in terms of their own thinking about violence he was, after all, their major influence.

Although Sartre knew of their interest in his philosophy, they carried little weight. Thus, when Laing first wrote to the philosopher he couldn't even be bothered to reply, and when he did, following further letters, it was to turn them down on grounds that neither Laing nor Cooper found convincing. Berke then took charge of the enterprise, putting some mild pressure on John Gerassi, who it was presumed did have influence as his father Fernando Gerassi was Sartre's friend and he himself the philosopher's so-called 'non-God son'. 'What we had in mind was that he might come over for two or three days, during which he would reside at Rotherfield Hall', he wrote Gerassi at the beginning of December, thus before the country house idea had foundered. Sartre's speech, he added, would be widely publicised and televised. 'Either Dr Laing or Dr Cooper would be quite willing to go to Paris at any time at Sartre's convenience to discuss these matters with him.'[31] This approach also failed, however, with Gerassi replying that Sartre had already committed himself to going to Russia during the summer, making him unavailable for the Congress in any case.

*

Calvin Hernton was given the honour of informing the wider public of the Congress during the second half of January 1967, through the medium of *International Times*, like Kingsley Hall, an organ closely associated with LSD and the drug culture. Hernton, having left Kingsley Hall for Sweden during the summer of 1966, had returned to London around Christmas, attracted by Berke's suggestion that he should take on the role of 'court reporter'.[32] 'This summer, in July, the Institute of Phenomenological Studies will make the move. A congress will convene in London on the Dialectics of Liberation', he said 'The entire world as we "know" it must be demystified.[33]

He then revealed the new list of principal speakers, including Laing and Cooper themselves, who the group planned to top and tail the Congress. 'But', he added, 'the list of names on the present announcement is far from complete: writers, artists, intellectuals, scientists, poets and scores of people who are concerned with and involved in the liberation of modern man will be on hand, both as participants and delegates from all over the world.'[34]

'Right now, such individuals, along with the populations of Western societies are being systematically victimised, hounded and imprisoned and murdered. Malcolm X has been silenced. An army psychiatrist who refused to instruct American soldiers how to use gases and drugs to murder people in Vietnam is undergoing court martial for treason' — this possibly being a mangled reference to the celebrated case of Captain Howard Levy, who was indeed court-martialled, and eventually sentenced to three years of hard labour for refusing to train his fellow servicemen to administer drugs, and for fomenting 'disaffection' amongst his comrades.[35]

'There will be a 15 guineas fee to bear the expenses of the congress which at the moment are being met by the Institute alone. For those who want but cannot afford to attend [all of] the congress, fee reductions may be made,' he concluded.[36]

Some of these aforementioned 'writers, artists, intellectuals, scientists, poets and scores of people' who the quartet expected to contribute to the Congress were just as eminent as the speakers themselves. Certainly no one could ever accuse Berke or the others of lack of ambition. Once the organisation really got going, potential participants were invited from all over the world, though, naturally, the emphasis was still very much on the European and North American left, and then social scientists for the most part, many intellectually distinguished or tipped for intellectual distinction.

Some Laing invited, others Cooper or Redler, but by far the most part of the invitations were written by Berke, who must have spent hours at a time combing the pages of publications like *New Society, New Statesman, New Left Review* and the U.S.-based *Monthly Review* for appropriate candidates. He must have invited hundreds, and then some.

Some of these men — and they were almost all men — were friends of the quartet: the anthropologist (and Laing's near neighbour) Francis Huxley for one, was very friendly with Laing; the sociologist and writer Robin Blackburn was friendly with Berke. Other members of the board of *New Left Review,* upon which Blackburn sat, were very friendly with Cooper, who had indeed, like Laing, contributed to the magazine's pages, and who met with them regularly for discussions on historical and theoretical matters. And then *these* friends led the quartet to *their* friends, forming an ever-widening network of left-wing or at least left-leaning intellectuals.

Redler, perhaps the most socially concerned of the foursome, focused most of his attention on people in the peace movement and civil rights. He invited, amongst others, the folk singers Julie Felix and Joan Baez, the comedian and civil rights activist Dick Gregory and Stokely Carmichael, the increasingly radical chairman of the Student Nonviolent Coordinating Committee (SNCC), the body of civil rights activists that had supported him during his own days of activism as a student. Obviously, the quartet hoped that the entertainers amongst these figures would contribute their creative talents to the occasion. 'We are planning daily lectures and seminars and some weekend and evening events, but we look to the spontaneous development of discussions, poetry readings, singing, dancing and inner or outer directed "happenings"', he told Felix during February.[37]

Learning that Baez had recently co-founded an Institute for the Study of Non-Violence, Redler extended his invitation to the Institute as well, promising the presence of such luminaries as Laing's pal, Alan Sillitoe, and Peter Cadogan—secretary of the anti-nuclear Committee of 100—and of the African-American journalist and civil rights campaigner, William Worthy. Like Berke, he also picked up on many of his friends and associates back in the States, in particular those who had supported him in his anti-nuclear activities, reminding one eminent academic, the cardiologist Dr Quentin Deming, that Deming had signed a petition that he had prepared against the shelter signs on campus at Albert Einstein.

But it was to Carmichael that he sent one of the fullest descriptions of the quartet's hopes for the Congress, using much of the same language as Laing and Cooper had used in earlier letters and articles. They had set up the IPS, he informed Carmichael, with the express purpose of extending their work beyond the families of schizophrenics, as any progress achieved in that department would of necessity remain incomplete if the rest of society remained 'mystified'.

> In this congress we shall address ourselves to the need for demystification and liberation in a society permeated with violence—from the violence inflicted on the child in inducing him to sell out his possibilities of being, through the violence of the Bomb, Viet-Nam, and the socio-economic and political fact that is Watts or Harlem.[38]

'What we arrive at', Redler added, 'may be a possible point of departure. There will probably be some sort of direct public impact, but this will be inevitably short-lived.' A 'longer life', he then said, would be guaranteed, by a book containing some of the Congress's deliberations. 'But above all we must aim at a lasting trans-national nexus of insights into our condition that cuts across the divisions of East, West and Third Worlds. We must maintain this connection of insights as a basis for action — action that will clarify, inform and influence governmental policies all over the world. The precise nature of this potential field of action will be central to our deliberations.'[39]

*

Whilst the book mentioned by Redler was probably the most commercially successful direct offshoot to emerge from the Congress, it wasn't the only one; the men also planned a film and a series of long-playing records.[40]

Berke was initially keen to recruit a Polish filmmaker. In November 1966 he wrote to the film critic Peter Wollen, i.e., 'Lee Russell' of *New Left Review*, asking for advice, having already discussed the matter with Wollen and with another *New Lefter*, Alexander Cockburn. But Wollen was against the idea. Then what about someone or some group from the Third World, Berke suggested: 'Possibly Cuban, [or] possibly a group from, say, Czechoslovakia'.[41]

However, by February he had returned to the Polish option, contacting first Jerzy Skolimowski, then Andrzej Wadja, the first best known in England for his semi-autobiographical films and for his collaborations with Roman Polanski, the second for his series of 1950s anti-war films. 'I have been told of your work in the cinema by friends of mine in London, and I would be interested to know if you might be interested in making a film of this congress', he informed Skolimowski, on the 17th. 'The purpose of the film would be to disseminate, on a large scale, the work of the congress to people on an intellectual basis.'[42]

But nothing came of the idea. The quartet never appointed an 'official' filmmaker. Nevertheless, at least three films (of a sort) were made of the Congress: one by BBC filmmaker Roy Battersby, who also recorded the congress for the LPs with his friend Ben Churchill, one by Dutchman Robert Klinkert and the writer and filmmaker Iain Sinclair, and one — and the only one to be focused on the Congress exclusively — by freelancer Peter Davis for New York's Channel 13, where it was shown in a science series.

*

Late in December 1966, the quartet released a short leaflet or manifesto presenting their viewpoints and aims. It was probably this that alienated Goffman, as it certainly alienated others. If the style is anything to go by, it was probably a collaborative piece. And like most works of that nature, it is a hotch-potch, strident and awkward in tone, seemingly patched together from Laing's, Cooper's and some of the other speakers' leading ideas and perspectives.

'All men are in chains', it begins, thereby echoing the opening words of Rousseau's *Social Contract*. 'There is the bondage of poverty and starvation: the bondage of lust for power, status, possessions.'

> A reign of terror is now perpetrated and perpetuated on a global scale.
> In the affluent societies, it is masked. There, children are conditioned by violence called love to assume their position as the would-be inheritors of the fruits of the earth. But, in the process, they are reduced to little more than hypothetical points on a dehumanized co-ordinate system.
> For the rest, terror is not masked. It is torture, cold starvation, death.
> The whole world is now an irreducible whole.
> The properties of this whole world system force us to submit to the fatality of Vietnam, the starvation of the third world, etc.
> In total context, culture is against us, education enslaves us, technology kills us.
> We must confront this. We must destroy our vested illusions as to who, what, where we are. We must combat our self-pretended ignorance as to what goes on and our consequent non-reaction to what we refuse to know.
> We experience what is and what is being done through the filter of our socially approved lies. But what is, is not the limit of what is possible.
> We shall meet in London on the basis of a wide range of expert knowledge. The dialectics of liberation begins with the clarification of our present condition.[43]

Reading these words, one of Berke's correspondents, an M.H. Arnold, writing from Warrington, in Cheshire, observed that it all seemed 'uncommon nonsense' as it was 'certainly bad English'.[44] The folk singer Pete Seeger called it 'scholargok': 'I must confess that I feel strongly that whoever wrote it should learn how to write the English language more as it is spoken,' he suggested.[45] Another writer, Nigel Young, then a prominent peace activist, wondered why the quartet had omitted any mention of wars of mass-destruction. Surely, they were the 'great facts of our situation?';[46] whilst a B.L. Lewis, writing from Switzerland, thought the flyer 'provocative but obscure.' He, for one, he added, had '"no vested illusions"', so was it not presumptuous of the organisers to suggest as much? He then wondered if the group was connected with scientology, which was then associated with William S. Burroughs.[47]

During the spring, following Laing's return from a conference abroad, the planning for the Congress moved up another gear with puffing paragraphs in Sweezy's co-edited *Monthly Review,* the American *Humanist* magazine, the *East Village Other,* Paul Johnson's large circulation *New Statesman,* and elsewhere. Already *Peace News'* features editor Roger Barnard had jumped into the space opened up by Calvin Hernton's *IT* article, with a long, analytical, piece on the paper's front page, describing the speakers as 'brilliant but unclassifiable' and the congress itself as an absolutely necessary project of '*subversive re-education,* back to first principles!'[48]

Berke kept everyone on their toes, drawing in further help from Kingsley Hall and writing letter after letter, sometimes adopting a sour or hectoring note, as befitted a man with what was inevitably becoming a virtually all-consuming passion. He bugged editors of radical magazines all over North America and Europe to put something about the Congress in their pages. Thus he requested Paul Goodman to put some mild pressure on *Liberation,* the anarchist magazine with which he was closely associated: 'We have written on several occasions to *Liberation* magazine in the hope that they would print an announcement of the congress, such as I enclose—I have had no luck in this regard, do you think you might have a word with them about it[?]'[49]

He also used his burgeoning connections in Europe's and America's mainstream universities, calling upon a host of people to publicise the Congress, many of them either teaching or studying politics, psychology or sociology. Some, like Richard Clifton, the President of the Students' Union at Warwick, put up posters or dropped leaflets, as did Brian Showler at Hull, Nicholas Johnson at Oxford, and Philip Elliott at the Centre for Mass Communications at Leicester. Others formed discussion groups with the dual purpose of raising awareness of the Congress and of preparing themselves for the speeches and seminars.

*

As for the two main anti-psychiatric contributors to the Congress, to a large extent they were already happily promoting themselves, with Laing's slim book *The Politics of Experience and The Bird of Paradise* (Penguin) leaping off the shelves and Cooper's *Psychiatry and Anti-Psychiatry* (Tavistock) garnering mostly respectful reviews in both the psychiatric and the popular media. Both books were opportunistic, being mostly compilations of previous articles nipped and tucked to bring them up to date (both were published during the first months of 1967). The contents were thus angrier than on their first appearances, more in tune with the era's increasing rebelliousness.

Cooper, by far the less fluent writer, quarried his book from articles in *New Left Review, Views, New Society* and the *British Medical Journal*, the latter a co-authored account of Villa 21, which he wittily re-titled 'Appendix: The question of results. An ironic addendum', thus signalling his continuing contempt for the pseudo-facticity of positivist methodology.[50] Laing's book included amongst its most celebrated pieces yet another re-working of his influential 'Violence and Love' lecture. It now had a juicier introduction. The only really new piece as far as the larger public were concerned was *The Bird of Paradise* itself, a potpourri from his copious notebooks. If it shocked and dismayed Laing's orthodox critics, that was its intention. He bookended the volume with some of his most startling apophthegms: 'Few books today are forgivable'; 'We are all murderers and prostitutes'; and 'If I could turn you on, if I could drive you out of your wretched mind, If I could tell you, I would let you know.'[51]

The pair also brought Foucault's *Madness and Civilization* to the attention of English audiences. Tavistock published a translation during April, part of a series edited by Laing called 'Studies in Existentialism and Phenomenology', with an introduction by Cooper. The book, the first major work by the Frenchman to reach English audiences, was startling in its impact. Quickly, it established a wholly new historical orthodoxy. Briefly, that the eighteenth century had seen the medicalisation of whole areas of hitherto normal human experience.

This, of course, was grist to the anti-psychiatric mill. Both men foregrounded the resemblances, Laing in a glowing review of the book for *New Statesman* in June, Cooper in his introduction. 'Foucault', Laing said, 'does not "take sides". He simply brings into view a few turns of the amplifying spiral ... the madness of the apparent sanity of "reason"'. [52]

Widely reviewed, the book inspired a special edition of *Peace News*, in May, to which Cooper contributed the opening chapter of *Psychiatry and Anti-Psychiatry*. There he repeated his notorious praise of the French writer and mental patient Antonin Artaud from his 1965 *Views* article. Artaud's so-called '"delusional statements"' had more to tell us about madness, he said, than an entire library of psychiatric textbooks.[53]

With this going on and with the two men stepping on each other's toes in other areas as well, not least in the fall-out from a pioneering and popular BBC television play,[54] it is perhaps not surprising that Laing's son, Adrian, has written of a 'guru war' between the two men. He instances Laing's *New Statesman* review of *Madness and Civilization* as a prime example of Laing's need to exert his 'perceived dominance' over his avowedly more political associate.[55] Cooper's introduction was 'too short', Laing suggested, providing his own much longer account of the book's contents.[56]

Perhaps some degree of conflict was inevitable when the two men were sharing the same stages so much. Both, to give a further instance, took part in a free university at the LSE during Easter.[57]

Yet, as Adrian Laing also remarks, the two had a 'deep affection and admiration' for each other.[58] Laing would fall out with a lot of people, but never with David Cooper. He respected their differences. 'He was very quick, and was several degrees past most people. I don't meet many people like him and he didn't meet many people like me', are some of the words Laing uses of David Cooper in the interviews he gave to Bob Mullan, during the late 1980s.[59] He thus forgave Cooper much, particularly his criticisms of Kingsley Hall, of which Cooper was never an admirer.

*

Having received final confirmation, during the first few weeks of 1967, that Rotherfield Hall would not be hosting the Congress, the quartet were forced to look for another house where the speakers (and their families) could gather, sleep, and take part in other 'behind the scenes' activities. By this time, Redler had already contacted Muriel Lester, the generous and trusting owner of Kingsley Hall to ask if she knew of a house that the quartet could borrow, but this was unsuccessful. He did, however, find a large, terraced house in Elsham Road between the Shepherd's Bush and Kensington tube stations, via an ad in the personal columns of *The Times*, which he rented from July 13 to the 31st. Then he also booked further space for the participants in a slightly seedy hotel in Knightsbridge.

Most of the 'alphas'—as the quartet had now begun to describe the speakers to distinguish them from a group of younger people who had agreed to help with the running of the Congress (betas) and the 'registrants at large' (gammas)—started to arrive just before the middle of July; they therefore missed a press conference that the quartet had arranged as a further means of drumming up publicity. This took place during the second week of June at Laing's flat in Belsize Park Gardens. By then the quartet had at last established a more or less definitive list of speakers around whom the Congress would coalesce: Jules Henry, Erving Goffman (who as I've said withdrew), Stokely Carmichael, Paul Sweezy (editor of *Monthly Review*) and Gregory Bateson (anthropologist and co-developer of the, previously mentioned, 'double-bind' theory of human communication) for the first week, followed by an 'open forum' session on the Saturday. Then Goodman, Goldmann, Ernest Mandel (who also withdrew), Gerassi, and Marcuse for the second week, the whole event topped and tailed by an introductory speech by Laing on the 15th and a valedictory address from Cooper on the third and final Saturday, followed by a happening from Carolee Schneemann and a concert from the pop group The Social Deviants.

The happening was Berke's idea, of course. He had been booting it around for months, ever since the Roundhouse had been settled on as the focus for the Congress's activities, but it was only now that he was finally able to put some flesh on it, for as ever he had had problems finding the money to support it. But then Panna Grady had offered to help. So, the happening was on. The problem for Schneemann was then to work out what she was going to do, though it was always understood that it would have something to do with the speakers' words and how they could be challenged by a countering physicality.

The press conference at Laing's flat found the quartet in an exuberant mood. Laing joshed with the assembled journalists. When someone asked him what the 'dialectics' in the title of the Congress meant, he described it as a 'problematical, hackneyed, [and] tarnished' word.[60] And it was Berke who gave the proper definition, adding that the purpose of the Congress was 'the demystification of the circumstances in which we find ourselves.'[61]

Filmmaker Roy Battersby was there representing himself and the BBC, Richard Boston *The Times Literary Supplement*, Judy Froshaug *Nova* magazine, Paul Barker *New Society* and, another well-known journalist, Sally Vincent *The Times* (a few years earlier she'd had an affair with Laing and the two had remained in close contact).

Then there was director Mike Hodges for ITV, Tom Maschler for publisher Jonathan Cape, Allen Woods for the communist *Morning Star,* and Bob Overy from *Peace News*. Amongst the other famous or not-so famous faces at the event, Berke spotted Michael Abdul Malik, otherwise known as Michael X, the notably controversial activist and crook. For the most part, however, celebrities, journalistic and otherwise, were few and far between, and the broadsheets beyond *The Times* noticeable by their absence.

Fig 7. Congress poster. From Peter Davis's *Anatomy of Violence*, 1967. Courtesy Peter Davis, www.villonfilms.com

Amongst the betas who agreed to help with the daily running of the Congress were people from the United States, but by far the majority were London-based and of those most had connections with Kingsley Hall, either as residents or as allies in the Laing group's battle against conventional psychiatry. These were allotted various roles. Some were tasked with publicity, printing flyers, putting up posters, those sorts of things, while others were asked to set out the chairs or to help with the construction of a platform.[62]

The die was cast. Following more than a year of preparation, the Dialectics was about to become a reality.

4. Welcome to the Roundhouse

The Congress opened during the afternoon of Saturday, July 15, with the sun in the sky and with the prospect of several more days of fine weather. Berke hadn't been back to the States since the death of his mother during the Spring of 1966, so he must have been pleased to see some of his American friends either seated and chatting in small groups near the platform or milling about elsewhere in the building.

Although the Roundhouse had been used for other events since the fund-raiser for *International Times* the previous year, and most recently an 'Angry Arts Week' programme for opponents of the war in Vietnam, it was still in much the same state as when Berke had first seen it, which is to say, in filmmaker Iain Sinclair's words, a 'stone circus tent': vast, rusty, crumbling and dusty.[1]

Fig 8. The Roundhouse. From Peter Davis's *Anatomy of Violence*, 1967. Courtesy Peter Davis, www.villonfilms.com

Sinclair was there with his friend Robert Klinkert in hopes of speaking to Allen Ginsberg about a feature the pair wanted to make about him. But he wasn't entirely fixed on Ginsberg at that point, and he kept an eye and an ear out for other celebrities.

By mid-afternoon, there were over a thousand people in the building. Some, perhaps the majority, had bought a ticket for Laing's speech alone; others had bought tickets for a selection of the speeches or all of them. Still others had paid money for all the speeches and the panel discussions and the afternoon and evening lectures and seminars. This last group were the so-called registrants, a group of about two hundred and fifty people. Some of them wore little yellow badges with their names on them, proof that they had paid the £15 15 shillings that the IPS had demanded of them.

Inevitably, most of these people were British. But there was also a very heavy and vocal North American presence and a smattering of Germans, French, Italians, Norwegians, Danes, Indians, and other nationalities. Most of the North Americans were students from the United States, many with ties to the London School of Economics (LSE) or to one of the other London colleges. Others were conscientious objectors, while a still smaller number had flown into London, attracted by the advertisements the IPS had put in various radical publications.

Like the British and other foreign nationals, each of these North Americans brought to the congress their own concerns about violence. But the major ones they shared with almost everyone at the Roundhouse: the escalating Vietnam War, the 'racial' crisis in the United States' larger towns and cities, and the role or non-role of the working class and the so-called 'white liberal' in solving these issues. Then they were also motivated by some of the same educational ideas that had inspired Berke and the other members of the IPS to put the Congress together in the first place.

*

At about three o'clock, the major speakers and Carolee Schneemann introduced themselves to the audience.[2] Each took a couple of minutes to speak about their work and what they hoped to bring to the Congress. When his turn came, Stokely Carmichael read from the Martinican psychiatrist and philosopher Frantz Fanon's book *Black Skin White Masks*. Already feeling that he was a token presence amongst so many white, mostly armchair intellectuals, it was a strong signal that much of his contribution to the Congress would concern racism. But what set the event apart was not politics or social issues in the purest sense, but Carolee Schneemann's description of her plan for a closing night happening. This drew a loud protest from Paul Goodman.

Schneemann would, she said, develop the happening from the issues and debates that came up during the Congress. It would be a 'shared process' drawing on the full space of the Roundhouse and grounded in a generational shift in 'art-life attitudes', away from the notion of the idea of the artist as alienated towards a much more communal, integrative and trusting experience.[3] And she asked for volunteers from the audience, both for a core group of nine or ten performers and for a mass group of more than twenty.

Unfortunately, neither Laing nor Goodman welcomed her proposal. Goodman was particularly insulting. Springing up from where he had been sitting amongst the audience, he said that he and the other speakers should have been 'consulted' before she was invited. 'Why in the world would we want her to do this sort of thing?' he ranted.[4] His objections were probably partly based on the image he had of himself as a plain-speaking man of letters, with little time for a work that he didn't think was a proper happening anyway. But there was also an element of misogyny. For, on the whole, Goodman didn't like women and particularly not young, highly articulate and free-spirited ones like Schneemann.[5]

But, in any case, this question of the happening's validity would also preoccupy several other people at the Congress, including a group of students. They objected to the happening on the grounds that it was 'imperialistic' and far too individual.[6] Nonetheless, for now at least the happening would go ahead, though shorn, as Schneemann was furious to discover, of much of its budget.

*

Curiously it wasn't Laing or Cooper who kicked off the Congress proper that afternoon, but Gregory Bateson on the extraordinary grounds that both men were too shy to do it. This, of course, was nonsense. But it gave Bateson an opportunity to quickly introduce himself before any of the other speakers. 'My name is Bateson. And I work in anthropology, and I have worked in zoology, and I have worked in psychiatry' — and to set out his own position as a sort of 'referee' between the other speakers at the Congress.[7]

Bateson had arrived in London for the Congress from Paris, where he had stopped off after attending a symposium in Austria and had brought with him his third wife, Lois, and his teenage son, John, thus signalling that, for him, the Congress was also a family occasion. He was sixty-two in July 1967, an immensely intelligent yet modest man, whose accumulated wisdom and puckish wit would offer a stark challenge to the people at the Congress demanding quick or merely political answers to the world's problems.

Laing, as previously mentioned, had been familiar with Bateson's work in psychiatry since at least 1962, and like many psychiatrists working in the US though rather fewer working in the UK, he was deeply influenced by the concept of the 'double bind'. But there was more to Bateson than just one idea even on such a profoundly difficult subject as schizophrenia. As he said himself in his introduction, he was also an anthropologist and had been a zoologist, both of which fields, plus psychiatry, continued to influence his present work, not least in the interdisciplinary and interlinked fields of communication studies, cybernetics, and ecology.

The first speaker Bateson introduced was David Cooper, who he described as the IPS's director. Cooper's task was to give a brief outline of the ideas which had inspired the IPS to organise the Congress in the first place and to say something about what he thought the Congress might achieve, as a prelude to Laing's opening lecture.

Unlike Bateson, whose spoken English was authoritative, yet warm, Cooper's voice was unmistakably Anglo-Saxon officer class (despite his South African background), the words pronounced in sometimes unfamiliar ways, each syllable given its full fruity value.

In their practice of psychiatry—or of anti-psychiatry, he added—the IPS was, he said, concerned to understand madness as it was conventionally understood as a sane response to insane circumstances. Real madness wasn't in them, i.e., 'patients', or, to put it another way, 'scapegoats'; it was in us or rather in society's institutions and in the ostensibly powerful people who ran them. It was time to demystify the mystifications.

Assembled in the Roundhouse both today and over the following fortnight were some of the social sciences' greatest scholars, he went on, thereby tactlessly forgetting to include Allen Ginsberg and Stokely Carmichael, who though not scholars in the formal sense were undoubtedly men of great intelligence and distinction.

One of the main tasks before the Congress, he said, was to find ways of connecting the expertise that these scholars brought with them to the ordinary decisions of politicians.

Perhaps they could evolve an international network that would influence governmental policies, he suggested, and develop a form of guerrilla activity suited to the sorts of conflicts taking place in countries like Vietnam and Bolivia. They could also turn every school, university, theatre, and hospital into a revolutionary nexus.

Finally, he concluded his speech with brief definitions of dialectics, phenomenology, and liberation. Liberation was not necessarily better than the unfreedom it replaced, he said; in fact, sometimes it wasn't even progress. But it was 'real'. It meant living in and through the dialectics that ran like an electrical current through every single life, the duality of living life as both oppressor and oppressed.

*

Although Cooper's speech was applauded, the response was respectful rather than enthusiastic. It was therefore Laing who provided the first, genuine, intellectual excitement of the Congress. Not that his manner of speaking was perfect; it was hesitant and rambling. Partly this was because he spoke without a full script, often trusting himself to the thoughts and impressions of the moment.

Laing titled his hour-long speech 'Mediations between the Individual and Society' and began with the observation that what is obvious to one person is not necessarily obvious to another. For instance, Hitler thought it 'obvious' that the Jews were a plague on humanity and should be exterminated.[8] Jews naturally thought otherwise. 'There is nothing more dangerous than the obvious.' If one didn't recognise it, then one would likely fall over it. If one attempted to deny its existence altogether, then one might become involved in 'endless complexities of self-mystification.'

Time, he said, was short. The Congress was meeting at an historical moment that was so 'precarious and dangerous and confusing', that he would do nothing more than state what he thought was obvious. He would speak about the 'social fabric of reality', as it seemed to him, at the micro- and macro-level or, in other words, at the level of the individual and of society.

Now, this was not something that was easy to understand; one couldn't, for instance, isolate a feature of reality and expect to grasp it that way. Reality at that level was unintelligible. No, one had to see it in relation to sub-systems and the sets of contexts with which it was 'interlaced', both spatially and across the generations. And then those sets of contexts had to be seen within the contexts and meta-contexts with which they themselves were interlaced and so on.

This was dialectical thinking, a way of explaining what was going on in a person by what had gone on and what was going on both before them and around them. It was a method of approaching the truth of a situation that both he and Cooper had learned from their study of Sartre.

> What is terrifying is that as we move up through sets of irrationality, rationality, irrationality, rationality and so on and reach the total context, when we get there, we seem to — as far as one can see it - have a glimpse of a total system that appears to be dangerously and horribly out of any control from within any of the sub-systems or sub-contexts that comprise the social system. And we have a theoretical, logical, and practical dilemma of having arrived at an empirical limit which itself appears to be without any obvious intelligibility at all.

Unless, he added, we could understand its rationality from the point of view of some final 'cosmic' pattern. But then that would raise the issue of the sanity of God.

Such sickness as there was, wasn't in individuals, which is to say in people labelled patients: the neurotic, the psychotic, he continued; it was in us: friends, family, institutions, nations and so on, both in the present and in the past.

Psychiatrists weren't cynical; they were no less sincere about what they were doing than he was; they were simply deluded. Indeed, the more drugs they prescribed, the more people's heads they hacked about, the more scandalised they were by the minority of their colleagues who did not employ these practices. As one eminent psychiatrist had said to him during his own days of walking the wards and administering conventional treatments — and here he got one of several laughs, including a loud one from Bateson — '"It's the white man's burden, Ronald. We can't expect any thanks, but we must go on."'

Thousands of people, Laing went on, were involved in this process of social invalidation. In the UK, you were ten times more likely to be sent to a mental hospital than you were to attend a university. It could even be said that psychiatry was practised as a kind of 'guerrilla warfare', in which raids were made on the so-called mentally ill, removing them from their houses by physical force so that they could be attacked with biochemicals, electricity and knives, against which they had no recourse in law whatever. It wasn't those who society labelled sick who needed treatment therefore, but the legalised 'sane' members of society. Granted the former may have broken a few windows or screamed a bit, but most of them harmed no one. Contrast that, he said, with the behaviour of those responsible for the 'mass-exterminations of wars, declared and undeclared'. Their violence far exceeded anything that the mentally ill had ever been guilty of. These, he said, were simply facts, observations that were obvious to him. Yet those who pointed them out — such as himself — risked imprisonment as a danger to themselves if not to others.

He then speculated that perhaps the system's very survival depended on one in every twenty or thirty people being selected as some sort of 'human lightening conductors' and treated as patients accordingly — scapegoated in other words — and who would therefore focus the violence upon themselves, so to ensure the system's survival.

This was a picture of 'Us': Britain, Europe, North America, the West. But Laing went on: what of 'Them'? What of that mass of people living outside of the Western world, the majority of whom were peasants? They were engaged in a war, he said, in which we ourselves could not be neutral. Why? because we were located in a 'social context' that was defined in relation to that very conflict.

Suppose, he said, the Chinese had half a million troops in Mexico, that they had missile bases in Canada, Cuba, and the Pacific Islands, and that their ships and atomic submarines controlled the seas, and that their leaders told them that all of these forces were deployed for no other purpose than to protect the Chinese people from the United States of America. Well, if that was the case, he, for one, would easily understand any American anxieties.

But that was the easy bit, by which he meant that it was relatively simple to put oneself in someone else's shoes in that sort of situation. But what about situations that weren't so easy to understand? Such as the situation of those Americans who felt guilty if they weren't accepted for the draft.

And here he returned once more to the theme of his 'Violence and Love' lecture. Parents, he said, destroyed their children's potential through a process of terrorism masquerading as love. What was needed therefore was a better understanding of the so-called 'normal' individual. Like the mother he had been told about by one of his patients, who had held him out of a six-storey window. Why? Well, to convince her son that she loved him. 'Why else should she do it? That's what she said she was doing it for?' But then, what of her, the mother's mother? he asked. What had she done to provoke her daughter to act like that? 'Evidently [she] never held her out at arm's length and showed her how much she loved her as she should have done', he said to more laughter from Bateson and the audience.

He then riffed off on the psychiatrist Donald Winnicott's writing on the mirror role, the notion that the newborn when looking at its mother's face sees itself. That would be fine, Laing said, if it occurred. But what if the mother looking at her baby's face didn't see the baby, but herself? Just as her mother had seen herself in her daughter's face? What hope was there in that case that the baby would ever find itself?

It was situations like that, he added, which gave rise to the 'paranoid-projective system' through which babies developed a 'collective Us in relationship to a collective Them,' with all the mystifications involved in international relations and otherwise.

While Laing didn't offer a prescription for how the circuitry which maintained this situation could be broken, he thought that one possible remedy might emerge from the study of obedience. To which end, he concluded his speech with what he called a 'morality tale.' This was a long quotation from an academic article describing Yale professor Stanley Milgram's not-yet canonical experiments during which numbers of male volunteers administered what they took to be punishing electrical shocks to other human beings — despite the apparent victims pleading for mercy.

*

Previously, Bateson had asked for written questions only — presumably on the grounds that there were no travelling microphones at that point and that spoken questions would not be picked up by the recording equipment on the platform.

There were a lot of questions for Laing to sort through, so he put them into groups and answered them in clusters. Some people took him to task for underplaying the extent to which people 'chose' to undergo psychiatric treatment; while others wanted to know more about how the relationship between violence in an international context and family groups was mediated.

The fact that some people chose to subject themselves to lobotomies wasn't something that surprised him. Just as some psychiatrists were misguided, so were some patients. In any case, why should patients be any more enlightened than the doctors who treated them? As for himself, if ever he found himself in a situation where he was forced to choose between incarceration in a prison or in a mental hospital, he would choose the prison. After all, at least there, the 'integrity of his actual biochemical system' would not be violated.[9]

He was less articulate about the second group of questions, however. There he struggled, interspersing his response with more ums and ers than ever, revealing that he himself was presently unsure whether the relationship that he had described was more than a metaphor.

At first, he said it was: 'There is more than an analogy. I think on a certain level of schematisation, there is a microscopic, microcosmic, re-enactment of the macroscopic social deployment of forces within family groups.' But then instead of going into further detail, he detoured into the subject of generational conflicts within families, where he was clearly more comfortable.

There were also questions about who, ultimately, was to 'blame' for violence. But these Laing dismissed as beside the point. A 'guerrilla fighter' didn't need to concern himself with whether he hated his enemy or not. What was essential was that he killed him. He then touched on what would become one of the main themes of the Congress: the relationship between violence and counter-violence. For his part, the key to that, he said, was in the *Bhagavad Gita*, which taught that all mankind was one. So that if he killed someone because they were about to murder him, he would in effect be committing suicide and vice versa. 'So, it's six of one and half a dozen of the other, and it may even indeed show a soupçon of compassion if there is any difference to kill him rather than to let him kill me.'

The final question Laing chose to answer was one that he thought would best be answered by the questioner himself. The questioner wanted to know why people had laughed at the parts of Laing's speech describing maternal abuse and other enormities. But if he had to answer it, he would use the words of Nietzsche. He would laugh so he didn't have to cry. But then what did laughing have to do with humour anyway? 'I don't actually regard creasing my circumoral muscles up and emitting sporadic jerks of air which hit my vocal cords, which is called laughter, as indicating in the present state of affairs that I see anything funny at all.' It was simply a convention, he added, an example of a 'socially conditioned' pattern like 'what's a man and what's a woman.'

*

During the early evening, the IPS held a meeting for the registrants, where in *Peace News* journalist Roger Barnard's words, there was 'sharp disagreement' about how the Congress should be organised.[10]

Consistent with their radical educational philosophy and the spirit of the times, Berke and Cooper had dreamed of a free-flowing 'anti-structure'. In Berke's mind, the Congress would be something like FUNY, with everyone free to say what they wanted, when they wanted and to whom they wanted. In Cooper's terms, the pseudo-scientific and bureaucratised relation of teacher to pupil would be abolished.[11] All would explore the space and use it entirely as they wished, improvising talks and other events. But with such a large, disparate, and articulate range of opinion present, it was already clear that if the Congress was to have any hope of meeting its objectives at all then someone — most likely the IPS itself — would have to retain control of parts of it.

Some elements, after all, could not be improvised however radical the quartet's intentions. The lectures, for instance. They had been advertised to take place at particular times in a particular place. But what of the panel discussions planned for the afternoons and the informal seminars to follow them? Would they be similarly 'managed'? Many of the registrants had brought their own material along. They wanted to know when they could read it and they couldn't understand why the IPS thought it necessary to nominate 'conductors' to help them; 'still others want[ed] the Congress to broaden out' from the Roundhouse and make use of Primrose Hill and other green and built-up spaces. They wanted to 'initiate action and protest' in the local community.[12]

Someone even suggested that the roles of 'speaker' and of 'audience' should themselves be 'demystified'. It would have been much better if Laing had sat within the audience; the seats should have been arranged in a circle rather than row upon row. There were complaints, too, about the ubiquity of the microphone. Barnard again: 'There seemed to be many people [at the meeting] who were irked (rightly so, in my opinion) at the way the organisers of the congress were apparently trying to "structure" everything in advance, blocking genuine dialogue by means of a very effective tyranny of the microphone, instead of letting the whole thing just fall into its natural parts.'[13]

On the other hand, the arrangements, such as they were, did meet the approval of the educationalist Aage Rosendal Nielson. This 'distinguished Dane', to use the words of the anarchist Anne Maria Fearon, complimented the organisers on the *lack* of organisation at the Congress. 'I should like to congratulate the people who have dared *not* to organise this congress,' he remarked.[14]

Eventually, a compromise of sorts was reached. The evenings would be left open for spontaneous events and all arrangements would be reviewed on the Wednesday.

*

While Berke and Redler spent the following day finalising the arrangements for a dinner party for later that evening, the speakers were free to fill their own time. For Carmichael and his close colleague, SNCC activist George Ware, it was a chance to hang out with Michael Malik and his fellow black activists Obi Egbuna and Roy Sawh and for Carmichael to make a speech at Hyde Park's Speakers Corner.

The pair had intended to arrive in London on Thursday, the 13th. But Carmichael had been arrested in Atlanta, with the consequence that they missed their flight. Not that this particularly bothered Special Branch or the CIA operatives who had been briefed to follow them. They had simply changed their plans accordingly. But it did inconvenience the IPS who, short of money already, were forced to make a plea for donations to cover the cost of booking new flights.

For Ginsberg, this was also the Sunday of the Hyde Park Legalise Pot Rally, an event organised by campaigners Steve Abrams and Caroline Coon in hope of influencing the legalisation of hashish and marijuana. So, he, too, was at Speakers Corner.

'Flower Power', which Ginsberg had been associated with since the winter of 1965, had arrived in London. Ginsberg, drug taker and consciousness expander extraordinaire, was its poet, prophet, and starriest blossom.

He arrived at the rally during the afternoon, wearing black trousers, a string of rudraksha beads, a scarlet satin shirt and carrying a pink carnation and a harmonium. The shirt was a gift from Paul McCartney, with whom he had partied the night before. McCartney had drawn psychedelic patterns on it. 'A souvenir of swinging London', McCartney called it.[15]

The police, who were mostly unobtrusive on the occasion, had no objection to Ginsberg talking about mysticism, religion and universal love. 'Shiva, god of meditation, asceticism, birth, death, change, creation, destruction, and ganga.'[16] But they did object to him chanting and playing the harmonium.

However, all in all, it was an overwhelmingly good-natured event. 'If the demonstration proved anything for the believers in "pot",' wrote a sympathetic journalist for the *Birmingham Evening Post* in the following morning's newspaper, 'it also proved the enormous tolerance of London police and the unamazed park strollers who watched it.'[17]

*

The dinner party the IPS held for the speakers at the house in Elsham Road was designed to be one of those behind-the-scenes-of-the-congress get-togethers, an opportunity for good fellowship and deep discussion. With sundry family members there as well, it should have been a civilised event. But with various jealousies and animosities already brewed and new ones brewing, conversation turned out to be only one of the things on the menu.

It didn't help that a mysterious 'someone' had already put cat mess on Carmichael's bed. That could be dealt with as indeed it was by Berke. But then there was a kerfuffle involving Carolee Schneemann's invitation. She was invited. But to the wrong address, another Elsham Road—she thought deliberately. Furthermore, it was on this occasion that Laing decided to 'pull a number' and put Carmichael in his place, which he had decided was considerably below his. Why? Well, that is a matter of debate. But probably it was because with the equally handsome and charismatic Carmichael around, he was simply no longer the centre of attention.[18] 'Ah, Carmichael. A Scottish name,' he said, when the pair were first properly introduced. 'It must mean that one of my ancestors owned one of your ancestors.'[19] Not only was this remark stupid; it was also, of course, exceptionally offensive, as were other remarks that Laing is reported to have made to Carmichael that evening.

Naturally, following this, Carmichael decided that he didn't want to spend any more time either at Elsham Road or with Laing. He thus packed his bags and moved elsewhere, consequently limiting any further opportunities for the kind of informal dialogues between himself and the speakers that had always been a key part of the planning for the Congress. Berke, for his part, was mortified. As for Schneemann, when she did turn up at the party, she was cold shouldered and for some time she sat alone, aghast at the, mainly male, insularity of it all. Not surprising then that her written views of the occasion were caustic. The atmosphere, she concluded, was 'deadly, dull [and] egoistic'.[20]

*

On Monday morning, it was Bateson's turn to speak, a major event in itself, and one that Laing in particular had been looking forward to. Bateson was driven from Elsham Road to the Roundhouse by Jeremy Holmes, one of the 'betas' who was helping to run the congress and who, like several other young men at the Congress, had worked for David Cooper at Villa 21.

It was another bright day and as the sun warmed the pavement outside the building and the waste ground at the back, there seemed to be a more cohesive spirit amongst the registrants than there had been on the Saturday. In Anne Marie Fearon's words, people had begun to 'meet and understand each other.'[21] Over the weekend, little colonies had formed in the gallery that circled the building. As Iain Sinclair put it, the registrants had begun to make the Roundhouse their 'territory'.[22] Some had even brought mattresses and sleeping bags, turning the upper deck into what at times could almost be described as a rolling seminar.

Amongst the celebrities that Sinclair and his friends Robert Klinkert and Christopher Bamford spotted were Michael Malik and Alex Trocchi, Berke and Laing's old Project Sigma partner, the second 'tense, [a] bundle of papers & books under his arm: a street don looking for a guerrilla seminar.'[23] They also picked out Bamford's younger brother, Geoffrey, a hip yet somewhat cynical figure, distanced from his brother by his experience of LSD. Geoffrey had somehow convinced Sinclair that he held the key to the Congress's significance. Meanwhile, he too was there to listen to Bateson.

On Friday Laing had directed people who wanted to buy his books at the Congress to the anarchist bookshop Bookshop 85 on nearby Regents Park Road. Now, a stall had been set up by its pacifist rival, Housmans.

Besides Laing's books and those of Goodman and Marcuse, Ginsberg's new pamphlet *Wichita Vortex Sutra* was available, plus copies of *Fire* magazine, though not *International Times*. Apparently, the organisers had banned it.[24] And then at the back of the auditorium, facing the platform, a sandwich counter was now open, set up and operated by a couple of Berke's friends, Richard and Lesley Goldberg.

Bateson's topic was 'Consciousness versus Nature'.[25] It was a good choice, more philosophical than Laing's, and it tied his offering to the growing realisation that the human capacity for problem-solving might not be such an unmixed blessing after all. Indeed, that without some drastic change to the purpose-driven priorities which underlay consciousness mankind might be doomed to environmental catastrophe.

Five years had elapsed since Rachel Carson's *Silent Spring* had alerted mankind to the damage that pesticides were doing to the environment, and with the slow blossoming of other aspects of environmentalism on both sides of the Atlantic and the additional understanding that Western Man and Homo Sovieticus were really two sides of the same coin, it was a good time to articulate a vision that did not depend on any great engagement with Marxism or with any of the other political doctrines at the Congress.

Not that Bateson was an unpolitical man in the non-party political sense. His politics were rather like those of his late friend, Aldous Huxley: conservative *and* revolutionary, and underpinned by a deep sense of life's interrelatedness. Partly this last characteristic derived from his research in cybernetics—in 1946, he had been a founding member of the famous Macy Conferences with amongst others, Norbert Weiner—but it also owed a lot to his biologist father's pioneering study of genetics (he named the field), to his knowledge of Eastern religions and then to his reading of William Blake and of the other European mystics and visionaries.

*

Following Laing's rambling introduction, Bateson began his speech by referring to the age-old battle between the haves and the have-nots or, as he teasingly put it, between the Romans and the Palestinians. By the Romans, he meant the conquerors of most of Europe, North Africa and the Middle East, the builders of empire and of the Colosseum and stone aqueducts. By the Palestinians, he presumably meant the Jews of prophecy, and the Jews of the second temple period, and then, much later, the Jews of Marxist dialectics, and then possibly too, the Palestinians of the present-day Middle East. His point was this: one could either take sides in this conflict between the haves and the have-nots or choose a third way, the Greek.

That, he said, was his way. Rather than defend the Romans or defend the Jews he would examine the 'bigger problem', the 'pathologies and peculiarities' of the 'whole Romano-Palestinian system,' by which he meant civilisation.[26]

He then made a swift turn to the history of biology.

From the perspective of religion, the biological world, world, the world of animals, plants and *infusoria*, had once been rigid. Explanation was deductive. It began with God. Then the French biologist, Jean-Baptiste Lamarck, came along and turned this hugely influential system on its head by stating that the explanation for the vast abundance of the biological world began with the simplest life forms and that it was best understood through the study of evolution.

And there matters, more or less, stood, he said, until the Second World War. Then cybernetics came along. And we began to understand that natural selection, the engine of evolution, operated as a kind of 'self-corrective system'. It kept [the relationship between] the species steady.'

But then, of course, since then we had learned to recognise many other self-corrective systems, he added. The Congress was dealing with three of them: the individual, the social system, i.e., 'human behaviour', and the ecosystem. In other words, man's natural biological surroundings. Laing, on Saturday, had said that we often found it difficult to see the obvious. Well, why was that? It was simply because anything that disturbed the status quo, destabilised the individual system would be screened out of vision or otherwise isolated like a pearl, so it didn't 'make a nuisance of itself.'

It was the ecosystem that he went on to talk about first, asking the audience to imagine an English oak wood or a tropical forest untouched by spade or plough. 'I may say that very few of you have ever seen such a system; there are not many of them left; they've mostly been messed up by homo sapiens who either exterminated some species or introduced others which became weeds or pests.' Each, in its natural state, would support a variety of species. There would be balance in the 'combination of competition and mutual dependency' based on the 'sort of circuit-structures' that he had mentioned.

The only problems that would arise would be when man intervened. Then that equilibrium would be lost, and one or another species would start to increase exponentially.

For his part, it was a process that he saw happening in Hawaii, where he was presently studying the communicative behaviour of dolphins. 'It is called the population explosion, not inappropriately.' Why? Because it was a sort of chain reaction', he said. 'We are the atom bombs, you see.' Just as there were checks and balances in nature, so there were checks and balances in the lives of individuals and in society. But both could run out of control, a process that, later in the speech, he called 'runaway'.

He then began to talk about mind. Mind, too, was a kind of system. But a peculiarly compartmentalised one. Events that took place in one part of one's mental life were segmented from other parts. Take consciousness, for instance, and here he got to the nub of what he wanted to say. Consciousness wasn't all that the mind consisted of; it was simply part of it, that part of the mind that 'we are aware of', that which got us to where we wanted to go by the shortest possible route. And what it was aware of was just a tiny part of potentially useful information.

He asked himself how this selection was done. The best answer, he said, was that consciousness was guided by purpose. Not that this was necessarily bad. In some contexts, it was clearly not. In fact, it has served humans and possibly some of the other animals for hundreds of thousands of years. In medicine, for instance, purpose might guide us to discover a vaccine, as had been done to prevent polio. But still, it could tell us nothing about the 'body as a systematically, cybernetically organised self-corrective system'. Instead, we had a 'bag of tricks' impressive in their kind, but nothing that we could legitimately describe as wisdom.

What's more, it, purpose, our purposes, were now being augmented by high technology, 'by more and more effective machinery, transportation systems, airplanes, weaponry, medicine and so forth. And the moment you start to do that, then you're beginning to get into a rather serious state. A pathology is proposed, I may say, by this process.'

According to Bateson, it was 'reasonable to suggest' that the loss of balance brought about by man's overwhelming concentration on purposes was behind a 'very great deal' of what had brought them all to the Roundhouse in the first place.

> The systemic nature of the individual human being, the systemic nature of the culture in which he lives, the civilisation in which he lives, and the systemic nature of biological, ecological system around him; and too the curious twist in the systemic nature of the individual man whereby consciousness is, almost of necessity, blinded to the systemic nature of the man himself. That is, you pull out from the total mind sequences which do not have

the loop structure which is characteristic of the whole systemic creature, and you are left, essentially, greedy and unwise.

As on many later occasions during the Congress, Bateson referred to the Bible, refiguring the Garden of Eden as similar to an ecosystem. Frustrated by his inability to reach an apple high in a tree, Adam made a step out of some old logs. He then reached the apple. Adam and Eve then became 'almost drunk with excitement. By God! This was the way to do it ... . You make a plan. A, B, C and you get it.' They then applied this way of doing things to other things in the garden. And soon they'd lost the topsoil. Then Eve wanted a washing machine, 'and Adam therefore had to work harder to get one, and the sort of larger and more human aspects, shall I say of the systemic aspects of their life had gone dry a bit.'

As they had for that matter for most other people in modern civilisations, he said, including President Johnson. The polarised situation in Vietnam was also being treated with too great an emphasis on purpose and too little on the system of which it was a part. That was why the problems that had brought them to the Roundhouse were much more than choosing to support one side or the other, or of adopting this particular strategy or another one. 'The real problem was how to deal with the status and functions of mind and workings, and its pathologies and distortions, and especially ... the problem of consciousness.'

Bateson's solutions were the old ones of education and humility: build 'wisdom' in the 'total population' but particularly 'policymakers' and 'symbol-manipulators' and less scientific arrogance; more creativity, 'dreams, works of art, or the activity of art, or the perception of art, poetry, and such things. These are all ways in which knowledge may be a little bit developed towards wisdom, towards systemic wisdom', though he was notably less enamoured of LSD. 'I'm not sure there are short cuts to wisdom. Maybe I'm an old puritan.'

He ended with a story which he had found in James Stephens' *Irish Fairy Tales* about the Christian missionary Finnian of Morvilla and the reclusive Tuan Mac Cairill. Tuan explained to the missionary that he had two genealogies, that in the first he had been reincarnated as various animals. It was Bateson's way of emphasising that if mankind was to survive then he had to embrace his animal nature.

*

Although parts of Bateson's speech had been inaudible to parts of the audience, like Laing he received a long round of applause. Seemingly, most of the audience had enjoyed his wise, and at times, difficult and amusing presentation. Once again, people had been asked to submit their questions in writing. But after the first question, which was read out by Bateson, this method was abandoned, and people were invited to use a travelling microphone.

The first speaker to take advantage of this dispensation was a ginger-haired and moustachioed New Yorker, a mature student who was writing a book about the mathematical foundations of social psychology. He would often speak at the Congress. Initially inarticulate but determined to say *something*, he asked Bateson if the sort of 'runaway' situations he had described would have been better expressed not in biological terms but in terms of Marxism. After all, any 'imbalance' in a system was essentially a matter of perspective. One group's disastrous Malthusian growth was another group's opportunity.[27]

Bateson accepted that Marx had made a 'considerable contribution' to some of the ideas about interacting social systems that he had mentioned in his speech, but surely, he said, Marx's standpoint, that of a Victorian social scientist, was out of date. We should listen to contemporary voices, people like himself and others at the Congress who had 'sweated' on the subject.

Several speakers asked Bateson to say more about his attitude to illicit drugs, dreams, and art, and to the ways that they could be used to broaden consciousness beyond what was most purposeful. To the first, Bateson said a little more about LSD. Not that he could claim any great knowledge about it, he said, but what he had learned was that its effect was rather like psychoanalysis, in as much as it tended to insulate people from the world rather than encourage them to engage with it.

Dreams, like art, he thought, offered much greater potential for a broadening of consciousness. But it depended on the type of art. Take Haussmann's boulevards in Paris, he said. That sort of artistic expression could never be helpful. 'One comes away from it sort of in despair. And I must say if you look at the faces of the people walking in front of the buildings, that despair is not alleviated.'

There was also a striking question from a North American man about the relevance of Bateson's statements to black people in the United States and to the people of Vietnam. Talk of the 'wisdom of total systems' was all to the good, he remarked, but to these people it was a 'luxury'. One needed to find a way of integrating both perspectives. Perhaps surprisingly, Bateson agreed with him. 'I object only to the word "luxury", he said, He then ran through a number of ways in which during the next ten to thirty years 'with the implementation of purposes', there was an 'even chance' of mankind destroying itself. It could be done, for example, by a resumption of above-ground nuclear weapons tests, by nuclear war itself or by the burning of fossil fuels.

> CO_2 is transparent to light but is opaque to heat. If therefore we move up the CO_2 figure in the atmosphere, [then] long before we start to asphyxiate the temperature of the world will go up of the order of, average shall we say, 5 degrees. Somewhere at that point, the icecaps melt, the polar caps; the sea level rises of the order of 300 feet and agriculture goes out of business. Period.

Essentially, this was a version of the global warming thesis of the Victorians Svante Arrhenius and Thomas Chamberlain which had been revived recently in an appendix to a report by the US President's Science Advisory Committee, and then popularised by the biologist Barry Commoner, the author of a best-selling book called *Science and Survival*. However, neither the Advisory Committee nor Commoner were as pessimistic as Bateson. The Advisory committee, as cited by Commoner, said that the amount of CO_2 in the atmosphere might be enough to melt the Antarctic ice cap in either 400 or 4000 years—depending on the model used—whereas

Bateson as his estimates suggest thought a fraction of the first figure the more likely possibility.

But, in any case, the effect on many of his auditors, unfamiliar with the greenhouse effect, was electric, and it was repeatedly referred to thereafter, not least by Ginsberg, who elsewhere at this point, but having received a summary from Laing, referred to it several times in his own contributions to the Congress.[28]

Bateson ended the Q&A on an additional sober note. 'Now, it is also true that there are a very large number of places in the world where what is happening to human beings shouldn't happen to dogs. [But] it is happening to those human beings as a result of things which I have been talking about." That said, perhaps there were short-term things that people could do; they could, as he said, at the beginning of his speech decide to back the Romans or the Palestinians. 'But I believe the larger problem is one in which it is not a luxury to put attention to. I believe it is an urgent necessity to pay attention to the larger problems.'

*

After lunch, the registrants took their seats for the first panel discussion of the Congress. This was a 'private' event meant to bring Laing's contribution into dialogue with Bateson's. There were five men on the panel that afternoon: Laing, Bateson, Paul Goodman, Francis Huxley and Erling Eng, the latter a humourless psychologist from Lexington, Kentucky, with a deep interest in the phenomenologist and neurologist Erwin Straus, and an inability to enter into any of the other panellists' viewpoints.

Unfortunately, the chairman, a psychiatrist friend of Laing named Ross Speck, was unable to prevent the speakers from talking over each other, and Goodman from shamelessly playing to the gallery. Probably he felt intimidated. But, in any case, his unassertiveness and obvious modesty were a poor advertisement for his later role as one of the Congress's major speakers. Laing had persuaded Speck to fill the place vacated by Erving Goffman, even though no one, a few psychiatrists aside, had probably ever heard of him.

Eng kicked off the session by being rude about Gregory Bateson's contribution. He had come to the Congress expecting fresh thinking. But Bateson had delivered a lecture that would not have been out of place over a hundred years ago. What was all this talk about 'systems' he added? For his part, a system was merely something that he figured out 'in different kinds of situations'.[29] As for the system that some people thought was coming together at the Congress, he wasn't minded to think about that one at all, because it didn't 'please [him] to do so.' Bateson had spent far too much time talking about systems as structures when he should have been talking about systems and their 'meaning'.

Then Paul Goodman jumped in with two of his own criticisms. Not only had Bateson misdescribed the individual, as if he or she could ever usefully be discussed independently of any function, but much worse than that was his suggestion that one solution to the imbalance between consciousness and mind in its totality was to encourage policymakers to act more wisely. But the existence of a separate caste of policymakers was exactly what was wrong with modern civilisation, said Goodman. Far better that power should be decentralised. Take the Congress. Several young people had told him earlier that the structure of the Congress was shackling them. They wanted to know what it was they could and couldn't do without 'mortally offending' major figures like himself. It was the same point that he would make again nine or ten minutes later, following further exchanges with Bateson and Eng over the nature of consciousness and the relative place of thought as opposed to habit. Why can't we be 'really conservative and ... a little more neolithic about the matter' of wisdom and authority, he asked. 'See, and let the kids be. Let's not try to teach them some ecology. Let's maybe try and dissolve the university [and implicitly the panel] altogether.'

This was a cue for Huxley to join in, with a short discourse upon the nature of technology during the neolithic period. But this was far from Goodman's point. And after a few more or less bad-tempered exchanges about the value of making distinctions between objects and between types of consciousness, Goodman flew at him with one of his sharpest put-downs: 'The way I'm going to get out of that, Francis, [which was to say, Huxley's insistence on the necessity of making distinctions], is just to say that it's the manners of your conversation that you make that kind of point and it's the manners of my kind of conversation that I'll make an ad hominem point and say that you're not serious.'

Shortly after that Bateson told Goodman to 'shut up', a remark which received a round of applause from the audience.

And so, the conversation continued for over an hour in much the same vein, Bateson and Laing offering wisdom and humour, Goodman and Huxley offering wisdom and wit, Eng mostly sitting silent and with an occasional spoken intervention from a registrant. The panellists spoke about the relationship between the macro- and the micro-level, thus, again, picking up on Laing's presentation, about animals and games and about the 'revolting' nature of politics and about power and its relationship to money.

One of Bateson's stories about animals concerned their difficulty communicating intentions to others of their kind. Without language in the human sense, they were forced to rely on bodily hints. For instance, baring a fang to indicate their readiness for combat. But what if at the same time they wanted to indicate that they did not want to fight? In other words, to communicate two meanings? They lacked the means to do this. So, they would fight. 'And this', Bateson added 'is the old and royal road towards making friends at animal levels and primitive society levels and rather unfortunately it's in a mess among human beings.' Which, Goodman being Goodman and unlike Bateson a non-biologist, cheekily said was 'not quite accurate.' To which Bateson replied that animals 'engage in brawls and thereby get somewhere like you and me now. And we don't have to screw to do it!'

*

While the registrants dedicated the rest of the afternoon and much of the evening to their own seminars,[30] for which the IPS still insisted on providing 'conductors', there were two other major Congress-related events still to come that Monday, one at the Roundhouse, the other at the BBC.

The Roundhouse event was a speech by the Buddhist monk, scholar and poet, Thich Nhat Hanh, an exile from South Vietnam and the inventor of the term 'Engaged Buddhism', which he used to describe his and his co-workers' activities on behalf of Vietnam's suffering peasantry. By the summer of 1967, the Vietnam War had been raging in one form or another for almost twelve years. Hundreds of thousands of lives had been lost, millions of people had been displaced, and untold damage had been done to the two Vietnams' industry and agriculture.

In 1966, Nhat Hanh, who had studied at Princeton and taught at Columbia University, had met Dr Martin Luther King, an event which in itself was probably enough to compromise what standing he had with the Johnson administration and the South Vietnamese government. But, in any case, following his presentation, a day later, of a five-point peace proposal at a press conference in Washington, the South Vietnamese government refused to allow him to return to the country. Consequently, he moved to France, where he became chairman of the Vietnamese Buddhist Peace Delegation.

It's not clear who invited Nhat Hanh to speak at the Congress. He had been in attendance since the beginning. One possibility was the young American who briefly introduced him, though he didn't say much beyond the fact that he had been impressed when he had heard Nhat Hanh speak at Cornell a year or so ago and that the monk's recent book, The *Lotus in the Sea of Fire,* was useful for putting the conflict in context from the Vietnamese point of view.

Accompanied by another Vietnamese monk, who recited a poem, Nhat Hanh spoke in good English for about forty minutes in a cool, compassionate voice. He gave an account of the recent self-immolation of a Buddhist nun, a young friend of his named Nhat Chi Mai, and then moving on to how he and his fellow monks were convinced that Western modes of thought were at the basis of the Vietnam conflict.

But what he really wanted to get across was that the great majority of Vietnamese on both sides desperately wanted peace and national independence and that the best way to achieve those was to install a government in South Vietnam that was not in hock to the United States of America. Americans often stated that they were killing communists in Vietnam. But that was an illusion, he said. The victims were 'innocent peasants.'[31] Just as it was an illusion — and here was a link to Laing's speech — that China was a threat to the United States. 'I think that if we are to work for a long-lasting peace in the world, we have to pay attention to that ... and to fight that fear away' through education.

As to the possibility of a military solution to the Vietnam conflict, there was nothing to be hoped from that. It would simply mean the destruction of the entire country, conceivably by nuclear weapons. The only real victory would come through a negotiated peace, for which it was necessary for the government of the South Vietnamese leader Marshall Nguyen Cao Ky to resign. After all, it had no popular support; he was simply a puppet of American interests.

Till then the best hope lay with the people of Vietnam themselves and especially with the peace movement within South Vietnam, which was neither communist nor anti-communist, though many of its supporters had been 'liquidated, suppressed, exiled [like himself] or imprisoned'.

He ended his speech with a moving endorsement of what the Congress was ostensibly trying to achieve:

> We are very happy to be able to come to this Congress, of which we think very highly. ... I think something very important might come from this beginning. Although I have been here for [just] a few days, I feel that I am totally at home ... . The liberation of the world should follow the liberation of the mind. And the attempt of the Congress to liberate the human mind from the old way of thinking, of conceiving things, is what would seem to be the most important in the work to contribute to the building of a new and better world.

Thereafter, he spent a few minutes taking questions.

*

Very different to Nhat Hanh's speech was the BBC event. This was a discussion about violence on the corporation's flagship current affairs programme, *Panorama*.

Had the producers of *Panorama* had their way, it would have been Laing in the studio at Lime Grove alongside Ginsberg, Goodman, and Carmichael. But Laing having something else to do, John Gerassi was drafted in as a replacement. The programme was presented by Robin Day and James Mossman, two of the BBC's most combative and experienced journalists, and was in two parts: the first (presented by Day) about the leading Labour politician Richard Crossman; the second (Mossman's) about violence in general, hence its title 'The Faces of Violence'.

The first arrivals in the green room were Ginsberg, Gerassi and Goodman, each man arriving with an entourage. After they'd introduced themselves, Mossman took them through his idea of how the programme would develop, which immediately led to an impractical objection from Ginsberg. Why should they talk about violence at all? Why not love? Or yesterday's pot rally? Goodman expressed a concern that the programme would end up stereotyping Carmichael, who if the riots-cum-rebellions in the United States were mentioned, would feel 'obliged to go through all his professional loops' and end up looking 'like a man of violence', whereas he was 'nothing of the sort,' he added.[32]

But that was exactly what Carmichael did, present himself as a man of violence, for as soon as the programme began and the introductions were over, he went into a tirade against white people. The West had taken over the world 'through force and through violence,' and the only thing for black people to do, he said, was to retaliate.[33] That was the only way that 'non-white' people were ever going to free themselves from white oppression.

But what about violence in general, Mossman came back at him. Wasn't violence a part of human nature?

But violence in general wasn't something that Carmichael was prepared to talk about. He had come on the programme to talk about white violence. So, Mossman turned to Gerassi and then to Ginsberg. 'When a man in north-east Brazil dies of old age at 28 years, when a Peruvian mother has to sell her daughter into prostitution because that's the only way to guarantee three meals a day, that's [also] violence,' said Gerassi. Just as it was violence when a seventy-year-old Englishman died without ever having been in love.

Ginsberg then related how the media in Nashville, Tennessee, had whipped up a firestorm against Carmichael when the pair of them had taken part in a debate at Vanderbilt University with the white senator, Strom Thurmond, who certainly was a racist. The media said that Carmichael was a communist, so the event had ended with a riot, when all Carmichael had in mind following the debate was a meeting with 'some very polite, neatly attired Fisk [University] and Vanderbilt [SNCC] workers.'[34]

The amount of violence that black people perpetrated throughout the world was infinitely smaller than the violence that whites perpetrated in South Africa, Carmichael added. 'But the minute a black man picks up a gun', the West's media organisations say that 'violence has erupted.'

Goodman, who hadn't spoken up to that point, said that the major cause of violence in Western societies was the police; that they were the cause of most riots. Like other authorities, they were simply intolerant of any sort of disorder.

What do you think about that? Mossman asked Carmichael. 'It is absolutely the truth,' said Carmichael. 'Today in the newspaper there's a story of a cop being stomped to death into the pavement in Plainfield [a town thirty miles or so from Newark]. Now, the newspaper just neglects to say that that white policeman shot a seven-year-old black boy. ... What can a seven-year-old black boy do against the police?' 'It was good they stomped that white man to death,' he went on. 'They should have killed his mother, his father, his grandmother 'and every other white.'[35]

'Oh, rot', responded Ginsberg.

The conversation then turned again to other sorts of violence, with Goodman making interesting points about guerrilla warfare and the 'organised' violence of armies, Mossman about psychopathology and the violence of the Chinese Red Guards, and Ginsberg offering further support to Carmichael. But Carmichael didn't want his support, and he pushed it away angrily. 'I'm afraid, you see that Allen is white, so that he doesn't have to go through the persecution I go through all the time in the United States.'

He gave the same dismissive response when Goodman chipped in with the observation that both he and Ginsberg were 'queer' and that he could assure him that they too experienced 'plenty of indignities.' 'Oh, come on, you go through indignities. ... You're not going to compare that are you?'

After that, it wasn't long before Mossman brought the discussion to a conclusion.

All in all, it had been an informative yet cacophonous event, not least as the participants had repeatedly talked over one another, leaving, at least according to one television critic, an impression of 'marvellous viewing.'[36] That evening throughout Fleet Street and beyond, the word went out, 'Get to the Roundhouse tomorrow!'

5. 'Call me Mr Carmichael.'

It was impact that Carmichael wanted from the BBC, and it was impact he got. His face, philosophy, passion, and persuasiveness had been beamed into millions of the UK's sitting rooms.

Not that Black Power was entirely unfamiliar to British viewers. Nor Carmichael himself, for that matter. His 'invention' of the term at Greenwood, Mississippi, during June 1966, and his charisma and bravery had seen to that.[1] But *Panorama* took things to a higher level; it had done what even such an eloquent and mesmerising television performer as the black writer and intellectual James Baldwin couldn't do.[2] It had made the American experience that of the young, partly self-educated, black British too.

Here was a young man, denouncing white people in a way that no one had ever heard them denounced on British television before. Not speaking in beautiful, perfectly calibrated sentences like Baldwin, say, or with Malcolm X's slightly donnish eloquence. But in a sometimes angry demotic. Whites were murderers, rapists, executioners, oppressors of black people in the West and in the Third World. The non-violent philosophy of Martin Luther King, Ralph Abernathy and other figures in the mainstream of the civil rights movement was utterly futile. It was time to stop the talking, stop the marches and fight back against white violence.

*

Yet those who expected a similarly fire-spitting demagogue on Tuesday morning were disappointed, at least initially, for although the content of Carmichael's speech was equally uncompromising, what they got was a relaxed and urbane young man, speaking with wit, seriousness, and occasional humour. It was Carmichael at his ironic and sarcastic best: a man who smiled rather than snarled, without compromising an inch of his principles.

He wasn't even put off when, following a rousing introduction by John Gerassi, he couldn't get his microphone to work. He simply joshed with Allen Ginsberg and shouted an anecdote from his boyhood in Trinidad. In those days, he said, his mother often told him to quieten down. And he would do as he was told because he 'didn't want to be black.' Well, today, he said, he was going to be as black as he could.³

The Sketch had sent along one of its star reporters Brian Dixon, *The Guardian* David McKie, *The Morning Star* John Gritten; and *The Times* Stephen Jessel. There were other newspapermen as well, some drawn from the regional press, like Malcom Totten of *The Birmingham Post* and others from the United States. Dixon was there to do a hatchet job; the men from the broadsheets something more complicated. But all were there to give some account of Carmichael: the man, his appearance and his philosophy.

Not surprisingly, Carmichael's first major point was to distance himself from the first two speakers: Laing and Bateson. They were psychologists, psychiatrists, he said. He, on the other hand, was a political activist, whose concern was with the 'system of international white supremacy coupled with international capitalism.' This system, he said, was going to be 'smashed' along with the people who supported it—unless, of course, the smashers were themselves smashed.

All talk of the individual was a 'cop out', for not only did it leave unaddressed the socio-economic position of black people— and here he quoted one of his 'patron saints', Frantz Fanon. But, just as importantly, it allowed white liberals to claim that if they were not racist themselves, they were absolved from the task of dismantling the system.

But racism involved more than the overt acts of individuals; it was also 'institutionalised, a powerful yet 'subtle' presence baked into the very marrow of how the system operated. Take the case of the notorious terrorist bombing of the 16th Street Baptist Church, in Birmingham, Alabama, on September 15, 1963. That was an act of 'individual racism', he said.

> But when in that same city, ..., not five but five hundred black babies die each year because of lack of proper food, shelter and medical facilities; and thousands more are destroyed and maimed physically, emotionally and intellectually because of conditions of poverty and discrimination in the black community, that is a function of institutionalised racism.⁴

He didn't doubt that this form of racism was much commoner in the United States than it was in London. He conceded that. But wherever it was, it had to be destroyed.

He then moved on to his next major theme: the question of bias in white Western accounts of world history and the way that bias supported what he called white people's 'basic assumption of superiority.' 'The history books tell you that nothing happens until a white man comes along. If you ask any white person who discovered America, they'll tell you "Christopher Columbus". And if you ask them who discovered China, they'll tell you "Marco Polo".' The same, he said, was also true of the West Indies, where he was born. '[Sir Walter Raleigh] came along and found me and said "Whhp. I have discovered you." And my history began,' a remark which like many of his other remarks was received with applause and much laughter.

The very notion of Western civilisation was a lie. 'We are told that Western civilisation begins with the Greeks and the epitome of that is Alexander the Great', who 'wept because there were no other people to kill, murder and plunder.' As for that other, more modern, symbol of imperialist arrogance, the industrialist and politician Cecil Rhodes, he wasn't a philanthropist, as white British people and Americans liked to call him. He was a thief, a murderer, a rapist, and a plunderer. 'You can keep your Rhodes Scholars', he went on. 'We don't want the money that came from the sweat of our people.'

The West should get out of Africa, get out of all the countries it had invaded. He was tired of the way it had imposed its culture. 'I remember when I was a young man in the West Indies, I had to read Rudyard Kipling's *The White Man's Burden*. I thought the best thing the white man could do for me was to leave me alone. But Rudyard Kipling told them to come and save me 'cos I was half-savage, half-child.'[5] Such sentiments were, he added, 'very white' of Kipling.

Drawing again on Fanon, he stated that non-western peoples all over the world had had their minds 'messed up' by imperialism, while their own, often much older, civilisations had been obliterated. Japanese and Vietnamese women were cutting their skin to make their eyes look more Western, while black people were using hair straighteners, because they believed that only white people could be beautiful.

But much of so-called Western civilisation had been stolen from Africa in the first place. And here he glanced briefly at the Afrocentrist thesis which would later be associated with the Senegalese historian, Cheikh Anta Diop.[6] White historians had deliberately distorted history, he said. 'Pythagoras didn't give you geometry. The Egyptians gave it to you.' And then Western politicians had the cheek to suggest that they might 'grant' some African state or other independence. But independence wasn't theirs to give. It had to be taken, and would be taken, and, if necessary, through violence.

Naturally, he also devoted a significant part of his speech to recent events in the U.S., and especially to the riots, or rather 'rebellions', as he called them, noting that 'white flight' to the suburbs had effectively turned the centres of many American cities into 'colonies' of the United States government.

Regarding capitalism and racism more generally, the relationship was clear. 'The struggle for Black Power ... is the struggle to free those colonies [meaning the ghettos] from external domination.' Which itself would mean replacing capitalism in the United States with socialism; for 'capitalism, by its very nature' was exploitative. Blacks in the United States should become a 'disruptive force in the flow of services, goods and capital,' while their black brothers elsewhere in the world should work to 'sever the tentacles' of the imperialist colossus.

SNCC, the movement he represented, he said, had had no choice but to take the path away from non-violence and integration. Both ideas had been too middle-class and 'unconsciously racist', the idea being to find jobs within white society for black college graduates; not to challenge racism, but to prepare black students for a role in white society.

But such ideas had never appealed to most black people, anyway. Take the example of young working-class blacks. These young men had hatred in their hearts. It was the same hatred that Che Guevara had spoken about when he said that hatred of the enemy should be relentless.⁷ These 'young bloods' were the 'real revolutionary proletariat, not the working class. They were 'ready to fight by any means necessary, for the liberation of our people.'

Indeed, the United States was itself 'conceived in racism.' Witness its treatment of the 'red men'. It was racist then and it was racist now. You only had to look at the Constitution, a document 'guaranteeing life, liberty, the pursuit of happiness, and all that other garbage.' These weren't rights for blacks. They were 'rights for whites only.'

Every left-wing white operated on double standards. The labour movement in the US was more interested in raising living standards than in combating capitalism, and the capitalists paid for these wage increases by expanding internationally. 'The American working class enjoys the fruits of the labours of the Third World workers. The proletariat has become the Third World, and the bourgeoisie is white Western society.'

The time for talk about black violence was over, he added. White people were the most violent people in the world. There was violence in Vietnam, South Africa, Zimbabwe, Hong Kong, Aden and Somaliland, all with Western involvement. But all white people wanted to talk about was what was going on in the ghettos of America. Black people the world over had had enough of them. 'We are not any longer going to bow our heads to any white man. If he touches one black man in the United States, he is going to war with every black man in the United States.' The fight against racism in the United States would be extended internationally. 'We are indeed fighting to save the humanity of the world.' New Ches, new Fanons, new Maos were emerging. As far as he was concerned, the West could keep its Rousseau, its Marx and the 'great libertarian' John Stuart Mill. The black man had no need of them. Unlike Europe's Jews during the Second World War, the blacks would not go to their deaths without fighting back. He then paraphrased a line from a poem by the Harlem Renaissance writer Claude McKay, called *If We Must Die*:

> '[If we must die,] we will nobly die, fighting back.'⁸

If white people genuinely wanted to help the blacks in America, as many said they did, he said, they should begin by examining their own propensity for violence. It wasn't the black man who was sick; it was the white man. 'So, the psychologists ought to stop investigating and examining people of colour. They ought to investigate and examine their own corrupt society.'

Finally, having spoken for a little more than an hour, Carmichael ended his speech with a poem by his friend, SNCC activist Worth Long, titled *Arson and Cold Grace (or how i yearn to Burn, Baby, Burn*. The poem began and ended with the following lines:

```
WE HAVE FOUND YOU OUT
FALSE FACED AMERICA
WE HAVE FOUND YOU OUT [9]
```

*

This was the first speech to genuinely fire the Congress, and as Carmichael pulled his notes together, he received a standing ovation, not from everyone in the audience, mind, but from those, mostly black people and some whites, who supported his programme. Much of the radical wing of black activism was at the Roundhouse that morning, men like Courtney Tulloch, Darcus Howe and Michael Malik and women like Jessica Huntley. The eminent writer and historian C.L.R. James was there too, representing, as some would see it, the old guard, and there was Angela Davis, only twenty-three at the time, but an American woman who would herself go on to have an enormous influence not only on the activist wing, but on black people more generally.

Davis had heard about the Congress while studying philosophy at the University of Frankfurt, and learning that Herbert Marcuse, one of her former teachers at Brandeis University, would be giving a lecture there, she decided to stop off in London before returning to the States, where she hoped to play a leading role in the developing crisis. Carmichael's words, she wrote later, were 'like a switchblade, accusing the enemy as I had never heard him accused before', though she questioned his dismissal of Marx and his 'indiscriminate' portrayal of white people as the enemy.[10]

Thereafter, she spent much of her time, between Congress sessions, with Carmichael, accompanying him, Malik, and others to meetings elsewhere in London. For her too, the Congress was thus a defining experience. 'I learned more about the new movement there in London than from all the reading I had done.'[11]

*

Having introduced Carmichael, Gerassi took charge of the Q&A which followed the speech. There was no need for written questions, he said; people should just shout them up.

Predictably, some of the questioners referred to the situation in Newark. One asked him what he thought about the possibility of a third party in the United States and the likelihood of a black president (not much, he said). Others about China and Mao, Vietnam and the draft, Martin Luther King (no comment), white communists and Malcolm X, and — a very silly one — about what he'd say if God turned black people white again, thus alluding to the Biblical story of Ham who, some Christians believed, was the cause of the dark skin colour of Africans.

Nonetheless, Carmichael treated this question as indeed he treated almost all the questions, with honesty and, sometimes, with wit. 'All I can say about that to you ... is that ... I asked my grandmother ..., '"Mam, why does God treat us so bad? We ain't done nothing to nobody." And she said, "Well, God has his reasons" and I said, "I sure wish he'd tell me, 'cos I could out-reason him. That's how I feel about God.'[12]

To a young Canadian white woman named Marjaleena Repo who asked him if there was really no role in the black movement for white people, Carmichael responded that any help they received would have to be on their, i.e., black terms. But Repo was not satisfied, so she asked him again. 'The lady insists on the point,' said Gerassi. 'If white people want to help us, they should move to disrupt white Western society,' said Carmichael, speaking, as he often did where whites were concerned, very slowly. 'There is no need for white people to come and help me. I don't need help. White Western society needs help.'

In many ways, Carmichael's answer could not have been clearer. Nonetheless, Repo was hardly the only person at the Congress to ask the question. Indeed, it was asked again and again, notably by white women and hippies.

Yet it was this occasion that has gone down in the history books as one of the defining moments of the Congress. 'I can remember the crackling tension in the air and the scorn with which he dismissed a young white woman who questioned separatist politics from the audience', recollects the future academic, Sheila Rowbotham. 'Without any conscious feminism, I recoiled angrily from his refusal to listen to her and his disdain of her political support.'[13] Other women, such as the artist, actress and campaigner Caroline Coon and writer and academic Juliet Mitchell, bracketed Carmichael's response with other controversial remarks he made at the Congress, notably one on the role of women in politics more generally. The position of women was 'prone', he said. [14]

As for the hippies, Carmichael was utterly contemptuous. 'The hippies are okay, except for one thing: they're white, see. Now, they can play hippie for two years but when they get tired, they'll go home to daddy with all the money he's got.' If they really wanted to help black people, they should head off to Newark, he said, gather in front of the blacks when bullets were flying, and throw their flowers at the police. 'Let's keep [the cops] busy.' Probably he didn't intend this to be taken as a serious suggestion, but it did impress Allen Ginsberg who returned to the subject during Friday's and Saturday's sessions.

The only time that Carmichael got angry was when some pacifists in the audience challenged his advocacy of violence. He then became incoherent, muddling his words and concepts, accusing them of the very thing they reprobated. If they really cared about violence, he said, they would have stopped it in their own societies. 'The only time you talk about it, is when a black man talks about it' — which was patently untrue. Just as it was also untrue — another of his allegations — that the British peace movement was insincere in its opposition to nuclear weapons. 'You cannot even recognise your 'self-conscious racism' (sic).

*

After the Q&A, Carmichael spent ten minutes taking questions from the press, who he asked to address him not as 'Stokely' but as 'Mr Carmichael'.[15] By this time, he was tired, so most of his answers were short, very few running to more than thirty words or so.

Malcolm Totten of the *Birmingham Post* asked him about a subject that was on many British people's minds during that long hot summer of racial violence in the United States: how long before the violence came to English cities? 'It won't be long. You can answer the question better than I,' said Carmichael. Which organisation did he associate himself with in England? asked another man. No one, in particular, he said. Then someone else: But he'd had discussions? 'Yes, I have. We're beginning to join hands not only in London but the Caribbean and in Africa in Asia and Latin America. This is the beginning.'

Another Brit asked him if he'd had trouble getting past officialdom at Heathrow Airport. No, but he had noticed the presence of CIA officers. 'We all got met by them,' said Gerassi. 'Yeah', said Carmichael, 'They're all over the place, aren't they.' But, naturally, most of the journalists focused their questions on events in the United States. Why had he resigned as head of SNCC. He hadn't, he said; he had chosen not to run. Did he seek separation from white people? White people had answered that question already. Were the disturbances in the United States organised? 'Well, last night six cities rebelled at the same time.' Only when he got onto the violence in Newark did he let himself go a bit, emphasising, once again, that the disturbances were 'rebellions', rather than 'riots' or 'racial flare-ups'. The cause of the violence, he said, was Democrat mayor Hugh J. Addonizio's policy of displacing the city's black poor from their neighbourhoods. 'He's not finding them new houses. They'll have to find new houses. It is a rebellion. I do not stop rebellions. Number one. And number two. If a white man hits a black man in the United States or anywhere in the world. If I am there, I'm gonna pick up a gun and shoot the white man.'

One of the 'gentlemen of the press', happened to be the student leader Tariq Ali. Having already asked Carmichael questions about black soldiers in Vietnam, he caught up with him and his entourage again, this time outside the Roundhouse, in the sun, where the two men spent a few minutes swapping political insights and pleasantries. Both had recently sat as part of the Russell Tribunal investigating United States war crimes in Vietnam. So, their meeting was also a chance to catch up on other matters.

Although Ali too was impressed by Carmichael's speech, he wondered, like Angela Davis, if his hopes for a specifically 'black' revolution weren't quixotic. After all, black people in the UK were in a completely different position to blacks in the United States, let alone in the Third World, whether independent or colonies. He asked him what he thought of the Congress so far. Not much, Carmichael replied. He had hoped to see more 'representatives from liberation movements in Africa, Latin America and Asia.' This was another objection to add to the one he had made at the beginning of his speech: the Congress was far too parochial for his taste.[16]

Later, Ali drafted a short account of Carmichael's speech and of their meeting for the *New Statesman*. 'As a speaker, Stokely Carmichael is very impressive,' he wrote. But he didn't think that Carmichael would ever have the stature of Malcolm X. 'To blame him for the violence at Newark or Watts is like blaming the Jews for the concentration camps', he went on. 'He merely articulates what growing numbers of Negroes are beginning to feel.' Yet, he also thought that his analysis of their situation simplified it unnecessarily.[17]

He ended his article on an ominous note: 'He admits in private that he expects to die a violent death, but stresses that it won't matter since the movement will still be alive.'[18]

*

After lunch there were two further panel discussions, plus a lecture from the American historian George Rawick, all linked to Carmichael's presentation. However, none proved as memorable as a speech from a former United States Air Force (USAF) lieutenant named Gregory Berglund. This was about nuclear war and psychosis and took place during the hour or so before midnight.

The panel discussions were chaired by Berke and Cooper. The first carried the title 'Mediating Potential conflicts between Minorities in the Liberation Movement', the second was on the theme of imperialism and revolution. This one, which included contributions from C.L.R. James, George Rawick, John Gerassi and, intermittently, Stokely Carmichael, was prefaced by a short speech by Michael Malik and a minute's silence for the jazz saxophonist John Coltrane, whose sudden death from liver cancer at the age of forty had reached the Congress the previous evening.

After Cooper's introductions, C.L.R. James began the second discussion with a few carefully chosen words about Stokely Carmichael. Though James's politics were profoundly different to the younger man's, not least in the emphasis he placed on class struggle, James knew a winner when he saw one, and he praised Carmichael accordingly. Carmichael, he said, represented a new stage in the history of the 'negro movement'. He was in the great tradition of Marcus Garvey, W.E.B. Du Bois, George Padmore, Malcolm X and Frantz Fanon.[19]

George Rawick, when he spoke, echoed this sentiment. But he also made a larger point. He said that American blacks were in the 'vanguard' of 'oppressed peoples' everywhere. He also had kind words for SNCC. Much could be learned, he said, from the way that the organisation had dealt with the problem of bureaucracy. The organisation had built itself up from the grassroots, he said, rather than rely on a cabal of intellectuals.

Neither James's nor Rawick's speeches impressed Gerassi, however. These were mere platform speeches, he said, fit only to rally the faithful. He, on the contrary, was concerned with practical action, by which he meant the practical action that whites could take in the First World and revolutionary cadres in the Third. Inspiring words were all to the good, but how could they be translated into guns and explosives?

Part of the problem for white people, he said, was that unlike the black youngsters mentioned in the morning speech by Carmichael, they hated intellectually and not with their guts. 'We talk like revolutionaries. We approve of revolutionaries. We cheer as revolutionaries. But we don't fight as revolutionaries ... How can the white become revolutionary in a context where it is the white and it is the white's class that is the oppressor?' he wondered.

Intriguingly, he also put in a word for the revolutionary potential of white-collar workers on low incomes. Seeing as the traditional working class had proved such a disappointment, perhaps the clerks could become the 'new proletariat'.

Rawick asked Carmichael to comment on how SNCC had transformed itself from an organisation advocating non-violence to the foremost black power movement in the United States. Although Carmichael didn't quite do this, he did give a gripping account of his own and others' experience in the organisation.

Like most of his friends in the SNCC, he was, he said, a first-generation college student. His parents had struggled economically, but they had 'bourgeois ideas': they hoped that their children would become doctors or lawyers. But by the time he and his friends had gone to college they'd already picked up certain habits from the street: they'd learned to hustle, to steal and shoot crap; and they were comfortable in their blackness. They thus resented a system that seemed designed, consciously or not, to 'whitewash' them, to turn them against the values with which they'd grown up. So, many of them rebelled. 'Most of us just said to hell with it.'

They had joined SNCC despite its philosophy of non-violence, he said. 'None of us believed it. I never did.' But, in any case, one day he got tired of being kicked and spat upon by white people. 'I just grabbed a white man and beat the living daylights out of him', he said. 'He ain't never come back, no more to bother me', a remark which he delivered with a slight theatrical emphasis, and which was greeted by laughter and loud applause from the audience. It wasn't just in the United States, he added, that a black man could be jailed for life for winking at a single white woman; the 'same thing' also held true for London.

*

When Cooper asked for questions from the floor, several people picked up on Gerassi's point about the traditional working class.

One man said that the British working-class was the 'most deluded' the world had ever seen, while Peter Cadogan, a well-known anti-nuclear activist, denied that they even existed. He wanted to address the question of power. 'The answer to power is the elaboration of anti-power and unless we say something significant about anti-power in this fortnight, we should not have done our job', he added. It was the sort of intervention that would have pleased Paul Goodman, assuming he was listening.

But other than several irritable jabs between James and Gerassi and another intervention from Carmichael, the session was really only notable for a speech by a white activist from Detroit named Frank Joyce, who represented an organisation called People against Racism (PAR).

This organisation, he said, worked amongst the white working class in order to counter white race hatred from within. It also provided support to white professionals working in liberal organisations, like charities, federal programmes, and churches, to discourage them from taking on the values of the organisations they represented.

Like Carmichael, Joyce spoke with passion about the insidious nature of 'institutionalised racism'. The question to an individual, he said, should never be, are you racist? But is society racist? And the fact is, it is, he said. 'We move then to the question of resistance. How do we as whites begin to function in that society to make it dysfunctional?'

But this was not a subject for a large public forum, he added. He would address it in the relative privacy of a seminar with John Gerassi, if people wanted that.

Finally, he ended with a warning: if his fellow Congress-goers couldn't move on from the 'petty prides and disputes' that he'd witnessed today, then he was going to replace his twenty-one-day excursion plane fare with one for nine days. Which is exactly what he did, but for another reason ironically. For five days later, Detroit too erupted into a riot-cum-rebellion, and he returned there as soon as he was able.[20]

*

Bearing in mind that a writer in *International Times* described Berglund's speech as 'one of the most poignant moments of [the Congress's] language spectacular'[21] and another writer as 'quite exemplary', it is unfortunate that, like the Berke-led panel discussion, it was not recorded.[22]

Berglund had been drafted into the USAF after graduating with a degree in Russian. Following Officer Training School in Texas, he had then been posted to the UK where he worked on NATO's nuclear deterrent. A few years after that, however, as he prepared for deployment in Vietnam, he became concerned about deficiencies in the command-and-control structure, so he resigned. Thereafter, he was hospitalised as a paranoid schizophrenic.

Titling his speech 'Psychosis over Pacifism: My Experience with the United States Air Force', Berglund described how US air force personnel were psychologically prepared to launch nuclear weapons; how pilots became mentally unbalanced if they were not allowed to take part in bombing missions; and how the state mobilised a 'psychiatric-repressive apparatus' to deal with dissidents like himself.

Unfortunately, that was the last that the Congress heard from him. He was arrested as soon as he'd finished his speech. At least that is the memory of one participant, a young man named Adam Saltiel, who had been drawn to the Congress to hear Laing and Cooper. According to Saltiel, Berglund was escorted out of the Roundhouse by military police.[23]

6. A 'Self-Governing' Congress

Following the previous day's excitement with Stokely Carmichael, it was inevitable that Wednesday morning brought a feeling of anti-climax. Jules Henry, that morning's speaker, was many things: anthropologist, sociologist, and economist among them, but a Black Power activist and scintillating orator he was not; and it was probably Carmichael that most of the participants were talking about as they filed into the Roundhouse.

Both *The Times* and *The Guardian* ran with sympathetic summaries of Carmichael's speech and of the question-and-answer session afterwards. And both provided glowing profiles. 'Mr Carmichael is a tall, lithe man. He is as cool as they come, totally "hip" (which is not the same as "hippy") and has, in the American phrase, great charisma. He is 26, and is one of the most influential men in America' was how Stephen Jessel described him in *The Times*.[1] As for *The Guardian*, good liberal flagship as it was, its journalist David McKie noted Carmichael's 'gaiety, wit and good humour', but also the 'cold contempt' with which he had treated those white people who had offered him their support. '"Come inside the ghetto ... if you all believe in that love power and so on, come inside, and when the cops are shooting at us, throw your flowers at them,"' it reported him saying.[2]

*

Laing's brief introduction of Henry was slightly slurred as well as halting (possibly the effect of alcohol from the night before), but it got across the main points: apprenticeship under the great American anthropologist Franz Boas and fieldwork in Brazil, Mexico, Argentina and in the United States of America. This latter, *inter alia*, was a reference to Henry's studies of American family structures and children in various states of mental breakdown; of the aged and their experiences in residential homes; and of young people in primary and secondary education.

The last of these interests placed Henry squarely in the same stream as that occupied by Paul Goodman, whose *Compulsory Miseducation* (a sort of companion piece to *The Community of Scholars*) of 1964 had covered much the same ground but from an explicitly anarchist viewpoint. That the two men seem not to have engaged with each other during the Congress is telling. Perhaps it was because Henry was too 'straight' for Goodman, in the sense that on a personal level he was too middle-of-the road. Or perhaps it was because of Henry's apparently overly friendly assessment of the Soviet Union.

It wasn't so many years before the Congress that Berke had introduced Laing to Henry's best-known anthropological work *Culture against Man,* a self-described 'passionate ethnography', which pilloried American culture.[3] But, in any case, Henry was one of the few speakers at the Congress who Laing genuinely had time for. On one occasion during the Congress, the two men peeled off together and shared what Laing later described as a 'deeply heartfelt and human touching' encounter. 'I got Jules to tell me about some of his work. He had written *Pathways to Madness* and was the only person I knew who had actually gone and lived in the houses of these autistic or schizophrenic children. He said he was absolutely blasted by the experiences, he couldn't do it again, that it was just absolutely awful but no one wanted to know about it.'[4]

That perhaps makes Henry sound almost like an American version of Laing himself. But, alongside his occasional brashness and vituperative judgements, his deportment was very much that of the sober, well behaved, upper-middle-class American scholar. In other words, although his subject matter was ripe, the books and the man himself were solid, workman-like, and almost entirely free of Laing's intellectual brilliance and occasional epigrammatical exaggerations. And that was the way he delivered - or rather read - his speech. His wasn't a speech to fire up or to capture a fractious or uninterested audience. Rather it demanded patience, commitment, and total concentration.

*

Henry titled his speech 'The Social and Psychological Preparation for War', thus riffing off the first chapters of *Culture Against Man*. He took as his starting point the observations that under modern conditions, the enemy, however defined, was always an aspect of the system itself; that due to trade, cultural connections, diplomacy, etc, as well as various 'destructive chains of impulses and activities' that most modern wars, whether 'cold' or 'hot', were, in fact, to a large extent, civil wars; and that, as a consequence of this 'interdependent world political economy', people developed a 'psychological predisposition to accept almost any nation at all as inimical when the government chooses to so define it.'[5]

Even such new or 'emerging' states as Israel, North Vietnam and the Congo had been forced into this pattern. 'When we consider that *shalom*, peace, is the word with which ordinary Israelis greet one another, that they are a people who know, better than most perhaps, what war means and that only through incredible toil and peace have they been able to create a home in the desert', their war with their Arabs neighbours still made perfect sense. The 'configuration' of 'world society', with its constant and shifting need for enemies, had driven them to it.

But it was the United States and the corporate world, in particular, that occupied the centre of his analysis. That was where he focused his attention most, heaping up detail upon detail and generalisation upon generalisation.

It was a world where corporate executives worked hand in glove with other corporate executives and with politicians and senior military officers. Indeed, such was the interlocking nature of the American system of economy and government at the highest levels that they were often one and the same individual. He — and it was almost always a he — simply switched from corporation to corporation or to one of the other allied career paths, whilst cleaving to the same inimical and anti-social policies. What this added up to was an 'organisation' "in being"', which, once mobilised by government' could 'exert irresistible power for war or for peace.' Yet, it had 'never been mobilised for peace,' he added.

Yet, curiously, with all this power and with all the concentrated means to exert it at the maximal rate, ordinary Americans still felt vulnerable. Why was that? he asked. Here, he introduced the psychological part of his argument. It was because of the rise of socialism and the associated doubling of 'violent revolutions' since 1958. This wasn't just his view, he quickly added; it was also the view of United States Secretary of Defence, Robert McNamara. Corporate America had looked at Cuba, Venezuela, Colombia, Iran, Syria, Zanzibar, Bahrain, Vietnam, etc., etc., and at all the red hordes banging at the doors of democracy and shuddered. It then used television, radio, and the newspapers to communicate its fear and vulnerability to the American public, with the result that taxpayers were persuaded to pump 'hundreds of billions of dollars' into the American armaments industry — an investment that itself came back in higher rates of employment and affluent standards of living.

Communism, but especially the authoritarian Soviet version, therefore functioned as a sort of bogeyman, something that was used to frighten children and impressionable adults and to bolster social cohesion.

Finally, he turned his attention to the conformity and docility of American life, equally visible at the top of the corporate tree and down at the bottom in organised labour. 'The American population is one of the most docile on earth. This is ideal psychological preparation for war, for docile people make excellent soldiers,' he said.[6] This, of course, was also one of Laing's points, as it was also, in a way, one of Carmichael's and Gerassi's as well as many others at the Congress. They too saw the American working class as painfully compromised by consumerism and self-interest.

Yet, despite the depressive tone of most of his presentation, Henry ended his speech rather implausibly with uplift.

> Man is everywhere chained to a system in which he perceives no new options. Yet there are. For the vast and radical political changes that have occurred in the past two generations prove that man can create new options where there seemed to be none.

*

It was a dull speech, evenly and dutifully delivered, taking almost exactly one hour to the second to read, and though it was lengthily applauded and glowingly written up by Roger Barnard in *Peace News*,[7] there was much that was slightly old-fashioned about it, almost as if Henry had taken some texts from C. Wright Mills and then crossed them with Republican President Dwight D. Eisenhower's famous valedictory remarks on the danger of the military-industrial complex.

Not that that criticism would have bothered Henry. The intellectual's role was simply to speak the truth, and if that meant coming across as a cardigan-wearing, highly respectable uncle, then so be it. He had not come to the Congress to flatter the young or to burnish his intellectual credentials. But it did bother Bateson, who quipped to Laing that he hadn't heard such a speech since about 1932. But that was far too harsh.[8]

A confirmation of the old saw that you should never mention Israel unless prepared for a long diatribe on the subject came in the question-and-answer session afterwards. It began with a statement from a Jewish woman, who had grown up under the British mandate and who interpreted Henry's brief comment near the beginning of his speech as implying that before the foundation of Israel the region was virtually unoccupied. Well, she had grown up there, and such towns and cities as Jenin, Safed and Nablus were already populous and thriving. She called 'Ben-Gurionism' — the policies of Israel's first prime minister, Mapai leader David Ben-Gurion — the Jewish version of fascism.

The session then continued with a couple of questions about Stokely Carmichael, both of which as well as the former question, Henry refused to answer.

Curiously, when Henry did answer a question, he sounded out of his depth. Thus, he completely misinterpreted an intervention from a drunken Bateson, who handed him a lifeline of sorts by tying Henry's comments about the interlocking character of the American capitalist and government elite to the danger of the 'abstracted human being, cut off [from the full range of human awareness] at the level of conscious purpose.' Henry interpreted this as a hit against capitalism.

The session then continued with a series of further questions from Americans, one of whom said that he was puzzled by the optimism of Henry's peroration. His optimism was justified, said Henry, by the existence of an articulate, motivated, and educated upper-middle class. After all, it wasn't the working class at the forefront of most of the demonstrations against the war in Vietnam, but upper-middle class people.

It wasn't long after that comment that an also drunken Laing chipped in. 'We seem to be developing a discussion that is a sort of *adante cantabile*.' By which he meant that the session was boring. And a few minutes afterwards he closed the meeting.

*

Following the Q&A session, it probably surprised no one when some of the same people who had spoken up during the evening meeting on Saturday organised a general meeting to take place immediately after lunch to discuss the management of the Congress. Not that Henry's speech had been a disaster. It was hardly that. But coupled with the lacklustre Q&A and the prospect of yet another panel discussion, they wanted to pivot the Congress away from spectatorship and towards the sort of thing that the organisers had originally intended.

So far, there had been three panel discussions: the one with Bateson, Goodman, Huxley, Laing and Eng and the two that had grown out of Stokely Carmichael's contributions.

This meeting had the following results: henceforth, there would be no more panel discussions except for another one timed to take place later that evening, which would be led by Gregory Bateson; the afternoons would be devoted to 'informal seminars'; and a general meeting would be held every day at which 'complaints and suggestions could be made and the programme for the afternoons and evenings decided.' Thus, in the words of a writer in *Freedom* newspaper, the Congress became 'self-governing.'[9]

*

The event which prefaced that evening's panel discussion wasn't a speech, but a television documentary produced by Roy Battersby, the same man, who with Ben Churchill, was responsible for recording the Congress. The documentary, a review of the previous year's developments in medicine and science and titled 'Challenge', had first been broadcast by the BBC in its popular science series *Tomorrow's World* six months earlier on the 5th of January.

The subject matter was grim: air and water pollution, radioactive fall-out in children's teeth, the overuse of antibiotics, overpopulation, the rationing of access to kidney machines, genetic engineering, the annual slaughter of pedestrians on the highways and byways and the same prospect of global warming that Bateson had mentioned in the Q&A on Monday – these were some of the themes that Battersby, a life-long Marxist and critic of the thoughtless application of science to industry, had chosen to address.

No wonder the reviewer of the January broadcast in science journal *Nature* spluttered into his or her typewriter. A popular audience more used to scientific uplift than to scepticism should not be unfairly agitated. 'Wild talk about the potential hazards to society which may spring from recent work in biology is often simply wicked', the reviewer wrote. 'The real problem is to find some way of balancing the benefits of change against the nuisances which change may often bring, or to find some way of eliminating the nuisances. The doomsday view does not help but, rather, hinders. It is no accident that petrified is often used as a synonym for frightened.'[10]

Possibly more in tune with most people's feelings on viewing the programme was the writer and comedian John Wells. He addressed its philosophical and theological implications in his satirical *Spectator* column. Humanity clearly faced a very dark future, he wrote. But what could he, a mere individual do about it? 'Perhaps there *is* an old man with a beard up there in the sky; perhaps even a lot of old men with beards, all telling dreadful jokes with sicker and sicker endings. Let us hope the author of this particular one remains inactive and delays the punch-line a little longer.' 'Unfortunately, we shan't be there to laugh.'.[11]

Naturally, the documentary marked Battersby out as a troublemaker as indeed he was — not only a Marxist but an intellectual, who nonetheless went on to make several other controversial programmes for the BBC, including such classics of the TV drama genre as *Five Women* and *Leeds United!*

In fact, the only way that he had got away with the programme in the first place was by failing to complete it until a few days before its broadcast, by which time, it had already been announced in *Radio Times*. So, the corporation felt obliged to go ahead with it. But this betrayal on his part was not forgiven. When a few months after the broadcast, Battersby had tried to set up further science programmes, he and the head of the science and features department, Aubrey Singer, had been called in for a dressing down by one of the corporation's senior management team. They were told that the film was 'anti-science', 'anti-progress' and an embarrassment.[12] Fortunately, Battersby had already copied the film, and it was that that was shown at the Congress.

*

The panel discussion which followed the film was chaired by Bateson, sober now, with platform contributions from Battersby, Francis Huxley, Laing, and Allen Ginsberg. It was a quieter and more even-tempered affair than the one on Monday. This was probably down to the absence of Paul Goodman and Eng. Possibly they had other things to do; possibly they weren't invited.

Contrary to the reviewer in *Nature* and the top brass at the BBC, Bateson thought that Battersby's film was insufficiently pessimistic. It suggested that scientists could remedy individual mistakes by individual acts. But that was far too straightforward. A mistake, the over-exploitation of a single resource in one area, the use of a particular insecticide, could lead — and often did lead — to disruptions elsewhere in the ecosystem, which could not be remedied simply by removing the stimulus that had caused the problem in the first place. He used the example of over-fishing in the Humboldt Current, an area of seawater to the west of South America, and historically one of the most productive and diverse of the world's fisheries. In recent years, Peruvian trawlers had started to use echo-locating devices to increase their catches, which had led to a fall in the population of birds, who fed upon the sardines in the area.

But that was not the only consequence. In the longer-term man too would suffer. Because without the birds there would be no more guano; and upon that the agriculture of Peru depended. And without efficient agriculture, 'we may rapidly look forward to a severe economic disturbance', said Bateson.[13]

One man in the audience asked Bateson if there were books he could recommend that addressed the issues raised by Battersby's film. No great reader himself, Bateson came up with three: Rachel Carson's *Silent Spring* of 1962, Barry Commoner's *Science and Survival* of 1966, and a book that was still in manuscript: *The Magic Animal* by his close friend and neighbour, the writer and philosopher, Philip Wylie. Intriguingly, it was Commoner who had inspired Battersby to make his film in the first place, and it was Wylie's book that Bateson had had in mind when, his plane tickets booked, he chewed over what he wanted to say at the Congress. Carson's book, Bateson noted, with more than a nod to the reaction in *Nature* to Battersby's documentary perhaps, had been ripped apart by a 'gentleman from the chemical industry' in the leading journal *Science*, itself the American equivalent of *Nature*.

To a statement from a man in the audience about the difficulty of interesting so-called ordinary people in the perils of science, Bateson returned to an observation he had made on Monday; that science had developed since the mid-nineteenth century into a 'bag of tricks', each trick logical and effective on its own terms, but potentially disastrous from the point of view of the entire system.

Not that there weren't signs of a better way, he added. To illustrate his point, he offered the surprising example of a fighter plane, a machine that if it was to perform well did demand some appreciation of integrated systems. 'It's a funny thing about these mechanical predators, you know, that they are running evolutionarily ahead of other machines, just as the predators of biology on the whole have better brains and more intelligence than the herbivores.'

Referring to some of the things that Bateson had said on Monday, Huxley at one point wondered if there was a 'way of knowing' things which was not 'poisonous.' Perhaps raising children as ambidextrous would help? A better-balanced body, would be more psychologically attuned and thus less likely to sink into 'lopsided' thinking, he said. Take the composition of poetry, he added. Wordsworth wrote some of his best poems while walking up and down a gravel path, Coleridge some of his best while ambling over mountains. These modes of composition were reflected in the rhythms in their poetry. No wonder then that so much scientific thinking was tunnel visioned. It was because most scientists did most of their work sitting down. It was a 'prison' they put themselves into to concentrate.

For his part, Laing, picking up on these and other of Huxley's observations, spoke about the research of an American child-psychiatrist named Harry Weiner who had published a paper on the impact of ectohormones on the social behaviour of rats and other animals. Perhaps, Laing wondered, similar ectohormones regulated human social life. After all, it was 'certainly true that smell is one of the first things repressed in the ontogenesis of civilised human development.'

The evening ended with a woman from the floor reverting to Huxley's point about sitting down being amongst the worst positions for thinking and feeling. 'And what have we been spending the whole evening doing — sitting and talking.' 'Time to stop', said Bateson drily. At which point, Ginsberg, a mostly decorous contributor up to that point, let rip with what sounded like a revocation or exorcism.

*

While Laing's rudeness to Stokely Carmichael probably stands alone in the annals of bad behaviour during the Congress, it wasn't the only event at Elsham Road that needed to be forgiven and forgotten. There were also incidents involving Gregory Bateson's son, John, and Paul Goodman.

John Bateson was sixteen during the Congress, a bright young man, who helped look after his father's dolphins at the Oceanic Institute at Waimanalo in Hawaii; and who would subsequently go on to Antioch College, in Ohio, where he would be remembered as a dab hand at growing marijuana plants. One evening he drank wine from a jug laced with LSD. No one knows who put the drug in. It seems very unlikely to have been Ginsberg or one of the Congress organisers. But, in any case, John was frozen with terror until the morning. The upshot of that was that Bateson removed him from Elsham Road and sent him to the home of one of his oldest friends, the botanist Nora Barlow.[14]

The other incident involved a 'wild woman' who, determining to 'cure' Goodman of his homosexuality, sneaked into his bedroom and threw herself on top of him. Apparently, Goodman's shouts woke up the whole house, while Laing, from whom the anecdote derives, yelled at the woman, 'You stupid fucking cow, that sort of stuff.' 'Paul was trembling and Jules Henry came down from upstairs, where he was trying to get some sleep', Laing recalled for one of his interviewers.[15]

*

Following Henry's speech, Thursday morning brought a return to militancy with a rousing and impassioned speech from John Gerassi. Of all the major speakers at the Congress, bar possibly Bateson and the 'indefatigable' Laing,[16] Gerassi had probably been the most active by this point, speaking at the Carmichael Q&A, the panel discussion which followed it, and at many of the seminars.

That said, Gerassi wasn't just a political activist and a writer and a journalist of distinction — although that's how those at the Congress knew him; he also possessed an extremely interesting back story. His father, Fernando Gerassi, was a painter and a friend of Picasso, who had studied philosophy with Edmund Husserl and Martin Heidegger and art history with the eminent Heinrich Wölfflin, and who had fought for the Republican side in Spain, where he reached the rank of general. His mother, a Ukrainian-born writer named Stepha Awdykowicz was a Catholic runaway who, at one point, lived in Berlin with the musician Alban Berg, the composer of *Wozzeck* and *Lulu*.[17]

John, or 'Tito', as most of his friends called him, was born during the summer of 1931, in France. The story goes that his birth took place at a clinic opposite the famous La Closerie des Lilas, in Montparnasse, while his father got drunk, and it was his father's best friend, Jean-Paul Sartre, who announced the baby's arrival.

Thereafter, until 1936 and the outbreak of the Spanish Civil War, Gerassi's parents lived a bohemian existence, drinking and gambling in the cafes of Montparnasse, and commuting between Paris and Barcelona. Then in 1940, they left Paris for the United States, where they did their best to contribute to the war effort. Like Bateson and Herbert Marcuse, Fernando served in the Office of Strategic Services (OSS). They put him to work in Latin America and sent him to Spain to set up an underground movement. Nonetheless, the family was spied upon by the CIA. for which they eventually received an apology from Attorney General, Bobby Kennedy.

As for John, like many young immigrants, he was quick to take advantage of the educational opportunities that the United States offered. He studied at Columbia, then moved to the London School of Economics for his doctorate. He worked as a staff writer on *Time* Magazine, then a correspondent for the *New York Times*, after which he moved to *Newsweek*, before moving again to the radical *Ramparts*. He also published books, notably *The Great Fear: The Reconquest of Latin America,* a coruscating journalistic study of American policy in the area ('Latin America's social and economic structure is decadent, corrupt, immoral, and generally unsalvageable,' he wrote) and *The Boys of Boise*, a well-received in-depth study of homosexuality and political corruption in a city in Idaho.[18]

Indeed, no less a figure than the Cuban leader Fidel Castro was a fan. Apropos of whom Gerassi had another famous story which concerned the CIA and one of their attempts to kill the Cuban revolutionary. This attempt took place at a meeting of the Latin American press corps with Castro in Havana in 1964 — except that it wasn't Castro who was almost killed, but Gerassi. He ate the shrimp salad that the CIA had laced with poison — the Cuban leader, unstoppably garrulous, didn't touch his food at all.

Fortunately for Gerassi, an alert driver rushed him to one of Havana's excellent hospitals, where he didn't come to until a few hours later. 'The most beautiful woman I've ever seen in my life was standing above me: my nurse, dressed in white with a .45 ... and saying, "You are alive thanks to Russian medicine,"' he told one of his interviewers, the academic and thriller writer, Tony Monchinski, and doubtless more than a few of his companeros at the Congress, 'And 'I said, "*Ohhh*, thank you!"'.

*

Paul Sweezy, who introduced Gerassi that morning, seems to have been silent up to this point; at least, there is no evidence that he contributed to either the Q&As or to the panel discussions, though he had arrived with his wife on the 14th. Perhaps he had focused his efforts on the seminars. But, whatever the reason, he took the opportunity of the introduction to say a few modest words about himself: 'I'm Paul Sweezy. I've worked on various committees with John over the last year or so and I can testify that there's nobody who has more interesting and vital things to say about whatever subjects he chooses to emphasise.'[19]

Not unusually, when Gerassi readied himself to start his lecture, the microphone played up, which gave him an opportunity for one of his frequent digs. This time his victim was Paul Goodman. 'Did the mike go dead? The mike went dead. Paul Goodman must be here' — a foolish, unfair, and catty remark, but fairly representative of the contempt in which he held those he deemed insufficiently revolutionary.

Gerassi titled his speech 'Violence and Counterviolence: Dollars and Sense', thus signalling his intention of tackling head-on one of the key issues that had brought people to the Congress in the first place: dialectics, and more particularly the relationship between the powerful and the less powerful. Yet rather than jump straight into the meat of his presentation, which was largely an economic and military history of the USA and its involvement in South America, he began, like Carmichael before him, with brief comments on the divisions that had opened up within the Congress. It had, he said, split into halves. On the one hand, there were those, like himself, who were concerned with political matters; on the other, there were people concerned with the psychological aspects of violence. As for liberation, another of the concepts that had brought people to the Congress, that had still to be defined. Liberation from what, in other words? Those concerned with political matters saw liberation by and large as liberation from physical enemies, while the other half saw it in terms of 'liberation from an environment for those who live within the centre of that enemy.' At least they had one thing in common, he added: the 'underlying assumption' that the 'system' itself had to be destroyed.

He began his history of U.S. imperialism with the Monroe Doctrine of 1823, continued with Franklin D. Roosevelt's Inauguration Address of 1933 (which, officially, at least, turned the nation's back on imperialism) and ended with the Punta del Este meeting in Uruguay, which had taken place during April 1967. It was a story of political and military hypocrisy, of arrogance, self-righteousness, deceit, he said, and of filibusters like William Walker, who invaded Nicaragua in 1855 with a small force of fellow adventurers and who had set himself up as president.

Men such as Walker, despite what modern-day liberals supposed, were not working against the interests of the American system of government, he said; they were working for the profit of 'individual American companies,' companies which, to all intents and purposes, were more powerful than the State Department. The rhetoric of democracy so beloved of liberal historians and politicians was therefore sham.

To the American people of the nineteenth century as to the American people of today, he went on, there was and is only one definition of democracy worth the name: American democracy; only one definition of freedom: American freedom, which was and is to say the freedom which allowed and allows the Vanderbilts, the Rockefellers, the Guggenheims, the United Fruit Company, the Hanna Mining Corporation and the Anaconda Company to do exactly what they wanted.

As for the marine force, America's finest in most estimations, they were simply American democracy's shock troops. Historically, their role had never been to uphold democracy in the countries they had invaded, as liberal politicians liked to pretend, but to destroy it.

Fig 9. John Gerassi and 'gammas' listening intently, possibly to a lecture on Primrose Hill. By Ragna Karina Priddy. Courtesy Roger Priddy.

He gave a back-handed compliment to the arch-liberal President Franklin D. Roosevelt, 'the most intelligent imperialist the United States has had.' Roosevelt, as a liberal, 'knew the value of rhetoric', he said, while as a capitalist, he also knew that 'he who dominates the economy dominates the politics.' Roosevelt's contribution to U.S. imperialism was to recognise that U.S. economic interests in South America could not depend on the presence of the marine corps. 'You always see the marine. The enemy is always present, and there is no way of hiding him.' It had to depend on proxies: the police, local militias, the national militaries, whose 'loyalty to American commercial interests' could be guaranteed by economic self-interest. In other words, the U.S. insisted on political democracy in South America, but denied its economic underpinning.

But without economic underpinning, without the resources to mount and run campaigns, how could ordinary South Americans influence politics or get themselves elected? Most, after all, were illiterate. Many lived in slums, which meant they had no right to vote. In Venezuela, for example, forty percent of the people still lived outside the money economy, twenty-two percent were unemployed, while the country was forced to devote over $100 million to buying food from the US, although most of the country remained uncultivated. 'Who controls the money?' he asked. It certainly wasn't the trade unions. 'Even today only one per cent of unions in the underdeveloped world have check-off clauses because that little percent, whatever it is, those few pennies that would come off automatically out of the salary into the funds of the union make the difference between getting a glass of milk for a child a day or a week or not.'

Fortunately, said Gerassi, many South Americans had finally got wise to all this. 'They now know that the only way to break the structure is to break it, which means a violent revolution.' It was as simple as that: continue to do American's bidding or revolt. 'For Latin Americans—and I would conjecture that this is true for all the underdeveloped world—there is only one solution, and that solution is a violent revolution.'

But what about Western critics of American imperialism? What could they do? It was then that Gerassi turned to the most controversial part of his speech, the part that would most discombobulate the liberals in the audience. Western democracy, he said, was also bogus. Even in the United States, where so-called 'participatory capitalism' was most entrenched, ordinary people had very little influence on economic decision-making. And the much-vaunted rule of law was nothing such. On the contrary, it was used to justify 'repressions', rationalise 'oppressions' and codify 'frustrations.'

He gave as an example of the rule of law, a conversation that he had had in 1966, before he had embarked upon a fact-finding mission to Vietnam for the Russell Tribunal. One New York friend he had spoken to about the tribunal was Irving Horowitz, then a sociology professor at St. Louis University and, like Gerassi himself, an expert on South America and like him, too, a self-styled revolutionary. Gerassi had hoped for support of course. Yet, what he got from Horowitz was very different: a tirade again the tribunal on the grounds that it was designed to put morality—the people's justice— above the rule of law. This, Gerassi, told the audience, 'is the liberal position'. Even though it was 'under the rule of law that we butcher people in Santo Domingo, that it is under the rule of law that we go into Vietnam and try to wipe out a whole population with napalm, nevertheless his answer will be it must be under the rule of law that we must put an end to all these things.'

A nation whose young people were educated to believe something like that could never hate in the way that the South Americans hated. To most white North Americans, the sort of poverty endured by South Americans was merely an abstraction. How could they understand the poverty that led a peasant woman he had met not to feed the youngest of her five children on the grounds that she only had enough rice for four of them and that the child was already so weak that it was likely to die anyway?

To do what that mother had done, she had needed to hate. It was the same hate spoken about by Che Guevara when he said, 'Our soldiers must hate. A people without hatred cannot vanquish a brutal enemy.'

In the developed world, people didn't hate like that. There, it's an 'intellectual hatred,' Gerassi said. Yes, people were rejecting the system, but by dropping out. Hence the 'diggers, hippies, drug addicts and whatever else there is.' But they were not 'effective'. If they were that, they would be harassed; there would be jail sentences and lynching. Indeed, the fact that he himself was not in jail was because he too was not particularly effective. Ditto, the overwhelming majority of other people at the Congress. 'The fact that we can all come here and get our visas and our passports and go back [to the United States], and perhaps at the [worst] if we go to Cuba or if we go to Vietnam' lose our passports for a month is 'precisely because none of us are a threat.'

That was not the case with the blacks, however; they were a threat. But again, with what effect? With almost all the power in the hands of the government, they were destined to lose, unless they linked arms with the people of the underdeveloped world. This of course was Carmichael's view, he said, just as it was also Che Guevara's.

But it wasn't enough to link arms with the undeveloped world, the blacks in the US should learn from them too. There, as Che had made clear, the revolutionaries 'picked their battles'. 'The negro movement in the United States' should do likewise. 'When it attacks the white oppressor forces, it must be the one to decide when and how.'

They should also not act alone. The only realistic way forward was with a programme and as part of a nation-wide revolutionary organisation. Fighting had to take place on all fronts, blacks and revolutionary whites working together. Blacks doing one thing, whites something else. But methodically, intelligently. In Cuba, they'd found that the 'one way to guarantee that their people are genuinely free is not elections, is not a free press, is not all the trappings that we have. It's a hell of a lot better and it's a hell of a lot surer: they armed the people.' 'And when the people are armed, you can be sure that if the people don't like the government they sure as hell can get rid of it.'

The 'final bridge', he said, is an 'existential bridge' — and here he returned to Laing and Bateson's speeches — lamenting their 'preoccupation with consciousness'. It was a luxury that was only possible because they were 'dependent on the sufferings of others.'

He ended the speech with what was intended to be a rousing call to arms, but which, due to slight hesitations, fell flat, even though the speech as a whole was greeted with one of the longest rounds of applause that any speaker received at the Congress. In essence, it was this: if whites crossed that bridge, they could look forward to a most 'meaningful' kind of adventure.

*

Bearing in mind that Gerassi had explicitly and implicitly targeted Goodman during his speech, mocking him at the outset and making a couple of sly digs at his so-called utopianism and dislike of violence, it was appropriate that Goodman was the first that Sweezy called to respond. Though first he invited the Congress to voice their support for the radical French journalist Régis Debray who had been arrested by the security police in Bolivia.

Typically, Goodman's intervention was less a question than an attempt to trip Gerassi up. He picked up on Gerassi's advocacy of violence both during his speech and during Tuesday evening's panel discussion with George Rawick and C.L.R. James. Referencing Gerassi's advocacy of small bands of guerrillas and of arming entire populations, he wondered if the revolutionary cause in South America would be better served by inflicting massive casualties within and upon the United States. A team of electrical engineers, for instance, could sabotage the country's power supply or, if that wasn't good enough, why, a single biochemist (he didn't specify of what colour) could release a deadly pathogen.

Violence of that second sort was not, however, what Gerassi had in mind, so he didn't address Goodman's horrendous suggestion directly — or his first suggestion for that matter, though it was mentioned by other people as the session wound bad temperedly to a close. Instead, he said more about the situation in South America and continued his praise of Che Guevara. Che, he reminded the audience, had spoken of revolutionising all of South America, of creating, say, ten or fifteen additional Vietnams. Several Vietnams, Gerassi said, would force the government to draft middle-class white youngsters in their hundreds of thousands. 'And McNamara and Johnson know very well that when you alienate the mass bulk of the United States because you're killing their sons, then you have a revolutionary situation.'[20]

Naturally, as Gerassi made these comments, he addressed himself specifically to Goodman. But Goodman's attention was elsewhere; in fact, he didn't even bother to look at him. Most probably, it was a calculated snub. But Gerassi carried on, nevertheless, emphasising, again, the visceral hatred felt by South Americans and black people and, again, the importance of organisation. 'You oppose organisation', he shouted at Goodman.

> When you see the word communist, you see Stalinism or whatever it is. You haven't made that break which the new generation is making .... We don't give a damn about what is past. The New Left in Spain is not worried that there was a civil war. There wasn't a civil war. They're thinking about

> 1967. ... An organisation is judged by what it proposes, and the quality of the men and the standards of the men who fight that fight.

It was a tough, passionately delivered retort, particularly damaging for picturing Goodman as old-fashioned and out of touch with the very generation which the anarchist saw himself as primarily addressing. But Goodman ignored it, preferring, like Laing at this point, to heckle. Instead, it was replied to by one of Goodman's allies, the same ginger-haired and moustachioed Jewish New Yorker who had spoken during the Q&A with Bateson.

Assuming that the leadership of an organisation, any organisation, would quickly become well-known to the authorities, the New Yorker made the point that it could easily be picked off. Much better, he thought, that people acted independently and anonymously. Why not, for instance, put LSD in the water supply? 'Aren't you young enough to be in the New Left,' Gerassi snapped back. 'Why must you think that when a man says organisation it has to be published leaders and so on?'

Sweezy tried to bring the discussion back to South America by calling upon Laing to ask a question. But Laing too was only interested in probing Gerassi's attitude to mass murder in North America. The sort of person willing to use chemical warfare wouldn't have to hate like the blacks and South Americans hate; they merely have to think hateful thoughts, he said. They could be people like the upper-middle class intellectuals that Henry had spoken about on the previous day. They would base their actions on a simple cold analysis.

'In other words, what you're suggesting is that the revolutionaries wipe out Washington and New York and all that? And I thought that was the side of non-violence', Gerassi hit back. 'If your solution ... is to wipe out all of society, well then, fine, so you wipe out all of society. I presume that's one solution to the problem of Vietnam.' Which, of course, was the opposite of what Laing suggested.

When, following yet further angry exchanges, another close supporter of Goodman asked Gerassi, more or less, the same question again, Gerassi lost his temper, dragging Paul Goodman back into the argument by criticising his part in the campaign against the Bomb. Millions of people all over the world were dying from lack of food and water as a direct result of United States imperialism. 'But that's not casualties, no. Let's talk about atomic bombs, let's talk about the ten per cent that died in the Russian revolution, etc. If that's all you want to talk about then I don't know what this conference is for.'

It was the classic argument that structural or institutional violence is worse than physical violence. Yet, whether it changed any minds or not is moot. Some people may not even have heard it, for by this time the session had degenerated into a shouting match, with people pushing and shoving to grab hold of the microphone.

Eventually, Sweezy called on someone who hadn't yet contributed, his colleague, the economist Sean Gervasi, to speak. Put another way, he called on one of his own, for it was Gervasi who would introduce him before his speech on the following morning.

Gervasi summarised both sides of the argument, with the obvious intention of bringing order back into the proceedings. Thus, he spoke in a kind of academese, passing lightly over the personal rancour expressed by the speakers and resituating the problem as purely intellectual.

It wasn't long after that four-minute speech that Sweezy officially closed the meeting. However, the arguments carried on, presumably for some time afterwards. Not that that would have mattered much to Gerassi, for it was his final appearance at the Congress. Just a few hours later, he was on the first leg of his journey to Cuba to attend the first conference of the Organisation of Latin American Solidarity (OLAS). Others would follow him later.

*

Meanwhile, if Carolee Schneemann had learned anything from her first few days at the Congress, it was that very little would go to plan regarding her happening. She would have to fight her corner every step of the way. Not only had she had the contretemps with Goodman and the embarrassment of finding herself looking for a party on the wrong side of London, but Laing too had doubled down on his dislike if not of her then certainly of her intentions.

One undated example of his rudeness involved Laing's girlfriend, Jutta Werner. When Laing introduced Schneemann to Werner, he seemed to imply that the American was of very little consequence. 'He introduced me to [Jutta] as if since he had nothing to say to me [Jutta] might,' Schneemann recorded in one of her numerous notes about the Congress.[21] She wondered if Laing had taken against her because she was 'insufficiently respectful' to him, speculating too that it had something to do with his looks: 'Ronnie Laing, an extremely attractive man seemed to project a silly narcissism onto me.'

Nonetheless, despite these, sometimes, petty discourtesies, Schneemann was able to make good progress on her happening. By the 20th, she had the first bones of a 'core' group and a 'mass' group of performers and had already begun rehearsals. Much of the credit for this should be given to core group member and chief administrator of the Royal Shakespeare Company, Michael Kustow. He had become a fan of Schneemann very quickly. Other helpers were the composer Ron Geesin and the American filmmaker Steven Dwoskin. Then there was John and Barbara Latham, he 'utterly distracted', she, on the other hand, 'vastly practical', feeding Schneemann eggs one minute, searching for Latham's glasses the next, then phoning a junk shop on Schneemann's behalf and collating an essay that she had written.[22]

*

After Gerassi's contribution, there were two further important lectures that Thursday, both of which were recorded: one delivered by the American writer and activist David Horowitz (no relation to Irving Horowitz), the other by C.L.R. James. The first introduced a relatively new subject to the Congress: nationalism in the Middle East. The second took on the subject of the Western proletariat and examined its relationship with the peasants of the Third World.

Although Horowitz was new to the platform as a speaker, he wasn't new to London. He had been living in the capital since 1963, after moving from Stockholm to take part-time jobs with the Bertrand Russell Peace Foundation and an outpost of an American university and to pick up on the Tavistock Press's offer of a contract for a book about Marx and Martin Buber. This contract had led him to Laing who, acting as his editor, eventually became a friend, dropping in at his flat near Hampstead Heath and inviting him to give a lecture at Kingsley Hall about Paul Sweezy's economic theories.[23]

Like many Americans at the Congress, Horowitz was not simply left. He was left and Jewish, a fact which possibly led to some internal conflict about Israel. Regarding Israel, which just over a month earlier had defeated three Arab armies and captured four new territories, the position of most New Left thinking was clear. As no less an 'authority' as Che Guevara had recently put it: Israel was a colonial venture backed by Western imperialism.[24] Yet this neither did justice to the country's history nor to the particularity of the Jewish experience, which was that of a people with ties to the Holy Land since biblical times and who had been persecuted over many centuries.

As for the Palestinians and the Arabs more generally, most on the New Left inevitably saw them as the war's victims as indubitably they were, even though much of their propaganda revelled in the 'Final Solution' (or Holocaust, as it came to be called), and called for the total destruction of the Israeli state and of every Jew, man, woman and child, within it.

For many intellectuals who were both leftists and Jews, the war thus proved particularly stressful. The Israeli David had become a Goliath. It had taken on and destroyed three Arab armies while, at the same time, moved closer to the imperialist United States.

Horowitz began his speech with some observations about nationalism in general. It was, he reminded his audience, a concept, with a 'deeply ambiguous' relation to liberation. On the one hand, it could be a force for good, as it had been in the American colonies during the eighteenth century and as it now was in Vietnam and in the ghettos of the United States. On the other hand, it could licence unjustified feelings of superiority, as it had done in the Prussia of the nineteenth century and in the Germany of the Nazi period.

It was also easy for nations to cross from one sort of nationalism to the other. Witness, he said, the history of the Jews. 'Their national feeling, if you will, their nationalism against the outside world preserved them as a people over thousands of years without a territory and against the most extreme forms of persecution'. Yet, this same feeling, coupled with the certainty that they were chosen by God, was 'the basis of all the chauvinism and aggressive nationalism' that the Western world had experienced.[25]

Regarding nationalism, Marxism, he said, contained two schools of thought, one deriving from Rosa Luxemburg, the other from Lenin. Luxemburg had viewed the nation state as an 'anachronism', which would be succeeded by the 'liberation of the proletariat', while Lenin was more pragmatic. Thus, under the tsars, he had supported the right of national self-determination for the empire's minorities, as a bulwark against Russian chauvinism.

These same tensions were now posed in 'all their ambiguousness' in the Middle East, he said. Zionism, in its present, dominant, discriminatory, form, 'repulsed' him. Yet, at the same time, he was unable to argue that a Jewish state was not a necessity - the sorry history of antisemitism was proof of that. The present situation of the Jews of Israel was a bit like the position of the Puerto Ricans in New York. Just as the Jews had displaced the Arabs, so the Puerto Ricans had displaced the blacks. The difference though was that the Jews had become very powerful in the region.

He ran through the history of Zionism's relationship with the Palestinian Arabs: the Palestinians' exclusion from the national economy; the forced clearances; the purchase of entire villages from absentee landlords. The irony in that, he went on, was that these same landlords used the situation of the Palestinians, which they had done nothing to mitigate, to deflect attention from their own depredations. On a larger scale, this was also seen in the actions of Arab conservatives like King Faisal of Saudi Arabia and King Hussein of Jordan. Both stoked the fires of anti-Israeli nationalism not to help the displaced people of Palestine, but simply because it was in their interest to do so. Indeed, had it not been for the 1967 war, Hussein would probably have fallen.

The solution to the present crisis in Israel-Arab relations was socialist revolutions in the Arab countries and a more enlightened relationship with Israel. The Arabs should aim their propaganda not against Israel, but against British and American interests in the region, most notably in Aden and Saudi Arabia. The United States, he said, didn't have a single air base in Israel, but it did have a number in Saudi Arabia.

*

While Horowitz had also spoken about Cuban and Vietnamese nationalism during his speech, the first questions from the floor focused on Horowitz's claim that conservative states like Saudi Arabia and Jordan were the true outposts of Western imperialism. Quite the contrary, said a hesitant-speaking Roy Battersby, also from the audience. It was Israel that received vast quantities of American aid; it was Israel that was keeping President Hussein in power; and it was Israel that was the central block to 'social progress' within the Arab countries.

But what Battersby really wanted to talk about was a general point that Horowitz had made about the Jews supporting the British against Germany during the Second World war. 'This was not precisely true', said Battersby. In fact, in every country that the Germans invaded, Zionists had worked hand in glove with Nazis. This was why ordinary Jews had allowed themselves to be corralled into the cattle trucks that had taken them to extermination camps like Chelmno and Auschwitz. Their leaders had told them that they were being taken to work camps.

To support his contention, he mentioned a high-profile Israeli court case of the early 1950s, without giving it its name. This was the so-called Kastner trial, a case brought by the Israeli government against a Hungarian-born Israeli named Malkiel Gruenwald. Kastner, Gruenwald argued, had known about the death camps. Yet he had negotiated an agreement between his fellow Zionists and the Nazi bureaucrat Adolf Eichmann which spared a small number of Hungarian Jews, including members of his own family, from the fate of so many others.[26]

The court case, which opened in Jerusalem during the beginning of 1954 and was settled during the summer of 1955, raised enormous moral questions. Should Kastner have acted differently? Would it have made any difference to the fate of the vast majority if he had? The verdict? The judge cleared Gruenwald of almost all the charges but accused Kastner of having 'sold his soul to the devil.' The attorney general's office immediately launched an appeal to the Supreme Court, with the intention of delaying any possible prosecution of Kastner as a collaborator. But before judgement could be given, Kastner was shot outside his apartment in Tel Aviv; he died of his wounds ten days later.

In his response to Horowitz, Battersby gave an extremely muddled account of the case, confusing, for instance, Hungary with Austria. More significantly perhaps, he then linked it to other examples of Zionist 'collaboration' with fascism and to the modern state of Israel. 'I mean it's quite obvious that Jewish nationalism in this respect has been the most reactionary thing. And also that Mussolini trained the Stern Gang ... . It's in the interests of Western imperialism, U.S. imperialism in particular, to have the State of Israel there.'

In answer to Battersby and another questioner, Horowitz repeated his assertion that it was Aden and Saudi Arabia which were the major facilitators of Western imperialism. It was again left to the same ginger-haired man who had spoken at the Bateson and Gerassi Q&As to reply to Battersby's assertions. By and large, he agreed with them. The Zionists, in the form of the Jewish Agency, had collaborated with the Nazis. But he then went on to make a qualifying point about the essentially communist nature of the country's kibbutzim. They were not a tool of Western imperialism. This point, in its turn, was then picked up by Berke's old Free University of New York friend, Allen Krebs. He made the point amongst many other points, that, despite their economic structure, the kibbutzim were 'essentially military'. Indeed, a good number of them, he said, were originally developed as forts. In fact, that was why the Israeli government had tolerated them in the first place.

Horowitz concluded the Q&A by reverting to the point he had made in his introduction: that nationalism was both a revolutionary and a deeply reactionary force; and that the 'German disease' stood as a 'warning to everybody', including, he implied, the Black Power movement in the U.S. 'The banner of nationalism is not clarifying like a class banner is,' he added.

*

Following David Cooper's introduction of C.L.R. James on Tuesday, this time the veteran historian and philosopher was introduced by Laing with a slightly perplexing endorsement. Most of it was boilerplate: 'one of the leading scholars ... socialist movement ... colonial independence ... *The Black Jacobins* ...'. But, when he got to James's other famous book in Britain, his *Beyond a Boundary* of 1963, he aimed a weak witticism at David Cooper. The book, he said was a 'study of cricket or non-anti-cricket.' Then, he mispronounced the name of one of James's intellectual heroes, calling the Pan-Africanist George Padmore, 'George Padmon.'[27]

At this point, he sounded sober, which was not the case later, so presumably he had a glass or two on the platform. After giving the title of James's speech as 'The Dialectical Relationship between the Proletariat of the Advanced Countries and the Peasantry of the Underdeveloped Countries,' he hardly spoke again until some way through the Q&As. Then he took James to task with a superficially simple question.

At the heart of James's thesis was the conviction that the peasants of the world had been unfairly marginalised by Marxist theory and historiography. It was this that gave it its bite and topicality. He began with a brief resumé of their role during the English Civil War, claiming, controversially, that they were the most 'powerful', 'decisive' and politically 'advanced' force amongst those that struggled for domination. He then moved on to their role during the following century, arguing that it was integral to the French Revolution and also to the Haitian Revolution, where an army of ex-slaves prevented the British army for five years from fighting against the French. 'It is an astonishing thing that people don't know that.'

Regarding the revolutions of 1848 and the Commune of 1871, the reason they failed was because the peasants did not play a noticeable part. Whereas the Russian Revolution succeeded because they did. One of the few Marxists who recognised their contribution to Russia's revolution was Lenin, he said. The two issues that preoccupied Lenin towards the end of his life did not include industrialism, as most people would have expected. But the nature of government and the education of the peasantry. The first task the revolutionaries faced according to Lenin, he said, was to alter the character of the Tsarist, pre-bourgeois government they had inherited. And the second was this: "The second [was] to conduct educational work among the peasants." He said that those were Lenin's actual words. The fact that by making his speech he was directing the audience's attention to what Lenin really said was very pleasing, he added.

So far, so logical. So, it was not surprising that when he turned next to India, then China, then Ghana and then the Cuban Revolution, James made the same point that he'd made about the English, the French, and the Haitian revolutions, praising Gandhi first, then Mao, then Nkrumah, then Castro for understanding that the peasantry was crucial to his success. 'The victory of the Chinese Revolution began as an extension of [a] peasants' revolt,' he stated. The proletariat became involved afterwards. Similarly, it was the peasantry which led the Cuban Revolution.

Finally, he turned to Stokely Carmichael and to the situation of black people in the United States and their relation to the black peoples of the Third World—and with this subject he became very passionate, departing from the refined and slightly self-mocking pedantry of the earlier part of his speech.

Just as Lenin and the Pan-Africanist and race separatist Marcus Garvey had led international movements, so Stokely Carmichael was leading one today, one that was reaching towards an 'international sequence and connection'. The fact that the movement still contained a lot of 'loathsome white liberals, white communists [and] white all sorts' was to be regretted, for, like Carmichael, James too had grown sick of the way that white liberals had been able to dominate the movement.

Yet to call Carmichael a black separatist was absurd. Listen to him properly, he said. He was leaving the way open for the white proletariat to ally with the movement. 'But he doesn't say we want you to come. He says you do something and then you will see that we will come with you. It is a remarkable piece of political manoeuvring' and in the 'very vanguard of political development in the United States.'

*

After the inevitable questions from various Marxists challenging or qualifying James's observations and a slightly mysterious question pondering why he wasn't at Brixton Town Hall (where presumably Stokely Carmichael was speaking), Laing too contributed.[28] He questioned what James meant by characterising the relationship between the proletariat of the advanced world and the peasants of the underdeveloped world in his title as 'dialectical'.

It was a fair point to make. And it immediately put James on the defensive. But before answering Laing, he made an important point himself. In contrast to the impression that most people had taken from his speech, he wanted to emphasise that he believed that within the advanced countries the proletariat was still the key revolutionary force. After all, who else could it be? (He did not mention the students let alone Jules Henry's upper-middle class. But then as he would later make clear he had absolutely no time for Marcuse or for his supporters).

He admitted Laing's point concerning the relationship between the peasants and the proletariat. But then posited that in China at least it was very possible that in the future there would be one.

However, it was hardly a convincing response. It left the road open for another speaker to describe what he thought *was* a dialectic relationship or perhaps, more correctly, a paradox. This was a development occurring in the 'ideological superstructure', both in the advanced and in the undeveloped nations and pertained to rationality, religion and other traditional beliefs and ways of living. Just as people in the underdeveloped nations were beginning to think like Westerners, Westerners were beginning to think like

Easterners. They were even becoming more 'tribal'. What, he asked, did James think of that?

It was not, however, a question upon which James was willing to be drawn. Speaking deliberately and at times even magisterially, he instead gave his views on the present condition of Western intellectual life in general. Western intellectual life was completely bankrupt, he said. There was a 'total absence of any sense of the development of human society.'

The intellectual who probably mattered most, James said, was Arnold Toynbee. Not that he himself had read more than a half of one of his books. 'I said that is enough for me. But I see he is very popular.'

He also noted that just as today there was a fashion for Zen Buddhism and Islam, previously Roman Catholicism had been popular. 'I haven't paid too much attention to [Western intellectual life] because I didn't see any point in it. I'm sorry I can't do any better.'

*

While Laing had apparently started the session sober, by this time he was again drunk and in no mood for observing pleasantries. When the ginger-haired and moustachioed New Yorker started on an involved speech about the character of the 'new' proletarian class, i.e., people like himself, people who did not live by bread alone, Laing interrupted him rudely. 'When you're ready to deliver a speech, you can deliver a speech. At the moment you're not. Don't poach[?] on someone else's. Ask a question.' This delivered in a slurred and irritated Glasgow drawl.

The New Yorker simply apologised and made a point based on his reading of Marcuse's *One-Dimensional Man*. It was the students in the United States who were the true revolutionary class. 'To think otherwise' was 'not to have your eyes open.'

This provoked a retort from Roy Battersby, insisting that he was wrong. Indeed, just the previous night, instead of sitting at the Congress, he had been talking to a group of workers in South London who were 'extremely revolutionary.'

Following some remarks about Marcuse and Goodman, neither of whom he rated highly, James concluded the Q&A with a long peroration, in which his voice, beautifully modulated, expertly surveyed the epoch of 'bourgeois degeneration.' In 1914, he said, the bourgeoisie 'controlled education. They controlled government. They controlled the press. They controlled ideas' and dominated the rest of the world materially and psychologically. But that world was now gone, blown apart by the First World War, the Russian Revolution, the emergence of fascism and the Second World War. Bourgeois society was now degenerating before people's eyes. In 1914, the bourgeoisie 'could have told you who they were, what they were ... , all they had, what were their prospects, what were their aspirations, what other people should look at.' But, 'what can they tell us today? Nothing at all, except to have a summit.'

'I needn't labour the point. There has been a total degeneration of bourgeois society during the last fifty years', he added. And here he paused to wonderful effect. 'Mr Chairman, I can't go any further.'

*

If Gerassi's speech had been lively and passionate then the first full week's final morning speech was more in the manner of a prayer meeting. Put another way, if Gerassi had proved himself one of the lions of the Congress: mercurial, eager, and quick to cause and receive offence, then Paul Sweezy would be one of its bovines. He was a tall, white-haired, rather spare, slow-speaking and donnish-looking patrician, whose reputation, first as an editor of *Monthly Review*, second as an historian and thirdly as a theorist of Marxist economics, was formidable.

Even Berke, not renowned for his interest in economics, had read Sweezy's book with Paul Baran, *Monopoly Capital*. But then why would he not? Like Laing's *The Divided Self* and George Woodcock's *Anarchism*, it was one of a small number of books that pretty much everyone on the youngish Left had read — or pretended to.

Sweezy was introduced by Sean Gervasi, who was dressed in a black suit, white shirt and dark tie, himself looking very much a picture of British academic propriety. Indeed, this was the flavour of almost the entire event. A rather ponderous, precise, ex cathedra, well-wrought, remorseless, speech from the platform. Then a series of earnest and occasionally ill-informed questions from hoi polloi below. No wonder some of the livelier types in the audience shuffled in their seats. Without any change of atmosphere, they could just as easily have been in a lecture theatre at an Oxbridge college or perhaps at a seminar organised by *New Left Review*. But that was Sweezy's style. He wasn't a rabble rouser or a theatrical personality, but a thoughtful and opinionated Marxist intellectual who fought his battles with insouciance, knowledge, theory, and statistics.

Taking as the subject of his speech the 'future of capitalism', Sweezy began by identifying the major approaches to the question. First, there was breakdown theory, which was characteristic of 'bourgeois economics' and of a 'certain kind of Marxism', he said; second, there was development economics, which was 'characteristic of the economic theory of the Soviet Union.'[29]

The first approach, he said, was deficient for treating the capitalism of the advanced economies as an isolated phenomenon, the second for picturing the pre-industrial world as in the same 'state of underdevelopment' as the present-day Third World. In fact, the Asian, African, and South American economies of the fifteenth and the beginning of the sixteenth centuries were extraordinarily well developed — and not just by their own standards. But by today's standards too.

He then described what happened to these continents with the advent of colonialism: robbery, slavery, genocide, economic ruin. The natives of South America forced down the mines; the natives of the Caribbean 'wiped out'; portions of Africa turned into 'hunting grounds for slaves'; and India — one of 'the most advanced civilisations in the world' — 'mercilessly robbed and turned into one of the poorest and most backward countries in the world'. While, on the other side of the coin, the slave traders of Liverpool, Bristol, Nantes and Boston grew fat. This, he said, was the 'economic and social basis' of the West's rise to global hegemony.

Thereafter, once the first few generations of conquerors had passed, the 'investors, the traders, the bankers, the administrators, and advisors' moved in; and it was to them that the world owed what became the pattern of normal economics, which placed metropolises and their peripheries 'in mutual and dialectical interdependence.' The peripheries produced raw materials, which were shipped to manufacturers at the centres, which then sold them back to the peripheries. 'The underdevelopment of the periphery was thus frozen and perpetuated, while the centre was enabled to continue to develop with the aid of the wealth drained out of its satellites.'

Fig 9. Paul Sweezy. By Peter Davis. congress still. Courtesy Peter Davis, www.villon films.com

This pattern of development and underdevelopment was not just characteristic of the relations between coloniser and colonised, he said; it was also true within parts of the developed and underdeveloped economies as well. So, for example, though Park Avenue and Harlem were just a few miles apart, one part was rich, the other desperately poor, while even Brazil, most of which remained underdeveloped, had its wealthy areas.

> This is the whole history of capitalism from the beginning, and it repeats itself on every conceivable scale. ... And until you learn this, and until you make it a part of your everyday thinking, you are going to be misled again

and again and again by the propaganda which comes at you all the time, and which attempts to separate things which belong together.

It was for this reason, he said, that, unlike some of the other speakers at the Congress, he was loath to use the phrase the 'Third World'. There was only one world, locked in dialectical interdependence, in which the stronger exploited the weaker. It was also the reason why the communist revolutions of the previous fifty years were not as 'bourgeois ideology' would have it, 'some kind of historical accident'; they were the outcome of the struggle of underdeveloped countries to free themselves.

One of these underdeveloped countries was China, another was North Korea, a third was Ho Chi Minh's Vietnam, and a fourth was Cuba, all countries that in their different ways were making remarkable progress, while those countries that remained within the Western orbit faced either overpopulation (thanks to the import of Western medicines) or a decade of revolution.

Naturally, for his part, he hoped for revolution. Yet, who was to say that the developed nations wouldn't blow the world up. 'I would only add to that, that if that should be the outcome, capitalism too would blow up. And that adds nothing whatever to the cheerful prospects for its future.'

*

Taking into account Sweezy's position on China, it was appropriate that during his speech a group of young people in the gallery above him unfurled banners with quotations from Chairman Mao's *Little Red Book* and some roughly sketched slogans on newsprint. This surely wasn't the first intervention from the small group of German Maoists who attended the Congress, but it was possibly the first time they were caught on camera, in this case by a young English filmmaker named Peter Davis and his Swedish colleague Stefan Lamm, the pair having been tipped off about the Congress by Davis's friend, Roy Battersby.

One of the newsprint posters contained words which could just as easily have come from a John Gerassi or a Frank Joyce: 'We need Strategy. Program. Coordination.' Another read, 'What is the Problem?' Then a third next to that: 'Fascism is evident in Europe and U.S.' While a fourth read 'Pacifists Liberals Anarchists failed in Greece Spain West Berlin'.[30]

Intriguingly, Davis's camera caught the expression of a smiling Tariq Ali as the first of these posters unfurled. As for Sweezy, he may not even have been aware of them, for he carried on in the same even, resolute tone that marked all his speech.

After a five-minute break during which the Maoists distributed copies of the *Little Red Book*, a clearly flustered Sean Gervasi called the assembly to order - flustered because the microphone wasn't working again. As he waited for written questions to come up from the floor, he mentioned a seminar that he and fellow economists Robin Blackburn, Bob Rowthorn and Ajit Singh were holding later that afternoon. Their subject would be ideology and economics, the North American economist J.K. Galbraith and the question of 'underdevelopment' as it had been described by Sweezy during his presentation.

Then Joe Berke intervened with an announcement that Julian Beck of The Living Theatre would be arriving at about the same time for a seminar in the annex.

The first two questions to Sweezy related to his analysis of capitalism: how did he account for the fact that Spain and Portugal, colonisers both, were themselves underdeveloped? And what did he think of Max Weber's thesis on the rise of capitalism? Neither of them impressed him very much. The first question brought forth an irritated assertion that his speech wasn't intended to be comprehensive. Capitalist development was complicated, so, of course, there were all sorts of contradictions. How could he possibly go into all of them here? Weber was plain wrong: he had attributed capitalism to the puritan ethic when, in fact, the puritan ethic was itself a response to developments in the economic base.

Another questioner wanted to know if capitalism would collapse because of its own contradictions or because of a challenge from the Third World? Probably from both, responded Sweezy. As he'd said in his lecture, capitalism was a global system; and it had been a global system 'from the beginning'. Another asked him about the Soviet Union. Was it or was it not an imperialist entity? It was not, said Sweezy.

One of Sweezy's lengthiest and most involved answers came as a response to a questioner asking him to predict how developments in the US economy over the next few years would alter the American way of life. Not that he answered the question directly. Instead, he began by looking at how developments in the world at large were transforming the United States into a 'militarist, imperialist society'. This was a path upon which it was 'irrevocably' embarked, Sweezy said, and which would see it impose its hegemony not only on the underdeveloped world but on its capitalist rivals in Europe and in the rest of the world as well.

A more surprising intervention came from Peter Cadogan towards the end of the Q&A. He gave a long statement doubting the usefulness of economics as an explanation of anything. What did Sweezy's thesis matter? The foundation of politics was politics, not economics, he said. Instead, the Congress should address itself to the gigantism of the world's major corporations, both East and West. 'We are facing the heresy of size. Everything has to get bigger; everything has to get nationalised; everything has to get amalgamated ... [which] is the very thing which is common to all the capitalist and so-called socialist systems.' Everything he had heard from the platform had been about the 'adulation of size'. But size was violence's 'quantitative aspect'. 'We have to assert what we can do at the individual level to take power away from the centre politically and economically and we have to begin to appreciate that the foundations of politics is politics!'

Meanwhile, an unimpressed Sweezy sat stony-faced, smoking a cigarette; while also unimpressed was Sean Gervasi. 'Thank you very much, Peter. It's very kind of you'.

*

During the afternoon, while the participants waited for the arrival of Julian Beck and the start of the afternoon's seminars, someone called an additional meeting to complain, once again, about the organisation of the Congress. This one was chaired by an American friend of Berke, a graduate student in mathematical logic, named Joe Rosenstein. During Berke's Columbia days the pair had roomed together. Since then, Rosenstein had gone on to play an increasingly active role in protesting the Vietnam War.

One speaker used the occasion to complain, once again, about that 'bloody thing, which is a horrible thing', the microphone.[31] But he also made two positive suggestions: first, that Francis Huxley should deliver a speech on the following Thursday, this being the space that had been vacated by Gerassi (who had taken over the absent Erving Goffman's spot); and second, that the Congress should have music of some sort.

Fig 10. Allen Ginsberg with Congress registrant Marjaleena Repo. Friday afternoon. By Peter Davis. Congress stills. Courtesy Peter Davis, www.villonfilms.com

But the main point of the meeting was to settle a seemingly foolish argument about the use of space. One small group of participants insisted that Sean Gervasi and his fellow economists held their afternoon seminar away from the area in front of the platform. 'If the circle was in the centre there [pointing away from the place where the Q&A had taken place], what would be the distribution of speakers? Here [pointing to the area around him] there are fifteen speakers. Everybody is speaking here. The density of speakers is enormous here and over there none. ... Speak man. Create spaces on your own. Don't [take?] the spaces over here' — this from the ginger-haired American, who Laing had brutally scissored during the Q&A following C.L.R. James's session.[32]

Picking up on the suggestion of music, a diffident Ginsberg stepped in with an offer to perform a chant during that evening, which a portion of the participants eagerly accepted.

Overall, it was a disagreeable and unruly meeting. 'People are so violent to each other. This isn't funny', Marjaleeno Repo remarked to Ginsberg just after Rosenstein had closed the meeting.[33]

*

It was Michael Kustow who announced Beck's arrival. Taking the microphone from a confused and lost-looking Gervasi, he said that the maverick actor and stage director had just arrived from 'exile' in Europe and was about to start a talk about the 'relevance of a new kind of theatre' to violence and liberation.

Fig 11. Julian Beck. Friday afternoon. By Peter Davis. Congress stills. Courtesy Peter Davis, www.villonfilms.com

Due perhaps to the kerfuffle involving the economists and the ginger-haired American and company, Beck delivered his speech in the annex, a small brick building accessed from near the main entrance to the Roundhouse. Paul Zeal caught something of his appearance on the occasion in a diary entry he made a couple of days later. Beck was 'brilliant eyed' and 'vividly present', he wrote.[34] He could have added that the top of his head was completely bald; that what hair he did have cascaded luxuriantly over his thin neck and floral-patterned shirt; that he was thick-lipped; and that he spoke without notes in a fully rounded and educated accent.

Characteristically for a man who made a point of breaking down barriers between audiences and actors, Beck did not deliver his speech standing up, but from a sitting position. The first part is lost. But it seems he began with one of his major themes: the evil of money.

The Living Theatre was not a conventional theatrical troupe, he said. The thirty or so actors lived as a commune. Some had part-time jobs or other sources of income. But one of the major ideas that sustained the group was that mammon was the cause of almost all the world's ills. 'We cannot continue to live in a world which is enslaved by money for very much longer', he said.[35]

Kustow asked him to describe the work which the troupe were currently working on. It was a version of *Frankenstein*, Beck replied. Their version was based, he said, on what the troupe called 'the struggle': an admittedly bothersome but open-ended process in which the troupe talked at great length about their 'personal psyches', their 'personal dreams' and their 'personal artistic concepts'. 'But you go through it, he said, and finally 'it all coheres ... something more inclusive comes together than just another form of creative work', something 'perhaps more pure.'

He then went on to talk about the importance of sex to the company, itemising some of its permutations. 'There is a reasonable amount of multiple-party sex, of three, four, five, six people sex — there's a reasonable amount of male homosexuality, and a smaller amount of female homosexuality.' These sorts of sexual relationships were usually unproblematic, he said; much more unsettling to the troupe's *esprit de corps* was monogamy. In recent months, the company had been turned upside down by the ending of one such monogamous relationship. He had resolved the crisis, he said, by creating a ritual at the centre of which was a girl—he didn't say which girl or whether she volunteered or not. For thirty-five or forty minutes the troupe had been free to do whatever they wanted to her. 'That is, they could twist her head off, they could bend [her] back ..., do anything that they wanted to this person.' Some people watching the ritual, he said, were not even sure that the girl would survive the experience. He had gone through a similar trial himself, he added. 'When I came out of that experience, I felt that I had gained a year of life, that my body, my organs, things had been awakened in me.'

*

One Englishman asked Beck how he dealt with different forms of authority, then another man— a Scot—asked him how he could join the company. It's a very 'mysterious' process', said Beck. 'If you can get a member of the company to fall in love with you or if you're a chick and you can get impregnated, that's a very good way because we have a very bourgeois sense of responsibility.' A third questioner, another Englishman, wanted to know how long people stayed with the company. That depends, Beck said. After all, some of the people who joined the company were mentally disturbed. But he never assumed that they had signed a contract, since he was 'a very good orthodox anarchist'.

There were also questions about technique and the nature of the company's interactions with their audiences. Sometimes, Beck, said people struck out at them with their hands or kicked them. Some even tried to burn them.

The final question came from Berke. He wanted to know if Beck planned to spend more time at the Congress. He did, he said. He would be back later in the afternoon for a meeting. He also, he said, would like to bring the entire company to the Roundhouse one day. Indeed, he would far rather work at the Roundhouse than in a regular theatre.

*

By eight o'clock Ginsberg was back on the platform, this time sitting cross-legged on a blanket with a stony-faced woman named Maretta Greer and a young man. Ginsberg was living with both, not at Elsham Road, but in Panna Grady's summerhouse in Hanover Terrace. 'Rumour' had it that the young man had walked to London from Gloucestershire', reported Iain Sinclair in a short paragraph incorporated into a section of *Kodak Mantra Diaries*. 'But rumour is unconfirmed', he added.[36]

Fig 12. Allen Ginsberg, Maretta Greer and a young guitar player change the mood to something spiritual. By Peter Davis. Courtesy Peter Davis, www.villonfilms.com

Having changed from the light grey jacket and trousers that he had worn during the afternoon, Ginsberg was now wearing a loose white jacket, a loose-fitting white striped shirt, and a thick string of rudraskha prayer beads. The beads were a nod to the central theme of the evening's 'demonstration': mantras, which is to say, in Ginsberg's formulation, a 'short-form magic formula, prayer, invocation, hypnotic, repetitive, breathing exercise, chant.'[37] The trio performed half a dozen of these, Ginsberg patiently interpolating explanatory remarks, various political reflections and anecdotes. It was the sort of heartfelt and ramshackle occasion at which the charismatic poet excelled, so it is not surprising that it stuck in many people's minds for decades after.

Greer began the first mantra *Om Sri Maitreya* on Ginsberg's harmonium, setting up a drone. She started to sing, was joined by Ginsberg on vocals then finally by the young man on guitar. Then, over the following two hours or so, they played half a dozen others, including a Hindu one, *Hari Om Namah Shivaya*.

Sometimes Ginsberg clapped along to the vocals or clanged little fingers cymbals, these, like the harmonium, one of his long-standing trademark accompaniments.

Perhaps the most interesting part of the evening from a non-musical perspective came when Ginsberg spoke about the potential 'political applications' of mantras, in other words their use as a form of psycho-politics. Speaking with great earnestness, he wondered if Carmichael and his fellow Black Power advocate, the poet and writer LeRoi Jones (also known under his new name as Amiri Bakara), could be persuaded to join with 'people trained in meditation exercises and in making psycho-political sound' to calm the police. Then perhaps the hippies that Carmichael had mocked during the Q&A on Tuesday really could make a difference. He mentioned, without giving anywhere near the full details, an occasion eighteen months earlier when, with Ken Kesey, Neil Cassady and a bunch of other so-called Merry Pranksters, he had met with the Oakland chapter of the Hell's Angels. The bikers were threatening to break up a peace march organised by the local branch of the Vietnam Day Committee, and it was Kesey and Ginsberg's self-elected task to try and persuade them not to. And, in fact, with the help 'of a little LSD', they succeeded. 'This is an indication of possible political manifestation of psycho-political tactics', he added.

The 'demonstration' ended with Ginsberg repeatedly chanting 'om'. That said, it could also have ended *him*, for unknown to the poet or to anyone else on the floor of the Roundhouse, a resident of Kingsley Hall, a disorientated, 'terrified' and 'terrifying' young American man named Dag Kolderup was up in the gallery, apparently nursing the intention of hurling a brick at *someone* down below him.[38] He was confronted by an anxious Peter Davis who, finding no better way of lessening the presumed danger to the people below, lunged at Kolderup, who struck with the brick at Davis's right hand, then wrenched the camera off Davis's shoulder and threw it at the gathering below him, where it hit an 'inoffensive Indian'.[39]

But perhaps, as Davis now concedes, Kolderup hadn't intended to throw the brick at all; perhaps he was simply carrying it for his protection.

7. Stokely! Stokely!

The 'open forum', which took place on the second Saturday at 8 o'clock, was always likely to be something special. And indeed, it was, though only partly for the slight air of mystery that surrounded it. The posters billed the event as featuring Laing, Carmichael, Ginsberg and sometimes Cooper (who would act as chairman) 'and others.' But who were these 'others'? When the posters were designed the IPS didn't know. Nor perhaps did anyone else for that matter until the 15th or the 16th. But by the morning of the 17th, 'their' identity was common knowledge enough for Geoffrey Bamford to speak about how they were going to 'cut through' the Congress's 'garbage of words' at Iain Sinclair's Haverstock Hill breakfast table.[1]

But, in fact, there were no 'others.' There was only one 'other': Emmett Grogan, the twenty-four-year-old Digger, which is to say activist of free food and free everything in San Francisco's Haight-Ashbury's hippie paradise. And even he almost didn't make it. It was Allen Ginsberg's idea to invite him: 'Emmett Grogan brilliant activist Haight Ashbury SF Diggers Group interested in getting to Europe—check out situationists elsewhere & attend conference with us—I don't have money to finance it but it would be a great idea I think [if you invited him]—this in a letter to Berke on June the 14th.[2] But with monies short at the IPS, Berke apparently passed up on the idea, so Grogan had to find his own air fare, which (apparently again) he ponced from Edwin Fancher, the publisher of New York's *Village Voice* newspaper.[3]

Ginsberg did, however, arrange Grogan's accommodation. He persuaded his hostess Panna Grady to put him up in her grand house on Hanover Terrace, where Grogan was quickly introduced to William Burroughs and Alex Trocchi, though it was Grady who made the greatest impression on him. She introduced herself with a 'delicate whisper' before expressing her hope that his journey across the Atlantic had been a 'pleasant one', he writes in a memoir which appeared a few years after the Congress, called *Ringolevio*;

and adds that she had the 'grace and beauty of years of wealthy refinement.'[4]

*

Meanwhile, since the brouhaha provoked by the *Panorama* Programme and his speech on Tuesday, Carmichael had continued with what a Special Branch security briefing later described as a 'whirlwind 9 day crusade', during which he was trailed by various 'spooks' and a Granada Television film team.[5] The crusade included speaking engagements with black audiences, numerous house visits, a workshop discussion organised by activist and publisher John La Rose in Hackney and interviews with BBC journalist Andrew Salkey and *Observer* journalist Colin McGlashan.[6]

Not surprisingly, many black radicals have (or had) golden memories of meeting him at this time, always in a crowd, and naturally, with Michael Malik, arguably the clown prince to Carmichael's authentic revolutionary. Darcus Howe, Jessica Huntley, Courtney Tulloch, Roy Sawh, Obi Egbuna and Angela Davis have already been mentioned. Others to add to this list include Eddie Braithwaite, Stefan Khalifa, Sam Sagay, the novelist Samuel Sevlon and the filmmaker Horace Ové, plus Farrukh Dhondy and Dilip Hiro, who were both of Indian origin. And there were certainly many others as well: black, brown and, perhaps surprisingly, white; people obscure then and obscure today, but bowled over by Carmichael's fire, charm and charisma.[7]

As for Laing, Cooper and Ginsberg, they had naturally stuck with the Congress, spending most of their time either at the Roundhouse or the house on Elsham Road.

*

By half past seven the Roundhouse was beginning to fill up, not just with the usual crowd: the alphas, the betas, the gammas, Peter Davis and various London-based professional or semi-professional filmmakers, the interested but uncommitted; there were also several foreign film crews.[8]

Carmichael presumably arrived with George Ware, Malik and others in his entourage. Ginsberg came with Burroughs, Burroughs' friend Ian Sommerville and Panna Grady. Grogan, who was high on hashish and heroin, possibly with Trocchi or another of his countercultural heroes. Laing and Cooper, who knows? Probably, Laing arrived with his girlfriend, Jutta Werner.

The forum wasn't just an opportunity for the panellists to address the main themes of the Congress; it was also an opportunity to play at peacocks; a fashion show (or anti-fashion show) even. Thus, Carmichael wore a dark jacket over a collarless gold silk shirt—Mao-style to reflect his politics—, Grogan and Ginsberg wore necklaces, a snake tooth one in the former case. Then three of the men wore dark glasses: Carmichael, Laing, and Grogan. Was that because of the lights? Or was it because they wanted to look mysterious?

Before taking the stage, Ginsberg introduced Grogan to various assembled notables or notables-to-be, one of whom was Angela Davis; Carmichael was another. But Grogan was in no mood for pleasantries with a man that he had already decided he despised. So, when Carmichael smiled and put out his hand, he ignored it.

What Carmichael made of the insult can easily be imagined. According to Grogan's own account of the incident, he started "huffin' n' puffin' thunder and smoke about 'Who's that longhaired motherfuckin' hippie punk think he is ...!'"[9] But Grogan's motive wasn't racist; it was political. He simply hated politicians, by which he meant people who worked within an establishment, any establishment: conservative, 'radical' or whatever. Put another way, he would have been just as rude to President Johnson.

*

Cooper introduced the speakers to the audience with short, pithy, to-the-point biographies, and added a few lines about himself and the other men in the IPS. If Carmichael was a liberator, so were they. The difference lay in the fact that Carmichael liberated people every single day whereas with them it was merely sometimes. [10]

Ginsberg began his contribution not with a speech, but with a rendition of one of the prajnaparamita sutras, a series of texts from the Buddhist tradition, which teach, amongst other things, that the physical world is an illusion. He did this, first, in what he called 'Sino-Japanese', then second, in English. Carmichael, then Grogan, then Laing followed him with their contributions.

Fig 13. Saturday, Open Forum. Laing with his back to the camera, then Carmichael, then Ginsberg then Grogan. Ted Joans is on the far right. By Ragna Karina Priddy. Courtesy Roger Priddy.

Carmichael offered what was effectively a summary of what he'd said before, either in his plenary speech or in the Q&A that followed it. This was in spite of the fact that since his Tuesday speech, there had been more riots-cum-rebellions, this time in Nyack and Minneapolis, and the first National Conference on Black Power had opened in Newark.[11] The only new things were a sideways dig at his 'good friend Emmett', a short section on the draft— for his part, if the army tried to conscript him, he would shoot it out with them—and the lines with which he ended his speech, paraphrased from Bertolt Brecht's famous poem, *To Posterity*. 'Please do not judge us harshly. For those of us who wanted to make a foundation for kindness could not ourselves be kind,' he said.[12]

Grogan had forgotten the notes he had written for the occasion. So, with his brain still addled by heroin, he made very little sense, speaking elliptically in short, disconnected bursts that, in any case, many people couldn't hear due to a fault in the sound system. His main theme was autonomy. The 'white world', i.e., the world of school, employment, marriage, a settled home life, etc. was an 'unnatural myth', he said. White people were revolting against it by going mad, black people by exploring their identity.

Just to 'stand on a street corner and wait for no one' was 'powerful', he said, thus echoing a line by the beat poet, Gregory Corso.[13] If the changes that people had been talking about at the Congress actually came about, most of the people in the Roundhouse would not understand it. In fact, they would 'die'.

All sorts of people had offered all sorts of interpretations to explain why white people were turning against the values that they'd grown up with. But there was only one explanation: each person was seeking their own 'natural humanity.'

Black people were fortunate — they could recognise each other by their skin colour, whereas turned-on white people could only recognise other turned-on white people by growing their hair and dressing colourfully. These, however, were fads. 'But the new reason and the new sense of brotherhood' was becoming 'closer to being understandable.'

Grogan ended his quixotic contribution with a sentence the final clause of which quickly became a classic, repeated all over the Western world and emblazoned on T-shirts: 'Spontaneity, autonomy, seem to be the new type of humanity that's coming about, and today is the first day in the rest of your life.'

This time the applause was smaller than it had been for Carmichael. 'What's that guy on?' Iain Sinclair overheard an American journalist whisper.[14]

Whereas Grogan had spoken for six minutes, Laing, like Carmichael, spoke for ten, his delivery hesitant and slightly slurred, again perhaps the effect of alcohol. He began with a long quotation from the philosopher Simone Weil on the pitiless cruelty of the

Romans and then accused the west of far worse cruelty. Indeed, the present-day West was worse, far worse than the Nazis.

Eschewing the word play that had characterised some of his previous contributions, he repeated his earlier observation about the nature of violence and counter-violence. For the most part, there was nothing intellectually challenging about them: if people were hit, at some point they hit back. More difficult, as far as he was concerned, was understanding why and how violence was perpetrated both at the 'periphery' of empire and at the 'interface with subgroups' within it. During the past week, the Congress had heard all sorts of suggestions as to what could be done about those sorts of violence. You could hit first, as John Gerassi had said, or you could use 'flower power'.

For him, he said, the most interesting speeches — and here he must have had Jules Henry and perhaps Sweezy most in mind — were the ones exploring the tie-up 'between industry, the military, racist ideologies', and economics, and showing how these interests were mediated to 'smaller groups', families and so on. The task was rarely easy, however, particularly as the connections were often invisible. 'As far as I know there's no economist or intellectual in the whole of this country who has come out with a systematic detailed analysis.'

Laing then brought the audience back to the fundamental purpose of the Congress in the first place: the dialectics of liberation and the demystification of violence. He gave Hegel's famous example of the master and the slave, how the more the master enslaves his slave, the more he gets the slave to do things for him, the more helpless he becomes. He then referenced Marx's thesis about the inevitability of revolution and said that the exploited of the world had entered a period of revolution.

Unfortunately, like Gerassi on the Thursday, he muffed his closing lines, mixing up his words and losing himself in a maze of twisted syntax, all to make a point based upon a metaphor used by Jules Henry about how the United States had 'grown fat' on the fear of communism. Fat, he said, flipping the metaphor, was killing the middle-class American male at a higher rate and at an earlier age than had ever been the case, irrespective of country or epoch.

He ended with a cant phrase, hopeless in its utopianism: 'Until all men are free, none of us can be.'

*

Following Laing's anti-climactic contribution, many in the audience rushed forward to put questions to Carmichael, though, wearingly and inevitably, there were again problems with the microphones. One young man, picking up on Carmichael's statements about institutional racism, asked him about the Race Relations Act. Enacted by parliament in 1965, the act, amongst other matters, made racial discrimination in public places illegal. Would he say this was a negative act?' Carmichael nodded his head. 'Yes, I would', he replied.

Ginsberg's first extended spoken contribution came shortly after this and in response to a well-spoken, confident, young man, who complained that neither Grogan's nor Laing's speeches had taken propositional form. It simply wasn't enough to talk about violence; he wanted to know what could be done about it.

Like the earlier speakers, Ginsberg also spoke slowly, crafting his sentences as he went along, speaking about the 'breakthrough' that he and others of his generation and the next had experienced; and about the role of LSD in enabling them to share a 'common meat universe.'

What else could be done about violence on a practical level? Well, there was the example of the Diggers in San Francisco and similar groups in New York, he said, madcaps almost all, who also tried to live without money. These people were 'beginning to leave the money wheel' and the 'hallucination wheel of the media' to form their own kind of societies.

He also referred again to Carmichael's tongue-in-cheek suggestion on the Tuesday that hippies should go to Newark, stand in front of the police, and throw flowers at them when they were shooting at black people. That was 'one area' he said, where he 'did feel a desire for practical action.'

However, none of this impressed Grogan. Violence, he said, was necessary. If you wanted to change a culture, you had to use violence; it was as simple as that. The problem with liberals, he went on, was that they were afraid of it. 'Violence is and will always be necessary to tear away the shreds of myth and absurdity that we've been encased in since we were born.'

Fig 14. Emmett Grogan speaking at the Open Forum. By Peter Davis. Congress stills. Courtesy Peter Davis, www.villonfilms.com

A much weightier response came from a well-known activist and public speaker named Ajoy Shankar Ghose, who challenged Ginsberg on his knowledge of Hinduism and Buddhism. Speaking in a voice dripping with bitterness, he pointed out that the two religions were in contradiction to each other. He had, he said, been a Hindu himself. And the religion was 'trash'. Ginsberg, he said, was a terrible influence on young people, leading them to hashish and marijuana and a false view of life. He was a spiritual fake and a hypocrite who, instead of supporting Carmichael and practising asceticism, was spending his time with teenage girls.' 'And boys!', someone shouted from the audience, which provoked much laughter from the other men on the platform and a smile from Ginsberg.

But this was hardly the sort of discussion that most of the audience wanted to hear. And a leaf was quickly turned by an earnest young American, who expressed contempt for white liberals as well as hippies and pacifists. The correct way forward had been identified at the Congress many times already; it was the policy advocated by Carmichael: black and white working separately but equally. Thanks to Carmichael and other activists, the blacks already had a programme, a strategy, and tactics. The time was now ripe for Anglo-American youth to formulate theirs. He was sick of listening to 'high-sounding phrases.' Whites should 'begin to organise, to smash the kind of machinery' that was also oppressing the blacks.

Following further contributions, the same man who had complained that Laing and Grogan's speeches had not taken propositional form asked Laing to comment on the nature of personal violence: 'Why one man should desire physically to harm another? Why a G.I. should want to kill a Vietnamese? Why a lout in Somers Town should want to break a bottle over my head?'

Fig 15. R.D. Laing in full flow at the Open Forum. By Peter Davis. Congress stills. Courtesy Peter Davis, www.villonfilms.com

Laing didn't answer the question directly. Instead, he told one of his favourite stories, about a young man he had come across while doing the rounds one night during his National Service at a hospital in Hampshire. It was, Laing said, a very difficult period for him. He couldn't talk to his fellow doctors about the ethical issues that concerned him and there was no one else in the hospital he could talk to, except for this young man alone in a padded cell.[15]

This brought him to the subject of opting out. Perhaps the young man had simply opted out. Well, if that was the case, perhaps madness was a bit like LSD or hashish. Both could lead to a cessation of action from the ego. But they could also lead to constructive action on a more spiritual plane, he added. This, he said, was the message of the *Bhagavad Gita*.

*

After Laing's contribution, Cooper interrupted the flow of the forum to make three announcements. The first referred to some people who were soliciting donations to help cover the IPS' expenses, the second to the coming Monday. Ross Speck, himself, and Laing would all give lectures, he said, and the entire day would be devoted to anti-psychiatry. The third concerned Carolee Schneemann's 'happening', Round House, tickets for which, he said, were on sale at the back of the hall.

Whether it was this final announcement or something else that antagonised Ginsberg is difficult to say. But seconds later, he grabbed the microphone and jumped in impatiently. 'I came here today expecting some extraordinary political, psycho-political event would take place, that we would try to figure out *what's* going on, 'cos I don't know what the fuck is happening. Like my world system is crumbling.'

But, in any case, he quickly moved on to make another point. While Carmichael was correct to say, as he had on many occasions, that black people were on the receiving end of extraordinary amounts of violence, whites were victims too. A couple of years ago, he had visited Russia where he had been told that between 1935 and 1953 twenty million Soviet citizens had been sent to the

Gulag, where millions of them died. He then returned to Bateson's comments about the greenhouse effect and stated that the entire planet was under threat. The question for him was who or what was the priority? He didn't know.

Jarringly, this heartfelt outburst was followed by another announcement from Cooper in his nicest and most civilised manner, adding his voice to those asking for donations. The IPS had had significant additional expenses, including the extra plane fare for Stokely Carmichael, he said; and it was very short of money.

*

While no women (as far as we know) spoke from the platform at the Congress, several did, of course, speak from the floor. Some of these women were anxious; they spoke hesitantly; others spoke with confidence. In other words, taken as a whole, they spoke no better and no worse than the men at the Congress.

One startling intervention, following Cooper's second announcement, came from a young, obviously drunk, Englishwoman, who began by observing that Carmichael was dressed, by and large, like a typical Western male: was that not an example of cultural appropriation?

This was the same point, in a way, that had been made by Ghose against Ginsberg just a few minutes earlier and that would be made again, though in reverse and more crudely, by a South African man a few minutes later. That man suggested, with a heavy dose of irony, that Carmichael's true ambition was to get the black people of the United States to live in mud huts, to make spears and arrows, and to have himself appointed as chief. 'Yes. That's right. Next question,' Carmichael snapped back.

The reply that the Englishwoman elicited from Carmichael was more considered, this despite a number of people trying to grab the microphone from her and other people trying to shout her down. As far as his shirt was concerned, he wasn't wearing Western clothes, he said. But a type of garment pioneered by the Chinese communists. 'This is Mao. This is Mao. Dig it.'

But what about your trousers, the woman asked. Surely, they were Western?

Maybe they were, maybe they weren't, responded Carmichael. Maybe the West stole trousers from another culture. But assuming it did invent them. Okay, then in that case she was right: he was wearing a garment invented by Westerners. But what about Western white people and their sartorial habits? They should be wearing the clothes of the people that they had oppressed.

The next female speaker followed on from Ginsberg reading a chilling excerpt from Burroughs' novel *Nova Express* and a black nationalist who claimed that the only culture in the world was black culture. She also was English, but sober and composed.

Fig 16. An unnamed woman and Leon Redler at the Open Forum. By Peter Davis. Congress stills. Courtesy Peter Davis, www.villonfilms.com

She began by observing that self-determination, while admirable in some ways, was useless in teaching cultural and ethnic groups to live together. She then asked a couple of questions, one of which she directed at Carmichael. What would happen 'when and if' black people became 'supreme'? But that, said Carmichael, was not what he was arguing for — unless, of course, a fair share of the pie *was* supremacy. 'If that is black supremacy, I am a black supremacist', he added.

*

After another twenty minutes of further questions exploring similar themes and some entirely new ones: black people exploiting blacks, the fact that some black people in the UK didn't feel downtrodden, the failure of black people in the UK to organise themselves, the event took a surprisingly personal turn with an intervention from a young white Englishman, who had moved down from the back of the hall. He was about twenty-three or twenty-four, with dark, fashionably cut hair, an open-necked shirt, and the sort of gangly, loosely held together demeanour and speaking voice that quickly marked him as middle-class and possibly a journalist or a university lecturer.

His first point was that he did not believe that Carmichael was a violent man, this in response to an exchange that had taken place earlier. If he was a violent man, he said, he would not have spent the last week at the Congress; he would have been in Newark, supporting the riots-cum-rebellion. His second point was that Black Power was going nowhere; neither in its advocates' 'aspirations' nor in its impact on 'white liberals' fears.

He then began to make a third point, but before doing so he moved away from his position to his left of the platform, because several of Carmichael's supporters were gathered there, and he was concerned that someone might throw a punch at him. He then returned to his third point: 'Now, I may be a white liberal. But what I want to ask Stokely is, what are you?' He was not a 'black liberal', he said, but neither was he a 'black fascist', as some people had labelled him. Perhaps he was a 'black totalitarian.'

'President Ginsberg', he said, had mentioned 'feedback' a few minutes earlier, which was a subject that probably nailed the entire situation. Perhaps members of the audience had seen Kevin Brownlow and Andrew Mollo's film *It Happened Here*, which depicted a UK under German occupation during the 1940s. Well, if they had, they would know that the lesson of that film was 'if you want to beat something in terms of violence then you have to become a mirror image of it.'

He then made a further point about Carmichael's favourite subject of black cultural integrity. During the earlier part of the evening, someone had said in response to one of Carmichael's remarks that there was no such thing as white culture, and that black culture was the only culture. But that was little different to what Cecil Rhodes and the recently assassinated South African Prime Minister, Dr Verwoerd, had said, except the 'opposite way round.'

Finally, his voice beginning to rise, his finger jabbing violently towards Carmichael on the platform, he said:

> I think if Stokely wants to get anywhere, then he should do what he says, be a violent man. Only a few years back, Stokely was in SNCC, he was non-violent, he went down on the pavement, and he got arrested. What I want to ask. This is my question. Since you became a so-called violent man, Stokely, since you started advocating black power, have you been arrested? Have you got a rifle? Have you gone down on the streets of Newark and sniped from the windows with all the kids, who are starving?

His comments drew an angry volley from Carmichael: 'Yeah, I was arrested before I came here for incitement to riot 'cos I tried to kill a cop.'

'But did you have a rifle?'

'[Speaking confidentially] I always got my stuff with me.'

'I don't mind you advocating violence if you take the risk. The only risk you have is of becoming a martyr.'

This remark was met with applause from some, but with pleas to Carmichael to calm down both from Ginsberg and Tariq Ali, who was standing next to the young man with his camera. Carmichael then picked up on the young white man's reference to Cecil Rhodes, addressing his next few words to him excessively politely, in an obvious parody of a middle-class English accent: 'My good man', he said, when Cecil Rhodes said that white culture was the only culture, did you give him a 'tongue-lashing'? Then he became furious again. 'Did you talk to him? Did you tell him he was crazy and insane? Did you try?'

How could he? responded the young man. Rhodes had died before his time.

'Oh, he died before your time. What about the British troops that are killing people in Aden?' Carmichael shouted, 'What are you doing to stop that? They're here in your time. Are you stopping it? How? What about the British troops that are killing people in Hong Kong because they've taken their land and told some bullshit about leasing it for seven years? What are you doing to stop them? What are you doing to stop them? What about the United States of America with all of its violence in Vietnam? What are you doing? You haven't done a goddamn thing to stop white violence, have you? Have you? Have you?'

Fig 17. 'I may be a white liberal ... But what are you?' By Peter Davis. Congress stills. Courtesy Peter Davis, www.villonfilms.com

The two then continued speaking or shouting over each other, the young man accusing Carmichael of advocating murder, Carmichael asking him again and again to state what he had done to stop white violence, while several in the audience chanted 'Stokely! Stokely!' 'Oh, you don't want to stop white violence, do you? You don't want to stop it, do you? Why don't you stop it? Have you stopped any of it?' Carmichael said, his voice gradually increasing in volume again and his right arm starting to make chopping movements. 'You are the descendant of the violent society. Have you stopped it? Have you stopped it? Have you stopped it? Have you stopped it? Have you stopped it?'

The violence would only stop, he said, when white men realised that when they came after a black man with a gun, they too would get shot.

All in all, it had been a tense and exciting seven or eight minutes. The white man had made his points, but for Carmichael, like the *Panorama* programme, it proved another minor disaster, encouraging the idea in some people's minds that he was a simplistic advocate of violence.

It wasn't long after this argument that Cooper, in an incongruously jolly voice, closed the session. The alternative, he said, would have been to have gone on all night, such was the volume of questions demanding answers.

*

Following Cooper's closing remarks, one of the posters that had appeared after Sweezy's speech dropped down again from the gallery 'Fascism is evident in Europe and U.S.' it read. Ginsberg, who a minute or two later, would start chanting again, asked Carmichael to stay behind and chat. But it was not to be. Carmichael said he had work to do. He then exited the platform via the back, where in the words of photographer, Andrew Wittuck, he was 'immediately surrounded by ten huge guys.' 'It was a really shocking thing to see,' he said.[16]

As for Grogan, he apparently sat down next to Malik where the pair had a brief conversation about money. Seemingly, there were no hard feelings from that quarter about the way Grogan had treated Carmichael. Grogan asked him how well he was faring financing a 'political-education operation' that he was running in Brixton. Not very well, came the reply. So, Grogan gave him an 'angle.'[17]

After that, Malik brought Carmichael back to his house in Compaygne Gardens, where there was yet another meeting of black radicals. 'There were a number of people, people like Stephen Khalifa, Horace Ové, Eddie Braithwaite', recalled Braithwaite's namesake, Rudy Braithwaite.[18] Roy Sawh was there too, and probably

Ajoy Shankar Ghose and Obi Egbuna. Interestingly, someone decided to tape their discussions and George Ware was recorded talking about the Diggers, about how their ideas related to Black Power.

For Carmichael, it had been a hard evening's work. He now had tomorrow to look forward to.

*

If Saturday's open forum summarised much of the first week of the Congress, then the Black Power event which followed it on Sunday took that summary, emptied it of much of its content and twisted it in a single direction. So far, the audiences for events at the Congress had been overwhelmingly white. Sunday reversed this pattern. Black people and brown people were out in force, a fact which was reflected in the uniformed police presence at the door. Were they there to protect the event from racists or to intimidate the participants? Or both? It is impossible to say. But what is not in doubt is that both Malik and Carmichael interpreted their presence as a threat, both to them and to other black and brown people.

Although the event must obviously be counted as a Congress event, it wasn't organised by the IPS, though someone — probably Redler — must have given the organisers permission. The IPS had not planned any events for the first weekend; and this weekend, bar the open forum, wasn't going to be any different.

In fact, it was organised by Michael Malik in concert with activists Obi Egbuna and Roy Sawh, those two being, respectively, president and number two in the recently formed Universal Coloured People's Association (UCPA). This fractious organisation was designed to represent people not interested in Malik's own organisation the Racial Adjustment Action Society (RAAS). And at this point, its membership was open to white people. For both organisations, the event was a natural opportunity to boost their bona fides amongst radical and radically inclined blacks. Both, of course, determined to make capital out of it.

Presumably, the publicity for the event was mostly via word of mouth and flyers. In the time available — at most three or four days - it would have been virtually impossible to organise a conventional campaign with newspaper advertisements. Laing's brief puff just before his introduction of C.L.R. James on the Thursday seems to have been the extent of the publicity from the platform. Carmichael, he said, would be the principal speaker. The event would start at four and it would be open to the public.

*

We don't know precisely how Stokely Carmichael spent his time before the event at the Roundhouse that Sunday, beyond receiving a visit from a Special Branch officer and reading the *Observer*, which published an interview with him. According to Roy Sawh, by this time he was staying at a 'secret address', though if it was secret, it was clearly known to the authorities.[19] He opened his speech by telling the audience that he had decided to cut short his visit and leave the country tomorrow afternoon, instead of as had been planned on Thursday because he had 'something very important to do', he said, without however going into further details except to say that he 'probably' would not be allowed back into Britain again.[20] Possibly an invitation from an officer of the Cuban High Commission to join John Gerassi and other radicals at the first conference of the Organisation of Latin American Solidarity (OLAS) in Havana also had something to do with his change of plan. Possibly too his fear of assassination had heightened.[21] But, in any case, his decision was to have enormous consequences for Malik who stood in for him at the one engagement that, following Sunday, he still had to meet. This was at Reading on Monday at the West Indian Register, a 'survey and advice' centre co-ordinated by the prominent activist, Courtney Tulloch.[22] The idea was that Carmichael would visit the centre and make a speech in the evening.

Not only was Malik's speech widely reported, as he doubtless intended; it also earned him a twelve-month prison sentence under the Race Relations Act.

*

While Laing had advertised a four o'clock start to the Congress event, it didn't get going until an hour or so after four o'clock, a fact which inspired a neat anecdote from Malik, who introduced the session. A white man, he said, had made the following observation to him: 'It looks like you're operating on CP time today' — by which, Malik said, he meant 'C[oloured] P[eople's] time. The idea behind that being that black people weren't as punctual as whites. But, as Malik said, he did not see it as his job 'to have that sort of dialogue with a white man.' So, he pretended ignorance of the phrase's meaning.[23]

Ginsberg arrived chanting a mantra, which apparently led to merriment and some applause.[24] There were also several other familiar Congress faces present: Berke, Redler, Cooper, Zeal, Tariq Ali, Sheila Rowbotham, the New Yorker with the ginger hair, plus a number of other people who went on to play slightly-larger-than-life roles over subsequent decades. One was Eamonn McCann, a young Irishman, who would soon be devoting himself to improving civil rights in Ireland; others were the Germans, Bernward Vesper, Dieter Kunzelmann and Johannes Koch, the first of whom was the partner of the future Baader-Meinhof Gang member, Gudrun Ensslin.

The backdrop to the platform had changed since Saturday. Rather than just the usual white drapes, there was a banner stating 'Black Power', photographs of Malcolm X, and a poster advertising a slave auction. There was also a diagram of a slave ship, a small poster with 'Uncle Sam' and another poster, again, stating 'Black Power', pinned to the front of the table. From the audience's perspective, George Ware sat on the far left, then Malik, then Carmichael, then a friend of Berke named Phil Epstein, then Roy Sawh, then Obi Egbuna. They would be joined on the platform by other speakers as and when, including John La Rose and a Cuban writer named Edmundo Desnoes.

Having concluded the anecdote about the white man and CP time, Malik went on to address some of the same themes that Stokely Carmichael had spoken about, though he spoke more personally and was at times even more provocative than the American. In contrast to his appearance: black boots, black jacket and trousers, black hair worn high on the head and long at the back, black moustache and beard — collectively suggestive of militancy perhaps — his speaking voice was soft and delicate, the words flowing smoothly and easily, like butter through gall.

He described himself as a Muslim and a follower of the separatist American religious leader, Elijah Mohammed, and admitted that he was a racist: 'I am a racist because the definition of this racism, the fact as I understand it, is people who love their own. Well, I love my own, and I'm willing to die for my own.' He spoke of how frightened he often felt: 'I get frightened when I walk from my house to the tube station and all what I see are white men and it's late at night.' And he boasted that when he'd first come to Britain, he had pimped out white prostitutes.

Some people, Malik said, didn't like him speaking so frankly. But he'd met Malcom X and Malcolm had told him to always speak the truth. Black people should always speak the truth, he added.

He mentioned a young Scottish woman, who during the open forum, had made the point that violence, whether institutionalised or otherwise had to be confronted on all sides. 'Each helps the other to exist,' said the woman. Well, he had spoken to her afterwards and what he had said to her was this: 'She had to go home and kill her mother and her father' — a comment which, like other remarks he made, was met with loud applause from the audience. It was advice, he said, that applied to all white liberals. If they really wanted to prove themselves as genuine allies of black people, then they should go back home and murder their parents.

The young white man at the open forum who had accused Carmichael of not doing enough to help black people in cities like Newark was a 'fool'. Carmichael had already suffered more than enough, he said.

*

Unlike Malik, Egbuna who spoke next, was an intellectual, a playwright and a novelist, as well as an activist. Not that Malik wasn't a writer of sorts; he was. But he did not have Egbuna's gifts or his education. Malik was a creature of the street. He was a 'mixed-race' man who had grown up in a suburb of Port of Spain in Trinidad and Tobago. He was a villain and a scamp, always in trouble or six inches from it. Egbuna, on the other hand, was born in Nigeria and educated at the historically black Howard University in Washington D.C., which meant, amongst other things, that he had attended the same academically rigorous alma mater as Stokely Carmichael. And he was a persuasive and attractive speaker. Thus, he had the makings of a career in the establishment, had he so wished it.[25]

Arriving in London in 1961, he had first intended to make his mark as an electrical engineer. But literature called and before long he had built a solid reputation as a writer of reviews, plays and novels. In 1964, he published a short novel called *Wind versus Polygamy*, which was turned into a BBC radio drama and taken to Senegal, where it was performed at the First World Festival of Negro Arts. He contributed reviews to *The Sunday Times* and was published by the Oxford University Press as well as by Faber and Faber. He also travelled widely, meeting leading black activists and politicians, including the former Ghanaian president, Kwame Nkrumah, a totemic figure for all black nationalists, not least for his support of Pan-Africanism.

If anyone had the making of a London answer to Stokely Carmichael, then it was probably Egbuna.

Fig 18. From Left to right: Michael Abudul Malik, Stokely Carmichael, Phil Epstein, Roy Sawh and Obi Egbuna. By Peter Davis. Congress stills. Courtesy Peter Davis. www.villonfilms.com

He began his speech by promising to be brief—he was—and by praising Stokely Carmichael. He then noted the various origins of some of the men on the platform: Carmichael from the United States of America, Roy Sawh from Guyana. Himself? Well, he was 'from the jungles of Africa'. 'But I was here only one week, and I discovered I'd come from one jungle to another,' he remarked. The 'white man was dead' he went on, slipping in a passing reference to Friedrich Nietzsche. He had died in Hiroshima, in Nagasaki, and in Sharpeville, South Africa; and 'today he is dying in Vietnam' and in Newark, he added.[26] Carmichael, in contrast, represented a new beginning. He was a 'human being'. But also a 'new note in the dialectical progression of the black consciousness.'

Everywhere he looked white people were oppressing black people. For instance, black Africans were unable to enter Canada or Australia on the same terms as whites. Speaking for himself, he could go to South Africa, but that was only because the whites there wanted to 'sit on' him. The only proper response to 'international white power' was 'international black power', Egbuna said. Recently, during a trip to America, he had worn traditional African dress and had been feted by black Americans. At SNCC's headquarters in Atlanta, he had heard black youngsters singing, 'not about the Queen of England, not about the President of America, but about the [Kenyan politician] Oginga Odinga.' It was a 'fantastic' and 'beautiful' experience.

*

This time Carmichael dressed in a white shirt, open at the collar and cuffs, a dark tie and side-buttoned waistcoat and matching trousers and wore the same pair of dark glasses as he had worn on Saturday. He spoke slowly at first as if he had difficulty finding the energy, but got quickly into his stride, speaking by turns passionately and confidentially, using irony and repetition, plus all the other verbal and tonal tricks that he had learned from his years of experience as a platform speaker.

As if to draw the sting from those of his critics from within black circles, who called him 'Stokely Starmichael', he heaped lavish praise upon George Ware, one of his many 'young black brothers' whose hard work had made his own visibility possible.[27] Ware, he said, was amongst the boldest of the bold. He too had been arrested at the Nashville event mentioned by Ginsberg on the *Panorama* programme and again on Saturday. When in the dock facing a white judge and a white jury, Ware had talked so much, he said, the judge had threatened to hold him in contempt.

Carmichael then got onto the great American boxer, Muhammad Ali, this to illustrate a point about black people starting from a different set of assumptions to white people. Ali, he reminded the audience, had been given the name of Casius Clay — a 'slave name'. Yet even after he had changed it to Muhammad Ali, white people continued to call him by his original name. Then, when a couple of years later, Ali refused induction into the United States army, these same white people had stripped him of all his titles. But what right had they to do that? In his eyes, Muhammad Ali was still the heavyweight champion. After all, he had 'beat the hell' out of every white boxer that had been put up against him. And if the World Boxing Council wanted to argue with that, well, they should go in the ring themselves and 'take [the title] from him'.[28]

However, most of his speech, as he admitted himself, did not contain new material, so the high points — and there were many — usually owed more to the fresh emphasis he gave them either through his choice of words or to the way he elaborated upon them.

The English press, he said, had been calling him and other advocates of Black Power 'racist'. Yet, as far as he could tell, it didn't have a single black newspaperman. He hadn't seen a single black reporter at the congress. He wasn't racist, it was.

He had, he said, come to London in the footsteps of his idol, Malcom X. Malcolm's aim was to internationalise the struggle for black liberation. Oppressed people throughout the world had to come together and fight a 'capitalist' and 'racist' system that was itself 'internationalist.' Sartre, in his preface to Fanon's *The Wretched of the Earth*, had written one of the 'most hostile condemnations of white society' he had ever read, he said. But then he had copped out by suggesting that whites could reform themselves by taking on board Fanon's message.

White people, he said, had white-washed the black people of the world into accepting their values, their traditions, and their civilisation. 'Whenever you read a book of history, nothing begins until the white man' comes along. They defined who was savage and who was not. It was time to rewrite the history books the 'right way.' Just the other day, he had seen on the television a film with white people giving orders to 'little piccaninnies' 'I would think that by 1967 the dumb white man in England would come to realise that that's nonsensical. The days of Tarzan are over.'

Wherever white people went in the world, they impressed their own culture on the people who lived there. When whites settled in Africa, Africans were taught to speak English, French or Dutch. It should have been the other way round: white people should have been taught to speak Swahili.

He was shocked and disgusted when he discovered that Japanese women were undergoing operations to change the shape of their eyelids, shocked that black women were still straightening their hair to make it look more Western. Each country, each race, had its own standard of beauty, he said. An Englishman was always an Englishman, wherever he lived. Why then should black people have to conform to Western standards?

Picking up on India's widely discussed policy of encouraging sterilisation as an answer to concerns about overpopulation, he said that in fact there was enough food for everybody. 'The question of overpopulation only arises with the coloured peoples of the world. That is because the white man does not want the numbers to rise any higher. And look at the disgusting trick that he pulls—a transistor radio for sterilisation.' Just like the Jews during the 1930s, the black peoples of the world had been lulled to sleep by their enemies. Whites, he said, had 'dehumanised' blacks to such a level that they couldn't even rebel.

He then made a surprising turn into economics, with a brief discourse on the distinction between absolute and relative poverty. Migrants from countries like Trinidad often claimed that in moving to the UK, they were better off than when they were living in the West Indies, he said. After all, there they lived in shacks. Here, they lived in three-room apartments. But this improvement had to be seen against the average of what was normal for white people. Those same three rooms often had to accommodate one or two adults and seven children. Whereas white families, which were usually smaller, lived in houses with five rooms. 'You judge the standard of living. It is relative, it is relative.' Was it right, he added, that 'most families' in the United States hoped to have two cars, whereas in India, Africa and Asia people couldn't even afford bicycles?

He reiterated what he had said on the previous Tuesday about the distinction between 'institutionalised racism' and 'individual racism'. But instead of illustrating the distinction with American examples, he mentioned the case, first of an African student who had been beaten to death in north London, then that of a white mob, one hundred and fifty people strong, that had stoned the house of a black man. Those were examples of individual racism, he said. These were the sort of cases that white liberals would have black people focus on because they themselves could say, 'Not guilty'. As an example of institutionalised racism, he used the example of Cecil Rhodes. What Cecil Rhodes and his confreres had done to Zimbabwe was 'dirty, filthy, murdering'. And then, like Malik, he too referred to the young white man with whom he had sparred on Saturday. Have you ever heard a white liberal condemn white violence, he asked? What had they said about the violence of sterilisation in India? What had they said about violence in Malaysia and in Aden, where the British were fighting an insurgency? What had they said about the violence in Hong Kong and in Rhodesia? 'But let a black man pick up a gun and the whole white liberal structure comes down on that one black man.'

Like the hippies, white liberals were products of economic security, which meant that their so-called Marxism could not be relied upon. More so, it made them 'irrelevant'. The same was also true of the white working class. Their economic security depended on the economic 'insecurity' of black people. 'You don't expect the Labour Union in the United States to come out against the war in Vietnam. If it weren't for the war in Vietnam they'd be starving.'

The bombs currently dropping on Vietnam, would soon drop on South Africa, on India and on Latin America, he said. It simply made good sense for black people to ally with the Chinese; they too were victims of white people. 'The white man has been playing God for centuries. And the reason he's played God for centuries is because we've let him. It's time for us to tell him that playtime is over.'

Finally, he reached his peroration, a part of his speech that was especially notable for its powerful refrain: 'You had better come on home.'[29] Here, he made several summary points: about the black 'revolutionary consciousness', about black liberation, about who and who would not be counted as allies in the fight against white racism and imperialism. It wasn't enough to be black on the outside; black people should think black too. Thus, the very black Moïse Tshombe, the former president of the Congo and something of a poster boy for Western conservatives was really a 'white man': 'He will be destroyed', to which David Cooper, who was standing at the back, whispered, 'Then we [too] can be black.'[30]

It didn't matter, said Carmichael, that he would be killed in the struggle; of far greater importance was that black people continued the fight after him.

'We are going to win', he said. 'Thank you.'

*

Possibly, it was one of Carmichael's best speeches in London. It was certainly lavishly applauded, with shouts and a long, standing ovation. Many people rushed forward to the platform to shake his hand. Thus, it was curious that Roy Sawh moved the meeting swiftly on to another speaker, a young member of the UCPA. Doubtless, everyone in the audience appreciated what Carmichael had said, Sawh remarked. But there was a 'very black boy', a young man named Winston Weese 'from England, who wanted to say a few words.

The youngster, though nervous, gave a passionate and amusing speech, highlighting his role in the 'black youth struggle', castigating the various 'Uncle Toms' that he had spotted in the audience and warning black men against socialising with white men, who might, he said, put arsenic in their drinks to 'intoxicate' them. He cautioned against complacency and reminded the audience that although black people enjoyed the opportunity of 'bettering' themselves in the UK, they should not forget their less fortunate brethren. 'The cause is greater than the individual need'. That, he said, was the slogan of the black youth of Britain. If only the school curriculum taught history from a black point of view instead of depicting black people as 'savages', he went on. White men were 'lynching black men' not just in the United States, he said, but in Britain too. 'But you never hear of it.' Refreshingly, he also added a few of the sort of home truths that by and large had been and would be ignored by the other speakers: if he was to make a success of his job, taking the message of Black Power to the black 'ghettos' of England, then people had to come out and support him; too often they were penny-pinching and self-interested. 'They do not like dipping into their pockets to help black people.'

John La Rose spoke next but only to make an announcement. He was then followed by the writer Edmundo Desnoes, who gave a short but rousing speech about Cuba. 'The white man is dead in me. ... It is dead because I have lived through a revolution and I'm living through a revolution, the Cuban Revolution.' Then Philip Epstein spoke about the situation of poor white people on the north side of Chicago. Like the blacks, they too were rebelling, he said. But they were doing it from a white point of view. 'If you're black, it's black. And if you're white, it's white. You have to get to the roots of it and define yourself in that context.'

*

Roy Sawh began his speech by revealing that he, Malik and Egbuna had organised the event with the specific purpose of raising money to send a cadre of young radicals to the West Indies to 'preach an internationalised Black Power' and to arm them with guns and bullets. They had reached this decision, he said, following a 'serious and long' discussion with Carmichael and Ware. 'We are not begging for money for Oxfam', he added to much laughter. Oxfam, like other international charities of similar ilk, was a 'racket.' How many people in the Roundhouse, he wondered, remembered the dark days of the Second World War, when like other youngsters in the colonies, he had been encouraged to bring unwanted garments to school for despatch to their unfortunate 'brothers and sisters' in England? 'You know when I came to Portobello market and I went down there, I saw one of my shirts with my name on it. That's the kind of society we live in.'

It was, of course, just the sort of speech to fire up the Special Branch men in the audience. But Sawh had a history of provocative statements and indeed just a few weeks after making this speech, he would be charged under the Race Relations Act for suggesting that black nurses should give the 'wrong' injections to white people, that Indian restaurant owners should put 'something' poisonous in their diners' curries, and that black bus conductors should not take fares from black people or stop for white people.[31]

*

As various black 'sisters' moved, bowls in hands, amongst the audience, the Q&A began with a statement from the musician and actor, Ram John Holder. He was a cosmopolitan and a louche figure, who had moved from his native Guyana to the United States in 1962 where, as he went on to say, he had been a founding member of the Ohio branch of the SNCC. He mentioned that he had worked closely with the American Jazz poet, Ted Joans, who happened to be sitting in the audience between two very attractive-looking black women. The two of them, he said, had 'worked a lot' amongst the beatniks in Greenwich Village. It was thus curious, he said, that Joans hadn't yet been mentioned from the platform, for not only was he a great poet, but he had also been 'in the struggle' for 'a very long time.'

He went on to ask George Ware a question, the only one by the way, that Ware was asked to answer from the platform: why had the SNCC moved away from its position of non-violence?

The reason for that, said Ware, speaking in a confident and expressive Alabamian accent, was because they would never win their freedom that way. As the movement had evolved, they had realised that it would be much more effective to think in terms of 'power relationships.' 'No people had ever rid themselves of their oppression until they had the power to wrestle that oppression ... from the hands of the oppressor', Ware said.

Ajoy Shankar Ghose spoke next, reverting to Roy Sawh's statement about equipping a cadre to fight abroad. They should, he said, send volunteers to train in Cuba. Then send them to Vietnam. He asked Carmichael to say what he thought about the idea. For his part, he had 'sixty or seventy people' who were ready to fight at any time. Carmichael had merely to give the order.

However, Carmichael thought it best not to be drawn in public on such delicate matters. They could discuss them privately later. In the meantime, they should work to raise people's 'revolutionary consciousness', so that when the moment for military action arrived, people would be ready.

As for the other questioners, almost all were black men. Some of those were African and one or two American. But the majority, by the sound of their voices, were West Indian immigrants. Unusually for an event at the Congress, no women spoke at all, even though lots of black women were present. Of the white men who spoke, one was the ginger-haired New Yorker, and another was a German student at the Free University of West Berlin.

One black man asked Carmichael how he could persuade Afro-American businessmen to put their money into African banks, another, whether black Americans planned to break away from the union; a third complained about the attitude of Asian people. In his experience, Asians were just as prejudiced against black people as white people. In any case, why should black people fight for the liberation of the Vietnamese, when they themselves were colonised? While a fourth asked for clarity on the relationship between Africa and the Soviet bloc.

The German student asked him to comment about a 'fascist and racist' film about Africa that was currently being shown in Leicester Square. When the same film had been shown in Berlin last year, he and his friends had trashed the cinema, he said.

Yet another black man, again repeating a question that had been asked before, wanted to know about his attitude to Martin Luther King and other 'moderates'.

Carmichael dealt with most of these questions patiently, only inflating his rhetoric (and the volume) in his responses when it came to the black movement's relationship with China and the subject of nuclear bombs. The reason why Africans were having to think about foreign investment at all was because white people had 'poisoned' them with the idea that they couldn't 'do anything right'; a separate black state in the United States was a bad idea because it could easily be destroyed. While for blacks 'not to join hands with Asia would be to do what the white west wanted them to do, to play apart so [they] can continue to dominate us.' Russia wasn't going to give the Africans the H-Bomb. Neither was France nor the United States. But the Chinese would, he said, for their 'very survival.' He knew about Russia. He had noticed how its police had brutally treated African students protesting outside the Israeli Embassy in Moscow during the Six-Day War. In any case, the 1917 Russian Revolution was a failure. The Bolsheviks were mere 'revisionists.' They should have armed the people. The film issue would be better addressed by the people of London.

But what about Red China's domination of Tibet, queried an Indian national. He had witnessed its behaviour there himself. Surely it was imperialistic — an observation that was met by outrage and loud boos from many in the audience. The same speaker also questioned Carmichael's exclamation of horror at the fact of transistor radios being offered as a *quid pro quo* for sterilisation in India. He agreed that it was 'very immoral'. But what alternative was there?

Regarding China's occupation of Tibet, Carmichael pleaded ignorance. But Mao was a political and military genius. 'I understand his fight for cultural integrity with the Red Guards. I understand his fight against revisionism.' The fact that people were being offered transistor radios in return for sterilisation was an abomination. People should use condoms or the Pill. He had had sexual intercourse without producing babies. In fact, he did it 'all the time'. One day he hoped to start a family. Why shouldn't the people of India have the same opportunity?

There were also questions or statements touching on black women and beauty again; about 'retribution', by which the speaker (a black American professional) meant the reparations for hundreds of years of oppression; and on intermarriage: what should be done about black men who had taken white wives? The answer to the first question, said Carmichael, was for black women to form a proper estimate of their true value. Disappointingly he didn't address the issue of reparations, but a supplementary one. The United States rightfully belonged to black people, he said. 'If we can't enjoy it, we'll burn it to the ground!'' Only the final question seemed to flummox him. It was, he said, a question with 'profound implications.' He didn't know whether a black man and a white woman (or vice versa) could love each other to the extent that they could transcend racism. But speaking for himself, he didn't propose to find out.

*

It was Sawh who closed the meeting. He promised Carmichael that he and others on the radical wing of the black community would follow the example of what Carmichael and his fellow activists were doing in America. When you get to Washington, we'll get to London, he said, to ringing applause. Finally, he warned the audience to be careful of assailants when they left the building. 'Let us go out quite disciplined and if we're attacked then you know what to do,' he said.

Yet not everyone did leave the building. After all, why should they have done? Since the beginning of the Congress, coteries of young people had been living in the Roundhouse, and there would have seemed no reason why on this particular Sunday people shouldn't hang around and chat. One group that certainly stayed on was a group of black intellectuals. We know this because Sheila Rowbotham sat eavesdropping on their conversation. Like other women who would go on to form the bedrock of the Women's Liberation movement, her head was abuzz with a wild stream of her own questions: what did Black Power mean for white women? Why didn't any black women speak? What use to her and to other women was Carmichael's credo of finding one's own group identity? And listening to these black intellectuals talking was a way of at last starting to find an answer to them.[32]

*

Carmichael's flight out of England was not due to leave until the following afternoon, which left him time for at least one other appointment. This was at an opulent house in the centre of London, where a party was about to take place. The party was a black-tie event, one of those political-cum-literary parties that brought politicians together with writers and intellectuals, and amongst the guests were the novelist and journalist Kingsley Amis, the louche politician and friend of the Rolling Stones and Panna Grady, Tom Driberg, and the Tory journalist, Peregrine Worsthorne.

It isn't clear who invited Carmichael, but it was probably the film and theatre director Peter Brook or his close associate Michael Kustow. In 1966 Brook had directed the Royal Shakespeare Company in a theatrical piece about Britain, the United States and the Vietnam War called *US*, and the point of Carmichael turning up at the party was for a staged meeting with one of Brook's actors and a Vietnamese woman. These would then be included in a film that Brook was making, which riffed off the stage play.

Carmichael and Ware, who arrived at the house with a couple of black women, were wearing the same clothes that they had worn at the Roundhouse—Ware in dark trousers and a white ribbed pullover - though Carmichael had smartened himself up a bit. The tie that had hung an inch or so below the top button of his shirt was now knotted at the neck, and he was wearing a matching jacket over his waistcoat. The actor, Mark Jones, asked Carmichael a string of deliberately naive questions. To Carmichael's remark that white people were 'going to be blown off the face of the earth', he said, 'Who's going to do that?' and 'Why do you think that?' 'So, you think [that white people] should be squashed now?' he added. To which Carmichael responded using many of the same words that he had used at the Congress: 'White violence', he said, had bred 'coloured violence.' White people had 'plundered and raped the world.'[33]

This exchange was then succeeded by a slightly muddled conversation between Carmichael, Ware, and a Vietnamese woman named Jacqueline. To the woman's question, what should be done to end the war? Carmichael returned an uncompromising response: the Vietnamese should kill every American soldier that they could get their hands on. At one point, he seemed almost to be catechising her on the distinction between liberation and peace. At another, he offered a paraphrase of Rabbi Hillel's famous apothegm, 'If I am not for myself who will be for me?' a quotation which he had already used at Saturday's open forum.

When Jones suggested to Carmichael that his dogmatism and advocacy of violence could easily end up causing the deaths of others, Carmichael parried the suggestion by stating that he didn't believe that an 'act could be isolated from its reasoning.' People were killed in all sorts of ways, after all—some of which were clearly justified. To illustrate this point, he then got onto the subject of sterilisation again, the 'most dastardly act of violence that anyone can commit.' It was, he said, more violent than 'shooting a man.'

*

Thereafter, later that night, Carmichael dropped in on Panna Grady in Hanover Square, where he passed Allen Ginsberg on the heiress's stairway. 'Well, things aren't all black and white', he said, as he gave Ginsberg a wink. It was an incident that Ginsberg was still thinking and talking about on the following day. It was certainly an extraordinary coda.[34]

As it turned out, Carmichael left not in the afternoon, as he had suggested, but in the morning. He and Ware picked up an Air India flight to Prague at just before ten o'clock. Following which they caught another flight to Havana.[35]. It had been a tumultuous ten days. Carmichael hadn't changed much perhaps. But Britain certainly had, the huge publicity that his visit generated had seen to that. In addition to the newspaper items, both in the nationals and the provincial press, there had been numerous radio and television reports, plus—one can surely say—countless saloon bar discussions and family arguments. Within days, the Black Power speaker was named in Parliament by opposition leader Quintin Hogg: Was the Home Secretary aware that Carmichael had made some 'rather striking breaches of the Race Relations Act'?[36] The Home Secretary was. On the following day, July 27, having considered the report that Special Branch had sent to him, Roy Jenkins told the House that he 'did not propose' to allow Carmichael to 're-enter the country.'[37]

Also, within days, UCPA threw out all its white members, while Malik, who had already made a foolhardy and garrulous speech at the Reading meeting, reorganised RAAS in an attempt to inject some seriousness and credibility into the organisation.[38]

Although it's unlikely that more than a few people realised it at the time, the country had embarked on a new path. The age of identity politics had arrived in Britain.

8. Doctor Dog

Just as the first Wednesday of the Congress kicked off with a flurry of newspaper articles about Stokely Carmichael's speech on the 18th, so the second week began with another media intrusion. This time it was a full-page advertisement in *The Times*.[1]

Fuelled by the same energies that had inspired the Legalise Pot Rally on the 16th: anger at the jailing of *International Times* editorial board member 'Hoppy' Hopkins for the possession of cannabis resin and for allowing his flat to be used for the smoking of the drug, the advertisement argued that 'the law against marijuana is immoral in principle and unworkable in practice.'

It was accompanied by a petition offering five suggestions: first, that the government should permit research into cannabis use; second, that smoking of the drug in private should be decriminalised; third, that it should be taken off the dangerous drugs list; fourth, that the penalties for possession should be relaxed or done away with altogether; and fifth, that people imprisoned for possession of cannabis or for allowing their premises to be used should have their sentences commuted.

The petition's main interest from the Congress point of view lay in the fact that it was signed by Laing, Cooper, Francis Huxley, Michael Malik and Laing's social worker colleague, Sid Briskin. Other signatories included Tariq Ali, Peter Brook, George Melly, Jonathan Miller, Kenneth Tynan, Aaron Esterson and The Beatles. The only wonder is that Berke didn't sign the petition. But with so many eminent people on board already he probably wasn't asked.

*

Bearing the advertisement and the petition in mind, it would probably have been better to begin Monday's session with a lecture on the liberatory potential of illegal drugs. But the organisers had already committed the entire day to what was now billed, in contrast to Cooper's announcement on the Saturday, as 'Psychiatry, Anti-Psychiatry and Related Matters'. Presumably there had been some discussion about Cooper's announcement behind the scenes, for not everyone on the radical wing of British psychiatry approved of the term 'anti-psychiatry'. Laing, for one, didn't like it at all. He didn't use it to describe other people's practices and he didn't like people using it of his.

It was David Cooper who invented the term and Cooper who popularised its usage.[2] Nevertheless, the term stuck to Laing as it stuck to all the members of the IPS. 'Again and again, I had said to David Cooper—"David, it is a fucking disaster to put out this term,"' Laing told Bob Mullin. But Cooper, he said, had a 'devilish side'.[3]

It was how Cooper described all four of the organisers in his introduction to the Penguin book of Congress speeches, *The Dialectics of Liberation*. The choice of the phrase, Cooper said, was an example of counter-labelling.[4] And apparently, Laing didn't read the introduction before the book was sent for publication.[5]

Redler, on the other hand, seems to have been agnostic on the subject. In fact, after Cooper, only Berke seems to have run with the term, using it of himself and encouraging other people to use it about him.[6]

*

The morning began with a lecture on families, schizophrenia and network therapy by the Philadelphia physician, Ross Speck. A modest and liberal-minded man, he was on the bill as a very late replacement for the sociologist Erving Goffman. Clearly, these were extremely large shoes to fill. And it showed. Following a brief introduction from Bateson, he spoke haltingly; and it was not until he had been speaking for a good thirty minutes that he relaxed a little and left his notes behind him.

Berke had known about Speck's work on families and schizophrenia since 1960 or 1961. Redler perhaps a little longer. But neither man was a friend of Speck. Laing was. So, it was probably Laing who did the actual inviting. During a research trip to the States in early 1962, Laing had met Speck at the Eastern Pennsylvania Psychiatric Research Institute (EPPI) in Philadelphia, and they had immediately hit it off. 'There was something eye-catching and unusual about Ronnie in that first meeting in my office,' Speck recollected. 'He was talkative and friendly and he told of sleeping one hour, then being awake for four on a round-the-clock basis. ... He then warned me that a sleep cycle was coming on but that I should keep talking'.[6] Thereafter the pair met on further occasions, including at a 'Society and Psychosis' conference organised in the same city by the Hahnemann Medical College.[7] The conference was memorable for several reasons. Not only were Jules Henry and Gregory Bateson present, but following a debate on theology and ontology, Bateson told Laing that he had a '10 percent IQ advantage on him.'[8] It was an accolade that the Scotsman quite rightly appreciated.

*

Like Cooper in the short speech that he had given on the 15th, Speck spent the first part of his speech defining his terms — but not before saying that he didn't know which type of psychiatry he was supposed to represent. He defined 'nexus' as a group of people that someone is in regular contact with, the members of a family, for instance; a 'social network' as 'all the relations' that someone has 'over space and time'; and 'scapegoating' perhaps less clearly, as 'a seemingly universal phenomenon', where one person is acted on by another, either consciously or unconsciously.[9]

Stokely Carmichael, John Gerassi, and several others had spoken about the politics of large groups. Well, his talk, Speck said, was about the politics of small groups, from the dyad, i.e., 'the gruesome twosome' up to groups of a hundred people or so. As an example of the latter sort of group, he gave the formative components of the Congress itself. This was constructed from a variety of networks: existential philosophers, Marxists, biologists and other sorts of scientists, Black Power, Flower Power and Acid Power activists, New Leftists and Hippies, and 'probably about fourteen others which I haven't even mentioned.' Out of these, he said, a nexus was forming.

There were parallels between his view of dysfunctional networks, he said, and the effects of electronic media on 'literate' cultures. The media theorist Marshall McLuhan had written about how kindergarten-age children were 'imploded' through their exposure to television. 'Vietnam, human rights, civil rights, Ban the Bomb, the hippies, and Provos, etc.' were becoming theirs and 'everybody's problem'. Just as people were being 'driven out of their cultures' in McLuhan's formulation, they were being 'driven out of their minds' in Laing's.

'Changes in our world produce changes in our culture, which produce changes in our families which produce changes in the individual person,' he said. The goal of his style of psychotherapy was to try and bring change at the level of the social network.

His first experience of social network therapy was with the families of schizophrenics, he said, i.e., with people who had been scapegoated. More recently he had been working with the social networks of drug addicts.

Regarding schizophrenia, by and large he took Foucault's view, that it had been 'created by society to fill the empty leprosy hospitals.' Laing, he said, had defined a schizophrenic as someone who had avoided the 'social lobotomisation process'. 'You and I are the ones who have not escaped,' he added.

But the most engaging part of Speck's speech was when he left the schoolroom pedagogy and the compliments behind and spoke about his own experiences as a therapist back in his hometown, Philadelphia, and in New York and Washington. This is when it came alive. He explained the differences between the major sorts of social networks and how his therapeutic meetings were arranged. He tended to get to the meetings first, he said, so that he could watch people arrive. Sometimes people turned up at the meetings who weren't part of any social network at all, and if there wasn't space at the house where the meeting was being held, they would be turned away. It was 'very pathetic', he said, when people had to be told, 'gee, you've got to find your own [social network].'

He described driving to one session and being struck by the behaviour of a couple on the pavement. They appeared to be lovers. But, in fact, they were a mother and son, both on their way to the session. Naturally, they didn't like having their behaviour pointed out to them in front of forty or fifty people, he said. But they were willing to work on it and the meeting did indeed 'disrupt their particular gruesome twosome.'

Indeed, almost nothing at the meetings was out of bounds. 'Secrets', 'past hurts', the 'difficulties and the fun' between people were examined openly and with candour. 'Of course, that means you get into this little thing called Oedipus', he added. There was only one subject he banned: politics. If people started on about the Democrats and the Republicans, he would insist on them reframing the discussion in network terms. Usually, he said, he would stick around at a meeting for about an hour and a half, in other words, for just enough time for new, healthier, subgroups to form.

Speaking in this way, Speck could probably have gone on for much longer. His words were flowing, and his auditors were with him. But, catching David Cooper's eye, he wondered out loud if Cooper had something he wanted to add to what he had said. But commentary was not on Cooper's mind. Without apology or any sort of proper explanation, he embarked upon his own lecture, thus ignoring every word of Speck's presentation.

*

Having bought a mastiff a few months ago, Cooper said that he had come to believe that he was himself turning into a dog. Not that he found this transformation unduly worrying. In fact, he had turned into all sorts of things before and had eventually turned out of them. What did worry him, however, was this: when a month ago, Laing had come around to his house in Hertfordshire to discuss the Congress, he had overheard him make the following observation to his wife, Simone, as the mastiff bounded down the stairs to greet him: 'My God. I thought it was David!' He was very amused by that, Cooper remarked to laughter from the audience.

He described the case of a girl he had been introduced to at a mental hospital. The girl had been admitted to the hospital under section 135 of the 1959 Mental Health Act because she believed she was a plant. She didn't speak but moved around like one of science fiction writer John Wyndham's triffids.. He didn't think that she was mad at all; she was probably experiencing a period of growth But his colleagues diagnosed her as schizophrenic. They gave her pills and electrical shocks, thus reducing her to a state of compliance.

He, however, knew the rules under which psychiatrists operated better than the girl did. So, should a psychiatrist examine him, he would say that he wasn't turning into a dog at all. But that he, the psychiatrist that is, was suffering from a delusion. He would then rush to the telephone and have the psychiatrist compulsorily admitted. And he would probably get away with it, he said.

Fig 19. David Cooper enjoying a puff. By Peter Davis. Congress stills. Courtesy Peter Davis, www.villonfilms.com

During the previous week, Cooper said, there had been much talk of turning on with psychedelic drugs. But drugs were not the only method of turning on. A psychotic breakdown could be just as effective. But it had to be managed discreetly and in a disciplined fashion.[10] That being the case, one could, he said, leave behind one's ordinary, quotidian, existence and journey back into the deep past, to distant worlds of prehuman fauna and flora. One could even become a unicellular form of life struggling out of the primeval soup. And then one could travel backwards further still through the form of minerals until one reached the universe's starting point, the alpha moment, the origin of all things material and spiritual.

Such extravagant imagery may or may not have been meant wholly seriously. But he was certainly serious in what he followed it with: a comparison with Gregory Bateson's belief that human beings had lost touch with their animality, coupled with a sly or possibly ironic dig at Bateson for taking funding from the United States navy to support his work on dolphins. He then mentioned Carmichael, who had often described Frantz Fanon as his patron saint. Well, Fanon was one of his patron saints too, he said. Another was the French poet Antonin Artaud. He concluded with a long quotation from one of Artaud's letters, ending with the words, '"Madmen are above all else the individual victims of social dictatorship."'[11]

What Speck thought about the timing of Cooper's short speech is unknown. But there is no doubt about Bateson's response. He didn't know how to proceed. Was he to ignore Cooper's statement and ask the floor for their responses to Speck's presentation? Or was he to do the opposite? A speaker from the floor suggested a third alternative: they should consider the relationship between madness and society. And that was what the event settled into: a series of long statements on madness and society; and it was not until near the end of the session that Speck's speech was even mentioned.

Henry spoke about Erich Fromm's concept of 'socially patterned defect', Murray Korngold, a Californian friend of Laing, about the relationship between experience and the metaphors people use to describe it, and the Italian psychiatrist and close colleague of Franco Basaglia, Giovanni Jervis, about the psychiatric hospital as a focus of violence.[12]

Both Korngold and Jervis were passionate in their denunciations of conventional psychiatry, Jervis in words that could easily have been Cooper's. Psychiatry, he said, was in crisis. 'What is our Western white establishment' asking us to do, he wondered? 'It is asking us to readjust people. Is it right?' He wasn't interested in 'bourgeois' private psychiatry, he added. Only in the asylum could 'so-called psychiatrists' and 'so-called patients' confront the violence that society inflicted on everyone.

Speck only came back into the conversation when a non-psychiatrist asked him to comment on the observation that most of the white people at the congress had refused to apply Carmichael's strictures to themselves. But, discouragingly, Speck had nothing of substance to say to this. He did much better, however, when another speaker described psychiatry as anti-revolutionary. Well, that depended on what you meant by revolutionary, Speck responded. For his part, he would just continue 'trying newer and better and different' ways to help people discover their autonomy. If other people wanted to make a 'real revolution', that was up to them. He would rather do things another way.

*

Although the titles of the seminars which followed that morning's questions are unknown as indeed are most of those for the other days, we can guess at some, and we can be reasonably certain that they were guided by the IPS or by one or other of the 'betas', people like Jeremy Holmes, Morton Schatzman or Sid Briskin.[13] Erling Eng, who wrote an article about the Congress shortly after returning to America, singled out Marx, Sartre, Fanon, Artaud, Joseph Gabel and 'perhaps' André Breton as 'invisible figures' at the Congress.[14] And if we add the names of Foucault, Goffman, Jacques Lacan, Maud Mannoni, Eugène Minkowski, Wilhelm Reich and Laing and Cooper as well, we would probably be close to the content of some of that afternoon's offerings.[15]

Laing delivered several seminars at the Congress, but oddly enough, possibly not on the 24th. One of them was called 'On the "Schizophrenic" Experience'. But he did not deliver that until Wednesday, the 26th.[16] Presumably Cooper delivered something on Villa 21 or on anti-psychiatry more generally. Ditto Berke and

Redler. Both, of course, were more than competent to speak about Mary Barnes and Kingsley Hall. It's also possible that some of the IPS's 'patients' contributed seminars that afternoon, perhaps James Greene and Vickie Hamilton.[17] Certainly, if we take the meaning of 'Psychiatry, Anti-Psychiatry and Related Matters' to include seminars with a psychological focus, there seems no reason why we shouldn't include Vickie Hamilton's paper on Lacan.[18] Possibly this was also the day that the American psychologist Joseph Havens delivered his paper on 'Methods of changing Consciousness and the Relation of such Changes to a New Non-Violent Social Order'.[19]

*

On Tuesday, Paul Goodman took the platform with a speech that was by turns practical, lofty, freewheeling, and didactic. Ever since the opening of the Congress, he had, in Roger Barnard's words, been 'prowling around ... cutting in on speeches and seminars, criticising speakers, audience and organisers of the congress'.[20] Now it was his turn to occupy the limelight.

As usual, he was dishevelled — the very image of the mid-century North American male intellectual: the shabby, oversized, tweed jacket, the tangled mess of brown curls, the pipe, the tie, the glasses, all giving the impression of, to use a word that appears in the title of his later book of poems, 'homespun'. He carried with him onto the platform a small sheaf of papers; the pipe would be lit for the Q&As. The audience that he had drawn was one of the largest that the Congress had yet achieved, some 300 to 400 people.[21] As usual Ginsberg was there, this time in a dark anorak; less usually, he had brought with him, Panna Grady. Naturally, there was also a large anarchist-cum-left libertarian element present: Peter Cadogan, Peter Ford, John Mackay, Roger Barnard, a young man named Martin Small, who would write up the event for *Freedom* newspaper,[22] and presumably Anne Marie Fearon, Colin Ward and Nicolas Walter.

Following Leon Redler's brief introduction, which highlighted Goodman's querulousness, Goodman moved swiftly into the first of his themes: political action, or what he called the 'experimental side of the social sciences.'[23] Not that he worked through his subject matter in a systematic or academic fashion, like Jules Henry or Paul Sweezy; that was not Goodman's style. Instead, he swung with the moment, introducing other topics as he went along, interspersing his speech with sly, often ironic, jabs at Stokely Carmichael, John Gerassi and at the various Maoists present, as well as others at the Congress who had displeased or offended him.

Naturally, different groups had different views of what political action involved, he went on; that was simply common sense. But then, he added, that one of the curious things he had noticed about the Congress was that people weren't interested in common sense; whereas to him it was 'intensely interesting.'

Take a subject like nuclear weapons and the strong likelihood that the world would be destroyed within ten or fifteen years. What struck him about that was less the politics, less the rights and wrongs of the situation, than the fact that the people who controlled the weapons had profoundly similar attitudes; they were thinking in the same way 'because of the kind of people' they were.

How could they be opposed, he asked? One approach would be to take a leaf out of the careers of people like Gandhi and Martin Buber. Both were nationalists only for as long as it took India and, respectively, Israel to become sovereign entities. At the back of their minds was always the belief that national autonomy was merely a steppingstone to something greater. But this was a hard route to take, so he then offered another commonsensical path, one that he had tried just a few weeks earlier at a Quaker-sponsored youth conference in Hungary.

There, he had suggested that the young people adopt a 'common front' approach to nuclear weapons and organise simultaneous pickets outside the nuclear powers' embassies in, say, Warsaw and Washington. This seemed to him an obvious response to the situation. But the Soviet bloc nations plus the Italians were against it, the common sense of the Polish delegation being that the question of nuclear weapons could not be isolated from issues of foreign policy more generally. But that, he had said, was his point—to isolate it, so that it could be dealt with more easily. Yet the Italians, of whom two at least were Maoists, argued that the 'present necessity' was for the Chinese to develop their own bomb; and that it would indeed be better—and here he quoted—if '"all mankind were destroyed than that 700 million Chinese were disadvantaged."'[24]

This, he added, mischievously, was the same sort of extreme attitude he had heard from Malcolm X six or seven years ago, when the two happened to be travelling on a plane together: Malcolm had told him that he would welcome a nuclear attack on New York, even at the cost of over a million black lives, 'because it would be the vengeance of Allah.'

Goodman then moved onto another major threat to the world: rampant urbanisation, which was occurring not just in the west but in the communist countries and throughout much of South America. Once again, there were all sorts of views on this. But what struck him most was that the causes were the same, wherever in the world it was occurring.

The solution here, though again it was hard, was to decentralise power, to 'give more decision-making power to ordinary people', and, to get people to think seriously about rural reconstruction.'

He then referred to the situation of the underdeveloped nations. It was here that he targeted some of his choicest barbs at Stokely Carmichael. No one denied that this was the 'crucial revolutionary situation' confronting the world. But Carmichael was wrong on all the important points: in the way that he racialised Western technology as white; in the way that he characterised the needs of underdeveloped nations; and in the way that he confounded underdeveloped nations with people of black African heritage in the Western democracies.

The problem of the undeveloped nations of the world was not that they lusted after Western technology and thus had to be re-educated in their own culture, as Carmichael saw it, but that they wanted to adopt it wholesale, whereas what was needed was a more discriminatory attitude. 'They should be lusting for this piece of this package and this piece of that package, you know, and they should be very careful.' And here he offered some judicious praise for President Julius Nyerere of Tanzania and the Cubans; they did seem to be following this policy.

Carmichael's third mistake was to treat the black people of the world as sharing the same identity. But there was no comparison between the identity of a poor black person in Africa and that or a poor black person in the ghettos of London or North America. The first were no more without a culture, than a professor at Oxford, whereas the identity of the ghetto residents was inflected through a 'culture of poverty.' This was different. And 'this is what happens to a group within a high technology when it gets pushed out.' However, he agreed with Carmichael's remedy for their situation: hostile action.

The next part of Goodman's speech took on the limits of political action. 'I'm an old Jeffersonian', he told the Congress, 'way out of date.' By which he meant that people were far too ambitious about what they believed that government, revolutionary or otherwise, could achieve. The role of government was merely to 'guarantee a situation of minimum decency' in which perhaps some 'some good' could occur.

The 'great societies' of the world were not the ones with the highest GNP, he said, but countries like Denmark, Tanzania, Ireland and possibly Cuba, where, taken in the round, the standards of living were generally much higher.

He himself had lived in Ireland for long stretches. The people ate well there. Even the censorship was much lighter than people imagined—a comment which provoked an interruption from a woman in the audience. Why, she asked, were so many young people leaving it? 'I'm [simply] saying that compared to the United States, it ain't bad', Goodman responded.

Regarding the United States, much of what the Congress had been told about the situation there had been twisted to fit various Marxist interpretations. In some ways, the situation was actually 'much worse' than Carmichael and Gerassi had pictured it. But the major economic problem was not exploitation; it was exclusion. In other words, it wasn't black people's 'surplus value' that the capitalists were after. The problem was that the capitalist class would rather not bother about them in the first place. Indeed, if you looked at the amount of cash that the federal and state governments spent on services, including welfare payments, the money was travelling in the opposite direction.

Such exploitation as did exist had more to do with the fact that poverty provided job opportunities for various public officials and 'young youth workers from Harvard.' The Black Power activists were saying, 'For Christ's sake, give us the money to use our own way.' And here he did agree with Stokely Carmichael; they were right to say that.

But even then, the blacks and the Puerto Ricans were not even the largest excluded groups. A much larger group was the farmers who, with the turn to industrial methods, had been thrown off the fields. 'Farms out, processes and packages in.' And then there were the aged, the so-called insane and the delinquent, by which he meant the youthful and high-spirited. Goodman's guess was that most young people didn't need to be in school at all; they were there because the state could think of nothing better to do with them.

So too the nature of modern colonialism had been misdescribed and 'fantastically exaggerated.' Not that it didn't exist in some of its older forms; it did. But the 'character of modern domination' was different. The fact was that most of the previously mentioned groups just 'didn't fit into this lovely high technological, interesting system.' Both in Harlem and Vietnam, the 'real inner policy' of the United States establishment wasn't to exploit people; rather, it was to get people to 'shut up'. 'If only they would go in the middle of the Atlantic Ocean and drown. You see, that's different. It's a different attitude. "What a bore," you know, 'Why don't they go away?"'

As for the state's attitude to the hippies, it wasn't one of tolerance, as Gerassi had suggested. But the opposite. In fact, the police treated them worse than they treated the blacks. They were the group 'most beat up by the police, most harassed, most jailed.'[25]

A much more 'revolutionary' question than those he had heard at the Congress, he said, concerned what should be automated and what should not. The modern tendency was to automate as much as possible. But there was much in modern life that was done much better by humans. Related to this was the question of which areas of modern life should be preserved from technical organisation altogether. He thought that school children as far as possible should be protected from most technologies until their early teens, since they took away 'too many' of life's 'potentialities.' Also, more thought should be given to mitigating the impact of technologies where they were used. 'How can we alter the technology in such a way that people can run it according to their local customs, and can understand what they're doing, and not become processed by high-falutin engineering types. No matter what their politics.'

Finally, Goodman got on to one of his favourite themes: the importance of professionalism. Young people, he said, seemed to think that a 'good spirit and a lively heart, courage, pure aims' were in themselves sufficient to bring about a better society. But, without professionals, 'nothing [was] possible.'

It was for this reason that SNCC's decision to exclude white people from the organisation was 'tragic'. Many of those white people were 'professionally gifted'; they were high achievers. By excluding this group, the SNCC had cut themselves off from 'ever learning anything.'

The bother though — to use one of his favourite expressions — was that most professionals, in the United States at least, were 'finks', which was to say that they acted purely in the service of corporations. He had seen the consequences of this attitude himself in the various free universities which had sprouted up in the wake of his book, *The Community of Scholars*. The young people who taught there, didn't believe in the value of a professional training; instead, they focused on subjects like psychedelic drugs and Cuba.[26]

Marcuse, who would be speaking on Friday, he said, would probably tell them that professionals were simply technicians. But that was mistaken. 'If they're just technicians, we are doomed because no one will ever give them the right goals, because only professionals know goals. ... A professional is not a technician. I wish the young would learn that.'

*

Arguably, Goodman had delivered more of a fireside chat than a speech, but therein lay its charm: it was relatable. At no point did he give an impression of bracing himself. There were none of the verbal tics or irritating verbal mannerisms that characterised, say, Laing's contribution. Instead, he looked and sounded fully relaxed. Beyond the spoken content, his speech was therefore also a lesson in kinesics. This he seemed to be saying is how one simply is, on the platform and elsewhere. As Roger Barnard put it in *Peace News* a few days later: 'Communication was back, with a vengeance.'[27]

Goodman could have capitalised on this, but then he wouldn't have been Goodman. His first contribution to the question-and-answer session was to make a further, this time semantic, point about Carolee Schneemann's planned performance. He had seen the posters advertising it as a 'happening'; and he was confused. His understanding of a happening was that it was an 'exploration of chance, drawing on spontaneous community response to a concrete situation.' What was spontaneous about an event billed to take place at 9:30 PM on Friday, he asked? He trusted, however, that the money was well spent and that it would prove a 'worthwhile theatrical experience'.

The first question was a provocative written one from the floor. What did he think of the Congress as an 'educational experience?' Not a lot, he replied. In fact, it was one of the worst events of its type that he had ever attended. No one was 'authentic'. Speakers who could usually be relied upon to speak honestly to people they disagreed with, had at the Congress become 'woolly', out of fear of alienating people—by which he presumably meant Stokely Carmichael and his supporters.

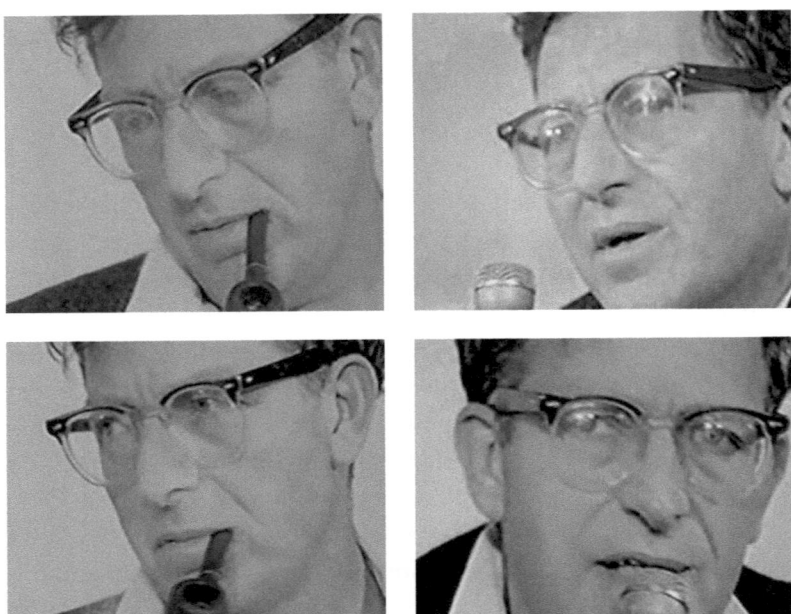

Figs 20-23. Anarchist of common sense? Paul Goodman taking questions at the Q&A. By Peter Davis. Congress stills. Courtesy Peter Davis, www.villonfilms.com

Laing asked him to comment about the problem of obedience. But first he began with praise: Goodman's speech was 'one of the best' he had ever heard: a model of 'sustained serious thinking', without omission or cliche. The best remedy for the problem of obedience was proper professionalism, Goodman responded. Which meant setting an example. Professionals should behave as professionals not as 'finks.' To illustrate what this meant in practical terms, he gave the example of the *Panorama* programme. Had he and the other talking heads had a professional organisation protecting their interests, they would not have been put in a position where rational thought had been impossible.

The black American who had raised the subject of reparations at the Sunday event objected to Goodman's view that SNCC's expulsion of its white members had been tragic. On the contrary, it was a necessity. It was absurd that in an organisation set up to represent blacks that, on his estimate, 75-80% of the decisions within the organisation, had been made by white people.

Here, Goodman corrected himself. Perhaps the black members of SNCC had made the right decision, after all. But he emphasised again that it had come at a cost. Something had been gained: black people had more autonomy, but the 'across-the-board humanity' by which he presumably meant certain humanist values that transcended race, had been lost.

Another American, this time a white speaker, then continued with a long statement on Marxism and economics, which concluded with a brief observation about the unequal relationship between the United States and Cambodia. But Goodman preferred to talk about an unequal relationship much closer to home, that between the United States and Canada. During the previous 15 years, American companies had bought up 65% of the Canadian economy. Now, you could call that what you liked, he said. But it certainly wasn't the sort of economic domination written about by Marx, or by Adam Smith for that matter.

Inevitably, there were also questions or statements about his attitude to technology and his notion of the immodesty of most political action. One that elicited a very interesting response came from a speaker named Richard, a veteran of the Free Speech Movement at Berkeley. It was about the organisers of the Congress themselves. He thought that Berke and Redler and company had been corrupted by the position of authority and control that their sense of their role had thrust upon.

Goodman disagreed with this. What happened was much less sinister. He didn't doubt for one minute that when the organisers had planned the Congress, they had started off with the best of intentions. But running a congress was expensive, so certain concessions to market principles had had to be made 'Then, when you have a crowd, you begin to get problems that make conversation impossible, and free interchange and changing the role of the teacher and student, which is all necessary, impossible because if the four do that, then the other two hundred and sixty can't hear, and don't get in. So then, having started in a nice way, you get tied up in an administrative hang-up just as if you were [former president of the University of California] Clark Kerr or somebody [laughter]. You know, as if you're a dean of students. And all that proves is that money is the root of all evil [laughter].

The final statement came from a scruffy, middle-aged Christian in a shirt, tie, and pullover. Earnest and nervous, he made the point that many institutions had yet to catch up with the great changes that had taken place in Western society. Goodman agreed with this. He did not however agree with some of the man's other points, and particularly not with the man's suggestion that the point of institutions was to make people happy. 'I'll take care of that myself, thank you, and I'd much rather not have this crowd taking care of it for me. I wish, however, if my water is polluted that this crowd would help me clean it up, you know 'cos then I can have a more interesting tragedy, see.'

*

The afternoon session that followed Goodman's speech had the appearance of a medley of dissonant voices. But that's because it was: a medley, pretty certainly put together solely to provide material for the long-playing records. The subjects covered: the New Experimental College, the anarchist Provo movement, the Free University of New York (FUNY), Maoism, self-realisation, the student movement in Berlin, community activities and peace action groups. These had almost certainly been explored in the seminars already and in much greater detail. Which was alright for the compliant amongst the participants — they would probably speak about or listen to anything — but an obvious source of frustration to those who were not and who were asked to sit through some inevitably boring presentations.

Berke brought the session to order with a piece of wordplay almost worthy of Laing. He begged those people who had agreed to help him with the session, but who had wandered off, to come back to the platform and help him do 'whatever' it was he didn't 'know [what he was] doing'.[28] This set the tone for the following five or six minutes. The Danish educator, Aage Rosendal Neilsen, started the session by pointing out that when people had something to say, that 'something' often got in the way of saying it. Which in his case *was* the case. He confessed that he had little appetite for saying anything about his ostensible subject at all. Perhaps one of his fellow collegians would give their 'version' of the New Experimental College, he wondered. But none of them would. 'New Experimental College does not have a story to tell, but we have work to do,' he concluded.

The next speaker, a German writer living in London, spoke about the situation facing students at the Free University of Berlin — not, of course, a free university in the FUNY, Trocchi or Paul Goodman sense, but an institution founded in 1948 by refugees from Communist persecution and with the strong support of the occupying United States authorities. There, too, students had set up their own 'kritische universite', which in some ways he believed went much further than the American free universities. And it was under attack, from the university, from the Springer newspaper press and from the city, all of them hysterically wedded to an 'unprincipled and primitive anti-communism'.

'If the director and senate of West Berlin university today want to repress freedom, they ... do so in the name of preserving freedom. If they want to take for granted the right of the West Berlin police or of imported American bodyguards to shoot down anyone who throws a custard pie, they do so in the name of responsibility for human life,' he said. This, incidentally, was an extrapolation from Herbert Marcuse's extremely influential 'Repressive Tolerance' essay of 1965, so it was significant that he went on to mention the man himself and to quote from the essay.[29]

The next speaker was a Dutchman.[30] He too didn't give his name, but like the previous speaker, he spoke excellent English. His topic was Provo, of which he was a former member — the movement having dissolved itself two months earlier, after being 'incorporated' into the Dutch establishment. Nonetheless, there was still much that the Congress could learn from the movement, especially regarding the police, who Provo had become expert at baiting. No representatives of state authority were more unpopular or more easily antagonised than the police, the speaker went on. All he and his fellow Provos had had to do was sit in the street or place a few flowers on a monument, and the police had rushed forward, 'grim-faced' and 'sirens wailing'. 'The police provoke[d] the masses just [as we did]', he said. 'They [did] it from one side, and we from the other.' 'Can one imagine a better comrade than the policeman?' Holland's democracy was nothing but a sham, he added. The brittle behaviour of the police force proved that.

Berke's FUNY campanero, Allen Krebs, took the microphone after the Dutchman. For almost two years, the two had engaged in an animated transatlantic correspondence. Of all the friends that Berke had left behind in America, Krebs was probably the one he respected most. So, it must have been painful to discover that acerbic former Adelphi University professor hadn't much liked R.D. Laing when he had met him with Jutta on a visit the couple had made to FUNY. Neither had he been impressed by Berke's thoughts on the predicament of black people in the United States in his Watts article.[31]

Had Krebs had his way, Berke would not have left the States in the first place. There was still so much to do at FUNY. With respect to the Congress, well, why hold that at all, Krebs had written during the summer of 1966? 'Why take what little sense we can make out of this madhouse and offer up instead 'COMPLETE AND TOTAL LIBERATION'?" Berke and the other members of the IPS should be reading Marx, not sitting about writing foolish letters to so and so. There was a 'blooming fucking bloody war' in Vietnam and the 'decolonization process' was not moving fast enough to save '1 or 2 billion people from incineration initiated by the psychopaths in Washington, New York and Los Angeles.'[32]

Not surprisingly then, Krebs did not take any hostages when given the opportunity to speak about the Congress. It was a mess, he said; a 'peculiar circus'; its various problems beyond his competence. Instead of wasting the Congress's time speaking about FUNY, he said, he would far rather hear more about the situation in Germany.

He ended his brief speech with another swipe at Berke and the other organisers. 'And if you have any further questions, I would be happy to answer them ... whenever the engines of power which run this carnival decide.'

Following further speeches by a young American man representing a Marxist-Leninist groupuscule called the Internationalists,[33] Peter Cadogan and Ginsberg (who more or less repeated the remarks he had made on Saturday about the Diggers and other American community groups), the event was brought to an end by another one of the Germans present.[34] This was Gabriele Kuby a sociology student and a leading member of the Free University of Berlin's students' union. Like the first speaker, Kuby spoke at length about the Free University of Berlin. But she went into much greater detail, giving examples showing how the administration had almost always taken sides against radical students. During April, it had tried to 'eliminate student opposition altogether' she informed the Congress, by punishing students at the behest of the city authorities and by allowing police onto the campus. She then gave a blow-by-blow personal account of the bloody events which had led to the killing of the student Benno Ohnesorg by a policeman at a demonstration against the Shah of Persia in June. This event was already widely known in England, but her personal involvement coupled with her rapid, earnest delivery must have contributed to its effect. Again, like the first German writer, she highlighted the insidious role of the Springer Press, which continually published lies about the demonstration. The university and the city were now in a state of crisis, she said. An emergency law was soon to be passed by the German parliament, which would have a further freezing effect on the students' movement, and she begged those at the Congress to do everything they could to help them.

*

Berke had always been active in one shape or another during the previous week and a bit, but he had not made a major speech. It was clearly with some trepidation then that during the evening following the anti-institutions seminar that he made his own hour-long contribution. Indeed, he was visibly and audibly nervous. His syntax and grammar were loose, his sentences rolled into one another; and he frequently repeated the same words and phrases. Much better then had he cut the speech down to twenty minutes, stayed with what he knew about and kept away from politics and sociology altogether.

His title was 'The Possibilities of Revolutionary Social Change in Post-Capitalistic Western Societies', which even he admitted was a 'mouthful.'

Most of the first half of his speech was mostly a summary of the previous speakers' contributions: Laing, Henry, and Goodman, in particular. But it was worth doing as these were the foundation stones upon which he built his hoped-for 'possibilities'.[35] The world was a 'single system'; it was 'fucked', and no part more so than the United States of America, he told the Congress. Various minority groups: blacks, students, mental patients, prisoners, the elderly were excluded from what the West had to offer, sometimes through overt violence, sometimes via covert measures. For instance, there were 'literally millions of people hidden away in bug houses', plus huge numbers in penal institutions and old people's homes, where most residents were already effectively dead, victims of a 'premature senility'.

There was no point in tinkering with the situation. What was needed was revolution, which was going to happen whether the middle and upper-middle technocrats who ran the system wanted it to or not. If only there were more people from the Second and Third Worlds at the Congress. Where were the Russians? The Chinese? Although the IPS had written to a few Russians, none of them had responded.[36] It was probably down to these absences that the Congress had taken on a 'schizophrenic' quality, by which he presumably meant the split already noticed between speakers with a theoretical bias and those, like Carmichael, calling for immediate action.

So, what to do about the system? How to bring about the 'possibilities' in his title?

The strengths of the present world system were also its weaknesses, Berke said. A) It was economically and politically centralised. B) It was complex. C) It was extremely bureaucratic and D) it was highly technological, as large parts of it were already automated.

Fig 24. Joe Berke. By Peter Davis. Congress stills. Courtesy Peter Davis, www.villon films.com

The task of the revolutionary, he said, was to exploit these features, either by working within the opportunities that the system provided or by doing the opposite and trying to undermine it by counter-measures. For instance, a centralised system was easy and relatively painless to drop out of. Revolutionaries could create their own social structures and still live off the fat of the land. They could set up a free university or some other kind of 'anti-institution'. 'By this, I mean people like the German students, the Provos, Aage Neilsen in his New Experimental College, the hippies, etc.' 'These people are beginning a cultural revolution ... which is a very political event', he added. Not only those, but in London, there was the example of Kingsley Hall and the other communities that the Philadelphia Association had founded. Then, in the United States, there was the commune movement, which was slowly panning out from San Francisco, New York, and other cities. People, he said, were finding new ways to live, confronting the 'fragmented alienated barbarism' of the family.

It was because he saw these actions as genuinely revolutionary that Berke was highly critical of Carmichael's position on the hippies, while at the same time remaining generally sympathetic to his analysis of the situation in which black people found themselves. 'I would say we are all subjected to the system.' The hippies were not merely dropping out; they were making permanent changes to their inner lives. Now contrast that with the Black Power advocates who were not undergoing genuine internal change. If they were in power, unchanged themselves, they would simply reproduce the pathologies of the old system.

It was the emergence of the anti-institutions, he said, which was the first phase in the overthrow of 'post-capitalistic' society. Put another way, in terms that he borrowed from Mao, it was the period of 'organisation, consolidation and preservation.' The second phase was to expand the reach of these anti-institutions, for anti-institutions to link up with other anti-institutions, which would again be 'a kind of group therapy in a psychiatric sense'. Finally, in the third phase, these linked-up anti-institutions would themselves become the 'major kind of [new] social structure'. This, he said, would be somewhat akin to what Marcuse had written about in his book *Eros and Civilization*, 'which is humane, which is decent ... [a kind of] ... erotic civilisation'. It might also resemble the culture of the Senoi people as described by the anthropologist Kilton Stewart in the article that Berke had reprinted in *Fire* magazine.

*

The Q&A which followed Berke's speech added little to what the American had said already, except for some disjointed remarks about group phantasies, authoritarianism, culture clash and the Bomb. More significant, at least in terms of the direction that the congress was about to take, was his mention of Herbert Marcuse. It was Marcuse who opened the following morning's session, having presumably arrived in London sometime during the previous day. This was for his close friend, Lucien Goldmann, a Romanian-born philosopher, and literary theorist, who was particularly influential in France.

Goldmann titled his speech 'Critique and Dogmatism in the Creation of Literature' and delivered it in French. He was then followed on the Thursday morning by the Yugoslav philosopher Gajo

Petrović and the Czechoslovakian writer Igor Hajek, both of whom were late replacements for John Gerassi—Gerassi having been moved to the 20th to take up the vacancy created by Erving Goffman.

Coupled with Marcuse, who gave his speech on Friday, each of these figures gave the final days of the Congress a European flavour, with Goldmann and Petrović both offering versions of a distinctively continental humanist Marxism and Marcuse's own version of Marxism reaching back to the Berlin of Walter Benjamin and the so-called Frankfurt School, of which he was still a distinguished member.

Goldmann, who Marcuse playfully described as 'engaged in fighting the new fashionable disease which has gripped the French intelligentsia, namely structuralism', yet himself a 'clandestine' structuralist, began his contribution by distinguishing between what was still valuable in classical Marxism from what the development of the consumer society in the western world had rendered obsolete.[37]

In the West, it no longer made sense, he said, to speak of the immiseration of the working class and the inevitably of a proletarian revolution. What did remain relevant, however, was the Marxist concept of reification, the idea that human relations had become quantitative relations, that men were in the process of becoming 'things', at best—for those who occupied professional roles—mere 'illiterate specialists.'

He spoke in a strong, rapidly delivered French, stopping every couple of minutes or so for a translator to rephrase his words in English, but making no other concessions to the difficulty of his argument.

What hopes now were there for man's liberation, Goldmann asked? 'Action', he said, 'would only be successful if it was carried out on two levels: on the "intellectual and cultural" level as well as on the 'social economic plane.' As for literature, the creative force behind a literary work or indeed any other 'cultural creation', could not be explained through the life of a particular individual or through any collection of individuals. Rather, it could only be explained as a product of a specific 'social group' in opposition to other social groups which 'through this opposition act on nature.' In most great works of literature there was a worldview, he said, 'but also an awareness of what this worldview rejects.' Thus, Moliere's *The Misanthrope* didn't just reject Jansenism, it also showed the 'human reality' that humans reject when they 'reject the misanthrope.'

He concluded with a few remarks critical about a book he had recently published in which he had praised the novels of Alain Robbe-Grillet for their realism and their 'coherent criticism of existing society.' He now, he said, saw that he was mistaken. For Robbe-Grillet's novels did not display the human reality that was rejected in a worldview that was reducing human relations to relations among objects. In other words, the novels had 'failed to see the sacrifices that that world view [was calling for] in respect of other possibilities.'

Although this was hardly the sort of speech to inspire a revolutionary consciousness à le Carmichael or John Gerassi, nonetheless it was warmly applauded and the questions it inspired were well-informed: what was Goldmann's position on Louis Althusser? Why was he critical of structuralism? How would he explain the development of Marxism in Sartre's *Critique of Dialectical Reason*?

*

Gajo Petrović continued in the same mood on Thursday morning, with a paper on the Marxist philosophical journal *Praxis*. This was at David Cooper's suggestion. Petrović, a professor at the University of Zagreb and President of the Yugoslav Philosophical Society, had arrived at the Congress towards the end of the previous week, expecting to deliver a learned paper on 'Philosophy and Socialism' at one of the afternoon or evening seminars.[38] His elevation therefore was not without risk. However, he rose to the challenge magnificently.

Perhaps inspired by Goodman's example, Petrović's adopted an informal tone for his speech, hedging his observations around with the sort of qualifications which could almost have been designed to subtly undermine his authority. This was an unusual approach to take. But coupled with his heavily accented and slightly abstracted delivery, it gave him a vulnerable, rather worried air, which somehow contributed to his authenticity.

Respectably dressed in dark suit and tie, he spoke for just under forty minutes on four major themes: *Praxis* and philosophy, *Praxis* and socialism, *Praxis* and Marxism and *Praxis* and internationalism.

He began his account of *Praxis* and philosophy with the common observation that quantity in any human endeavour did not have a necessary connection with quality. There were lots of philosophers, but too many of them were specialists, and too much of their work was ivory tower or worse. At best, they seemed only concerned with helping the 'existing world to function.'[39] The Praxis philosophers, on the other hand, wanted to change the world. The problems they examined were rooted in everyday people's lives. Indeed, as the word 'praxis' suggested, they considered their philosophising a kind of activism. In Marx's words, their aim was the 'pitiless criticism of everything existing,'[40] allied with, in Petrović's own words, a 'humanist vision of a better human future.'

He then defined precisely what Praxis meant by socialism, which of course was very different from what Stalinists both in and out of the Soviet Union meant by it. They spoke of it as the period after capitalism and before communism and from which it was separated by the so-called 'dictatorship of the proletariat.' But what did this 'dictatorship of the proletariat' mean? In practice, it often meant a period of intense violence, 'a period in which inhuman means are used for achieving human purposes.'

Additionally, most definitions of socialism put too much emphasis on economic factors—'socialism is defined as a society where we have distribution according to work.' But what is most characteristic of contemporary man, Petrović said, is that he is alienated from himself. The *Praxis* conception of socialism therefore encompassed the whole man, whereas economics would only ever form part of its definition.

He described how the Praxis philosophers had developed their philosophy from the early Marx and how they were interested in all sorts of Marxist and non-Marxist philosophers. There was, he said, no canonical list of authorities to which its writers were forced to pay obeisance. Of course, such a position was not without problems. On the one hand, Stalinists accused them of 'betraying' Marxism, while, on the other hand, they were attacked by people who saw nothing of value in Marxism, period.

Taking his final theme—*Praxis* and internationalism—at a swift pace, he emphasised that friendship between states was never sufficient; a truly humanist conception of international amity must also embrace individuals. This was why the editorial committee of the journal had formed an 'international advisory board' of forty or fifty figures. These figures were not chosen on the basis of the countries they belonged to, but on the grounds of their views.

*

Hajek spoke immediately after Petrović. In contrast to the Yugoslav, he kept his presentation short, speaking after Cooper's very brief introduction, for just twenty minutes about Czechoslovakia. He was a small, slightly elfin man dressed in a coloured shirt and dark tie who, in his opening remarks, described himself as a simple magazine editor. But that was misleading. In fact, the magazine that he helped to edit was *Literární noviny* [Literary Gazette], the official organ of the Union of Czech Writers, a famously liberal body which was struggling to broaden Czechoslovakia's intellectual and literary culture in the face of official opposition. In 1959, Hajek had introduced Beat literature to Czechoslovakia. He was also friendly with Ginsberg on a personal level, having helped to host the poet during his uproarious second visit to Prague in 1965. It was a visit that had ended badly for Ginsberg, but arguably far worse for Hajek, who was subsequently trailed by the Prague secret service and denounced by the Czechoslovakian president and the Communist Youth Organisation daily newspaper as an enemy of Communist morality.[41]

Hajek began his speech by emphasising that Czechoslovakia was a work in progress. It was a 'social experiment on a grand scale' and its many 'problems' (a word he used again and again) would not be solved without a great deal of further discussion.[42] Many people, he said, liked to use the word 'liberalisation' to describe what was happening there. But that was far too simple a way of looking at it. In any case, such progress as had been achieved could easily go into reverse, though, for his part, he remained optimistic that it would continue.

Just like Petrović, he divided his speech into a few linked themes: economics first, then political science, then what he called, with perhaps more than a nod to Ginsberg, the 'widening of awareness.'

In the economic sphere, Czechs were keen to get rid of the rigid planning system and to experiment with new patterns and structures, he said, while in the political sphere, people were talking about the 'responsibility of society to the individual' and not vice versa. The expansion of people's awareness, he said, had led to creative ventures in all sorts of fields, but particularly in film, literature, and theatre. Like the French, the country had even experienced its own cinematic New Wave. Many of these films, despite the criticisms of Czech society that they offered, had nonetheless been supported by the nationalised film industry.

He then mentioned Ginsberg. Not as a writer, however, but as a homosexual—this on the very day that homosexuality between consenting males was effectively decriminalised in England and Wales by the Sexual Offences Act.[43] He raised the issue, he said, not only because it was a good example of the positive role that intellectuals had played in Czechoslovakia, but to pick up on a throwaway line of Paul Goodman. During his speech on Tuesday, Goodman had asserted that it was Ginsberg's homosexuality that had got him thrown out of Czechoslovakia, in 1965. But the full story, Hajek said, was 'much more complicated.' Czechoslovakia had long been more liberal than the UK in such matters, he said. In fact, the Czechs had passed a similar law to the Sexual Offences Act about ten years previously.[44]

*

The questions that followed Hajek's presentation were almost exclusively aimed at Petrović. He was asked about Mao, Stalinism, the party system in Yugoslavia, the difference between bourgeois humanism and Marxist humanism, and what one speaker called the 'psychedelic revolution'. He could contribute nothing to the last, Petrović said. He was still in the position of a learner. Of Mao, he said, he knew little. But what he did know worried him deeply. An American friend of his had drawn a comparison between what the reformers were doing in Yugoslavia and the 'cultural revolution' in China. But he was not convinced. There was much about Maoism that suggested to him Stalinism, not least the 'cult of personality'. Only time would tell, he added.

Hajek was asked just one question—about the imprisonment of Jan Beneš, a writer and former paratrooper, who had been arrested on the charge of smuggling. So, no one asked him about homosexuality. Yet, the subject was often on people's minds, on the platform and off. Naturally, there were many gay people at the Congress. Some of them, consciously or not, looked to Goodman and Ginsberg for guidance and inspiration.

Goodman's pursuit of Gregory Bateson's son, John, has already been mentioned. But he was hardly the only young man to excite the veteran anarchist's attention. Goodman was often spotted 'cruising' the Roundhouse.[45] One participant remembers him telling her and other youngsters a story about allowing a vagrant to 'bugger' him. 'He went along with it out of the goodness of his heart, as it were. He was generous to an amazing degree!!' she recollected.[46]

Intriguingly, while Goodman must have forgotten much about the Congress on his return to America, he didn't forget his brief exchange about homosexuality with Carmichael on the *Panorama* programme. In an article published a few years after the Congress, he referred to the way Carmichael had 'blandly' put him and Ginsberg down by saying that they could always hide their 'dispositions and pass.' 'That is, he accorded to us the same lack of imagination that one accords to n--- ; we did not really exist for him.'[47]

*

While the speeches were the main offerings on Wednesday and Thursday, there were also a number of other significant events. These included poetry readings, a film show about Cuba, a panel discussion on art and violence, and presentations by Ginsberg and the Dutch poet, Simon Vinkenoog.

The best of the poetry readings took place on Wednesday evening. Sponsored and organised by the Caribbean Artists Movement (CAM), it included contributions by Evan Jones, Ted Joans, and the Movement's founders, John La Rose, Edward Braithwaite, and Andrew Salkey.

Though billed as a poetry event, it started off with C.L.R. James reading from *The Black Jacobins* and *Facing Reality*, his pseudonymous book of 1958, which he had co-authored with Grace Lee Boggs and Cornelius Castoriadis.

One of the best applauded poems was Evan Jones' evergreen *Song of the Banana Man*. But it was the 'fireball figure', as John La Rose put it, of Ted Joans who ultimately stole the show, beginning his energetic performance with *The Truth* and ending it with a poem written on the same day as Gerassi's presentation, entitled *This Poem Is*. The poem, which evoked 'guilty oatmeal faces', ended with a thunderous shout of 'Black Power!

This poem is

> This poem is Stokely Carmichael, he who never cowers for he is this poem with us at this hour

Together we are this poem

> Black Power! Baby, Black Power!'[48]

David Cooper led the panel event, which took place on Thursday afternoon. His own contribution was a learned discourse comparing a psychotic breakdown to the music of Luciano Berio and John Cage.[49] He was followed by Carolee Schneemann and then another friend of Berke, the poet and magazine editor, Susan Sherman. Other contributions came from the poet Jerome Rothenberg, the artist Gustav Metzger, and a middle-aged black South African musician named Moses Supola, who had published an anthology of African folk songs.

Sherman spoke about the way that the riots-cum-rebellions in the United States had desensitised people to much higher levels of violence than had been the norm, instancing the relatively muted public reaction to a recent outbreak in the Spanish Harlem district of New York, while Schneemann described the war in Vietnam as a 'huge fantastic happening' for hoi polloi. Ordinary people, she said, wanted to 'see' the violence that the conflict had unleashed, 'they wanted to feel it, they wanted to see those bodies crushed.'

Yes, but only if they were at a safe distance, remarked Rothenberg.

Figs 25-28. Art and Violence seminar. Participants included Gustav Metzger, Carolee Schneemann, David Cooper, and Susan Sherman. By Peter Davis. Congress stills. Courtesy Peter Davis, www.villonfilms.com

For his part, Metzger, gave a shout for his own practice of auto-destructive art. The looting and other attacks on property in the riots-cum-rebellions, he said, were a 'mirroring of the wastefulness' to be found in modern industrial society and its rapid elimination in wars. He also agreed with another point that Schneemann made, that the purpose of art was to 'protect' the individual. 'People come up to me and say, "Haven't you destroyed yourself?' I smile and say, "Don't be ridiculous. The idea of auto-destructive art is to destroy things, partly as a matter of protecting the individual."'

*

Ginsberg and Vinkenoog delivered their sessions during the late afternoon and evening,

Ginsberg, who was exhausted having already spent several hours with Iain Sinclair, began by reemphasising the difference between the unmediated human voice and electronic communication. What kind of 'reality' was the latter?[50] Perhaps it was merely someone's 'strange, nightmarish space-age hallucination'? He then read a passage from Burroughs' novel *Nova Express* on mind control. But it was 'praxis', i.e., 'consciousness and practical action, he really wanted to talk about, so he tried to keep his attention on that.

In one very powerful section, he, again, returned to Bateson's remarks about the greenhouse effect. So, what if the polar ice caps melted, he said? It might be the end of mankind, but the porpoises would benefit. 'Ultimately, the universe doesn't need our execrable howling for the continuation of its own life. Like porpoise power!', he shouted.

He then went on with a long section on conditioning and paranoia and the relationship between private fantasies and their public manifestation, arguing that if people really wanted to understand what was going on in the world, they had to get behind the image that people presented of themselves.

Imagine what effect learning that Hitler was a secret coprophile who had encouraged Eva Braun to shit on him could have on those middle-aged and elderly Germans who still hankered for the Nazis, he said. Hitler's public behaviour would finally make sense to them. 'The private must be made public', he added.

He gave another definition of flower power, similar to the one he had given at the open forum, restating that although it was a euphemism, the image it inspired was correct in terms of its 'origins' and 'techniques'. 'Don't escalate the hostility, don't escalate the anger, control your mind. watch what you're doing, be aware totally.' It wasn't love that the hippies were offering people, he said. But the possibility of becoming aware of their own feelings, including of how they were manipulated by language.

He mentioned a conversation he'd had with David Cooper earlier that week. Cooper had said: Don't give Che Guevara LSD. It might stop him fighting. Well, that was one point of view, said Ginsberg. But maybe the drug would have the opposite effect. Who could tell? But the main thing was to be active in some way: 'active black power, active flower power, active manifestation of the understanding ... not sitting around on your ass.'

Finally, he picked up on some of Paul Goodman's remarks on city life by counselling people to move into the countryside. We have to return to our 'tribal-mammal origins in the original ecology for which we are fit.' We should, he said, 'replant back to some sort of living delight, instead of dead vibrations.'

Fig 29. Allen Ginsberg and Simon Vinkenoog. By Peter Davis. Congress stills. Courtesy Peter Davis, www.villonfilms.com

Simon Vinkenoog, who came after Ginsberg, said that he'd keep his contribution short, which he did, speaking for just six or seven minutes. A poet and established provocateur, he was probably best known in England for a non-poetic contribution to the International Poetry Incarnation at the Royal Albert Hall during the summer of 1965. He had infamously interrupted a reading by poet Harry Fainlight by shouting 'Love. Love ... Come, man, come.' an episode which the filmmaker Peter Whitehead caught on camera for his film *Wholly Communion*. At that time, Vinkenoog was dressed formally in a black suit and tie, his blond hair cut short. Now, he appeared brightly clothed, with tousled hair and sideburns.

When Berke had invited him to the Congress in April he had been full of enthusiasm: 'Dear Connector ... . I think that your conference is one of the nicest things I have heard of recently, and I wish you all the realizations possible.'[51] Vinkenoog's experience of the Congress jaundiced him, however. There was talk at the Congress, lots of that, of course. But he was doubtful that it had contributed an iota to decreasing the amount of violence in the world. The participants, he said, had been swept into a 'collective hallucination called angst, anxiety.' 'We were run over by front-page news, old world power struggles, politicians, ideologies and we seem to have forgotten that the priest, the magician, the musician, the poet, the prophet, the artist may be the only real-lifelines man has got left to hang onto.'

He particularly regretted the absence from the Congress of the 'great Londoner' Elias Canetti,[52] Marshall McLuhan and the architect and futurologist, Buckminster Fuller, who just last week he had heard speaking in London.

Yet all was not lost, and he was careful to end his contribution on a positive note. People should try to be their 'beautiful selves', he said, to liberate themselves from all previous modes of thought and action. If they could succeed in doing that, then anything would be possible. 'All the rest is silence. I share my trips with innumerable others, and I shall see the last states disintegrate through love special delivery.'[53]

9. And then there was Marcuse

The car that brought Marcuse and his wife, Inge, to London had also brought him to Elsham Road, where his reception had possibly been 'interesting'. Not that he had been confronted by cat mess or any rudeness from Laing—apparently, the two hardly spoke to each other.[1] It had simply brought him face to face with Paul Goodman.

Marcuse didn't like Goodman. He didn't like his politics and he didn't like him personally. Forced to share a living space with the veteran anarchist, he was irritated by Goodman's habit of leaving the bathroom door open as he brushed his teeth—'flirting his buttocks' in his underwear, as he described it to the editorial committee of the *New Left Review*—as he wiggled his own bottom in imitation.[2] 'Too much civilization, not enough Eros', quipped Mrs Marcuse, punning off one of her husband's book titles.[3] Possibly, she meant that her husband could himself have done with loosening up a bit.

That was during dinner on Thursday evening. Now that it was Friday morning, it was Marcuse's time to address the Congress. He titled his contribution 'Liberation from the Affluent Society'.

*

Following Cooper's brief introduction and the inevitable problems with the microphone, Marcuse began his speech by remarking that he was pleased to see so many flowers in the audience. But flowers had no power of their own; they had to be protected by men and women. He himself, he said, was merely a 'hopeless philosopher' to whom philosophy and politics were 'inseparable' and for whom the word dialectics meant liberation 'by virtue of the contradiction generated by the system, precisely because it is a bad, a false system.'[4]

He wasn't a charismatic speaker like Carmichael, say, or an expert raconteur like Goodman. Instead, Marcuse spoke slowly and remorselessly from a prepared text in a heavily accented English, dense with multi-syllables and abstractions.

Fig 30. Herbert Marcuse. By Ragna Karina Priddy. Courtesy Roger Priddy.

To most of his listeners, he was probably best known as the author of two books and an essay: *Eros and Civilization* of 1955, *One-Dimensional Man* of 1964 and 'Repressive Tolerance' of 1965. But, in recent weeks, he had also become widely known as an activist, lecturing to and stirring up Berlin's student radicals with a series of lectures titled 'The End of Utopia'.[5] His present lecture carried echoes of all these works, including his lectures in Germany.

We have been too 'hesitant', Marcuse went on, too 'ashamed' of proclaiming the qualitative superiority of what a socialist society would offer, which was nothing less than the 'negation' of every other society and the construction of a truly free society. It was what the Communards had had in mind when they had shot at the clocks on Paris's public buildings. They were arresting the 'established time continuum'. So that a new time could begin, a time with new needs and new satisfactions and therefore new institutions.

Presently, most men in the advanced societies lived in a condition of 'voluntary servitude', he said. They were slaves to a capitalist system, which while satisfying their material and cultural needs did so 'in line with the requirements and interests of the apparatus and of the powers which control the apparatus'. The price for these so-called 'achievements' was exacted both from people overseas and from a 'substratum' of the populace who continued to live 'in poverty and misery.'

The so-called 'capitalist welfare state' was really a 'warfare state'. 'It must have an enemy ... a total enemy', to discharge the 'primary aggressiveness' which had built up within it. Fortunately, it had one: Russia, though the country's 'image' and 'power' had been inflated beyond measure.

So, who or what would bring about the liberation in the title of his lecture? It certainly wouldn't be the working class. That had been bought off by consumerism. It could be helped into existence, he said, by the intelligentsia. This was its vital, preparatory role. For, with so many intellectuals working in education, they were in an ideal position to influence the younger generation.

This was education, he said, in a 'new sense', meaning theory as well as practice, 'reason and imagination, the intellectual and the instinctual needs.' 'We must confront indoctrination in servitude with indoctrination in freedom,' he said. In short, education should be used as a kind of political therapy.

The new society, Marcuse said, would be an 'aesthetic reality — society as a work of art.' With the abolition of labour, life would become an end in itself. There would be a total trans-valuation of values. Which in concrete terms would mean, *inter alia*, new cities, the 'restoration of nature after the elimination of the violence and destruction of capitalist industrialisation; the creation of the internal and external space for privacy.'

Before concluding, he added a few words about the hippies and the Third World. Gerassi and Carmichael were wrong to dismiss the hippies, he said. Although in some cases, their behaviour was 'mere masquerade and clownery', there was also an inherently 'political element'. This was also true of the Diggers and the Provos. They all manifested a 'new sensibility' against 'efficient and insane reasonableness.' Their 'revolt against the compulsive cleanliness of puritan morality and of the aggression bred by this puritan morality' in Vietnam deserved to be taken seriously.

Finally, 'let us continue with whatever we can: no illusions, but even more, no defeatism.'

*

The applause which followed Marcuse's lecture was louder and longer than Goodman had achieved, partly because the audience was considerably larger and partly because people were simply in awe of him. Once again, the IPS insisted on written questions only. Consequently, the identities of the questioners were not revealed, except for the first which came from Giovanni Jervis. Jervis wanted to know what Marcuse meant by the phrase 'abolition of labour.'[6]

This inspired Marcuse to make a detailed, five-minute-long disquisition, touching on Marx, Nietzsche, and Charles Fourier. Marx, he said, had been far too cautious in most of his definitions of the concept. For his part, he was much more taken with Fourier's formulation. This was his 'great idea' for a 'society in which all necessary work could be organised in accord with the developing instincts and inclinations' of individuals, a society in which 'alienated labour' would be totally abolished.

Another questioner asked him to comment on the riots-cum-rebellions in the United States. What was their relationship to liberation? Then there were allied questions on the rioters' use of violence and on whether he expected to be banned from the UK, like Stokely Carmichael.

Marcuse thought that the rioters' violence was best interpreted as an example of counter-violence, in as much as they did not appear to be aiming at the overthrow of the system. As for violence, in general, he said that people had become far too lax in how they defined it. This perhaps was a gentle dig at the IPS. 'Authoritarian education', for instance, was merely an example of violence in a figurative sense; it could not be compared with 'mental torture' or the lynching of a black man.

Physical violence, he said, could also be divided, again, into two distinct types. There was violence in the 'protection and defence of life' and violence used in its 'destruction and suppression'. Regarding himself, he thought that he was far too insignificant to be considered a threat to anyone—'certainly not in the United States,' where he was free to teach in any way that he chose, though, later, he accepted that not everyone was so fortunate.

Fig 31. Herbert Marcuse during the Q&A. By Peter Davis. Congress stills. Courtesy Peter Davis, www.villonfilms.com

This final comment related to another question he was asked, this time on the desirableness or otherwise of the society described in Aldous Huxley's *Brave New World*, a society in which people were chemically engineered to achieve the maximum personal happiness consistent with their role in society. Except for the existence of the Epsilons, the semi-moronic worker caste, Marcuse didn't think there was much that was wrong with Huxley's dystopia at all. 'Here looms in the background' he added, the idea of an 'educational dictatorship'. This was an idea that he had discussed in *Eros and Civilization*, which also formed a part of 'Repressive Tolerance' and which he had glanced at in his lecture when he mentioned education as a kind of therapy.

He was also asked questions about the likelihood of fascism returning to Western societies and about the war in Vietnam, while one cheeky participant asked him sneakily from the floor why he didn't resign his job and join other people using the tactics of civil disobedience. He didn't resign his job, he said, because he believed that he was more useful in it, and, frankly, because he didn't feel that at his time of life — he was almost seventy — he could face living in poverty.

*

That wasn't the end of Marcuse's contribution to the Congress. During the afternoon, he returned to the Roundhouse for a further session, not from the platform this time but from the floor, where he sat at a table next to Joe Berke, with a book on the origins of science in front of him and a packet of cigarettes. The purpose of this session was to provide an opportunity for further questions, which this time could be spoken. Unfortunately, the preliminaries were so taken up with a debate about whether the question-and-answer format was itself authoritarian that much of the time was wasted.

Nonetheless, there were, eventually, one or two very good questions, including one from a young working-class man, who seems to have been a first-time visitor to the Congress. He made the point that if his fellow participants really wanted to change the world in the direction that Marcuse had suggested, then they should first learn to speak how ordinary, working, people spoke. 'You're doing the same thing as all these other people have done before,' he said, apparently indicating Arnold Wesker and his Centre 42 organisation, from whom the IPS had hired the Roundhouse.[7] 'You're just interested in yourselves.' 'Don't talk to me, 'cos I have seen the con. Go and make someone see the con who hasn't seen it. This is all chat.' At which point he jumped up from where he was sitting, laid the microphone down, and bolted out of the building.

In his reply, Marcuse denied that he had not considered these issues: indeed, what right did any of them at the Congress have to tell working people that 'their society should be changed from top to bottom', particularly as most working people were better off materially than they'd ever been. He admitted, however, that there was a language problem. 'How can we impose our language on them?' he asked. 'They speak correctly their own language. And our language is difficult for them.' The sensible thing for the people at the Roundhouse to do in the meantime, he said, was to remain 'conscious of the fact'. And then only speak to working people when they were clear about what they wanted to say in their own minds.

Fig 32. Telling the congress to get stuffed. 'This is all chat.' By Peter Davis. Congress stills. Courtesy Peter Davis, www.villonfilms.com

And the response to that? Well, the best response probably came from a gum-chewing local boy of about eleven or twelve, one of a small group of 'Roustabouts' who were helping Carolee Schneemann in preparing for her happening. 'I think this man here [meaning Marcuse] is absolutely right. And I do really think this because he's got, well, I can't name the word, 'cos I don't know one. But he's right. That's what I have to say.'

Perhaps, as Roger Barnard said of another occasion, it was a pity the Congress didn't end there and then.[8] But there was still another day to go.

*

Come Saturday afternoon, the Congress embarked on its final timetabled events: a valedictory speech from Cooper summarising everything that the Congress had achieved and what it could still hope to achieve, followed by a short Q&A, Carolee Schneemann's happening, and a set from the hippie rock group, The Social Deviants.

Apparently, the group, though it seems unlikely, was Schneemann's idea. 'Some idiot' told her — according to the source of the anecdote, the band's vocalist Mick Farren — that they were an 'electronic wind-chime ensemble' or an acoustic version of The Fugs, and that was what she expected.[9]

Then there was also one other significant event, which was not on the bill. This was a lecture by Emmett Grogan.

*

That afternoon, Cooper started his presentation by pointing to the various dialectics that had played out during the previous two weeks.[10] These included the undulation between theory and activism, and between the individual, his or her small networks and much larger, anonymous, social and political events, by which he meant the war in Vietnam and the riots-cum-rebellions in the United States.

He said that he hoped the registrants had endured rather than enjoyed the morning lectures, the Q&As and other events and that they had discovered the ability to be alone with their thoughts while still open to others, for that was probably the perquisite for rational conversation. He then got on to Stokely Carmichael, recalling the moment during the open forum when he had confronted the white liberal with 'What have you done? ... What have you done?'

The task of whites, Cooper said, was not to try and 'help' Carmichael, but to erode white power. That, he added, was not a racist position, as some people at the Congress suggested. It was simply based on fact: imperialism in the world, as it was presently constituted, was white power. That said, white people too were oppressed by whiteness. Not in the same way, mind. But they were oppressed. They should feel the oppression, experience it, then act on it, he said, not as the inspiration of hare-brained schemes such as putting LSD in water supplies or blowing up factories, but as a challenge to their pessimism.

As rootless intellectuals, inescapably marked by their bourgeois and colonising outlook, they were all called upon to take action of a different sort: to demystify their ruler's mystifications; and to demystify and deinstitutionalise themselves, their families, the schools, the hospitals, the factories, and the universities. In other words, Cooper made some of the same points as he made in his circular letter of 1966 and in his speech at the opening of the Congress. Each registrant should begin preliminary work on themselves. Each of them should strive to integrate the various dualities within themselves: winner/loser; lover/hater; perpetrator/victim; murderer/murderee; and so on. And not split off and externalise the unwanted parts of themselves in others, as the people of the United States had done to the people of North Vietnam.

Cooper also commented, again, on the nature of schizophrenia, what he had previously described as a publicly stigmatised yet liberatory madness. The true lunatics were those with their fingers on the nuclear triggers. He then recalled witnessing a happening during which a pile of scholarly-looking books was burnt. He described it as an entirely reasonable response to pseudo-authoritative scholarship [11]. It might be better, however, to focus on more obvious vehicles of mystification, he suggested, to tear up newspapers and ballot papers and burn radios and TV sets.

Finally, he had been deeply impressed, he said, by Marcuse's remark about the Communards shooting at clocks. For Marcuse, the shooting signalled a fresh start, a break in the 'established time continuum.' Which was precisely what was needed today: a new beginning. '

*

The chorus of approval that greeted Cooper's final speech was only half of that afternoon's story. There was also a Q&A to follow it. Roger Barnard caught one of its spikier moments in an article he wrote for *Peace News*. He hadn't enjoyed Cooper's speech at all, and he clearly didn't like Cooper personally. He noted Cooper's contemptuous response to a questioner who asked him why the IPS had not permitted people without money to sit at the back of the hall during the major speeches. Cooper's reply, he said, was 'Tough luck' — which was 'hardly the tone of an educator or liberator.'[12]

Another questioner picked up on the issue that had come up during the second Marcuse Q&A and asked Cooper how the participants could communicate with people who had been brainwashed by the mass media.

Cooper's response to this was to continue with the infiltration of media organisations that had already occurred. To illustrate the success of this strategy, he instanced the case of David Mercer's play, *In Two Minds*, which had been broadcast by the BBC the previous March, which critiqued conventional psychiatry, and which had been a massive hit.[13] They could also, Cooper suggested, stage happenings.

Another question Cooper read to the Congress himself: why, the questioner asked, had he, the questioner that is, been brainless when some time earlier he had asked Cooper whether he considered Cooper's theory of schizophrenia to be 'falsifiable' or not?

Many of the participants clapped and laughed at that. Which Cooper remarked was an excellent answer, the clapping and laugher, that is. But, he also offered an olive branch. He would meet the questioner after the Q&A was over and discuss the matter privately, presuming he wanted that.

Cooper's best answer was also his last — at least as far as the recordings are concerned. This was in response to a string of questions read out by a drunken Laing: 'Can you tell us about the Institute of Phenomenological Studies? What will its activities be in the next month? ... Can one be on its mailing list? Become a member?'

Here Cooper really got into his stride. The IPS, he said, didn't exist. So, consequently, it didn't meet either. It was merely a kind of anti-committee. It would, however, stage further events, he said, probably in the near future.[14]

*

Grogan's speech came next on Saturday's agenda. Like the Black Power event, this wasn't an official Congress occasion. But an ad hoc personal contribution. Probably, it was motivated by Grogan's guilt at having performed so badly at Saturday's open forum. This time, he did not take drugs. He was simply himself: a trickster and a moocher, with a devastating sense of humour.

Following the open forum, he had spent the previous week on a lightening tour of London and of half a dozen other European cities. He had visited Kingsley Hall and the Exploding Galaxy commune on Balls Park Road, the Shakespeare and Company bookshop in Paris and Kommune 1 in West Berlin.[15]

Leaving nothing to chance, he had memorised his speech the day before and he went over it again before delivering it. Not a difficult task perhaps as it wasn't his own work but a speech by Adolf Hitler. Not that he told the audience that. He simply delivered it and awaited their response, which, apparently, was rapturous. He then told them who the author was. 'His name was Adolf Hitler, and he made his delivery of these same words at the Reichstag in, I believe, 1937. Thank you, 'n be seeing you.'[16]

*

By the 29th, Schneemann had been preparing her happening for almost two weeks, with more downs than ups, including numerous vocal interruptions from students and other young people, and some not entirely helpful interventions from Laing and Cooper.

One of their interventions related to a court case following on from a performance by the Vienna Institute of Direct Art during the Destruction in Art Seminar (DIAS) series of September 1966. The performance had involved the evisceration of a dead lamb and the display of a film showing male genitals.

Just a few days before the 29th, the organisers of the Congress, Gustav Metzger and John Sharkey, had finally come up for trial at the Old Bailey, with the result that Metzger was given a £100 fine and Sharkey a conditional discharge.[17]

For the IPS, mindful that Schneemann had mentioned that she wanted to show an erotic film as part of her performance, the verdict therefore raised a particular dilemma: would the IPS too face prosecution?

Fig 33. Poster for Carolee Schneemann's 'Kinetic Theater' performance. Private Collection.

Eventually, following discussions with lawyers, the IPS and Schneemann came to an agreement. The performance would go ahead with the film, but if there was a prosecution Schneemann would bear responsibility.[18]

*

With her core caste of eight, including herself, plus a mass group of over twenty people and the 'Roustabouts' and other helpers, Schneemann delivered a performance that night that was almost certainly nothing like anyone at the Roundhouse had witnessed before. It was loud, sensuous, and visceral.

On the first Saturday of the Congress, she had described her intention to incorporate and challenge the 'dominant issues and elements' of the Congress, and that's exactly what she did: incorporating Congress flyers, seminar papers and other literature, the spoken words and kinesics of the speakers and other participants into a maelstrom of tangled limbs and debris and challenging them through the writings of Wilhelm Reich, Simone de Beauvoir and Antonin Artaud and her own proto-feminist and highly individual creative consciousness.[19]

The performance began with the entrance of a wooden cart piled high with the core group, foam blocks and other rubbish. Helpers unloaded them into the performance space, which was covered in white sheets and on the same level as the spectators. Then for the next twenty minutes or so, they squirmed and coiled, pulling or pushing each other's grease-covered bodies up or down, moulding them into various shapes and wrapping them in aluminium foil.

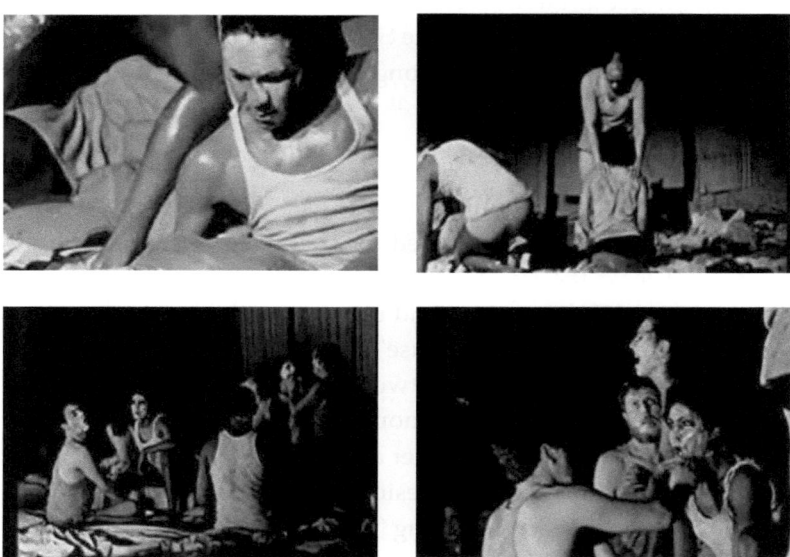

Figs 34-37. Carolee Schneeman's Round House happening. By Peter Davis. Congress stills. Courtesy Peter Davis, www.villonfilms.com

Meanwhile, the mass group ran around the balcony growling or humming and occasionally showering the core group with debris — all this part and parcel of the 'kinetic theater', which Schneemann had spent the past couple of years evolving.[20]

Besides the film, there was recorded music from the Beatles to whom she dedicated the performance, slides including one of the Pope delivering a blessing, the aforementioned film and newsreels showing atrocities committed in Vietnam, and flashing strobe lights.[21] The performance climaxed with the core group lying in a disorganised heap, upon which film of the atrocities was projected. They were then loaded back onto the cart with the foam blocks and led off the performance space.

Considering Schneemann's intentions in creating the piece and the problems she'd had during the rehearsals, it was perhaps not surprising that the response of part of the audience was aggressive. Repeatedly, the performers were interrupted by heckling and yelling. It was thus with some relief when they were trundled off the stage. As Jean Michaelson, one of the core group, remarked to Schneemann as they lay in the cart, 'Carolee. I'm glad you had the foresight to get us out of here.'[22]

It wasn't long after that the Social Deviants, under-rehearsed and out of key, 'howled [the Congress] to a close' with one of the worst sets they had ever played.[23]

*

Even before the Congress ended, people talked about its significance, not least the speakers, the registrants, and the organisers themselves. Was the expense and trouble worth it?

On the Friday after Marcuse's speech and the first or second Q&A, Peter Davis interviewed two of the registrants on the wasteland at the back of the Roundhouse. One was a woman in early middle age named Jane, the other an American woman aged about thirty named Joan, who was a resident or former resident of Kingsley Hall. Jane confessed to feeling 'confusion. Massive confusion.'[24] She had arrived at the Congress expecting a measure of clarity about violence and liberation. But what she'd encountered was the 'superficiality' and egotism of intellectuals. Except for Marcuse, she didn't think the major speakers had communicated well at all; they had simply got up on the platform and 'said' their 'discrepancies'; there had, she said, been no 'bringing together'.

She was also struck by how insular Monday's psychiatry and anti-psychiatry event had seemed; most of the participants had appeared to be only interested in the views of their fellow professionals. And she connected this observation to Carmichael's condemnations of white liberals: that they were self-regarding and almost entirely ineffective. But then, what was the alternative to the white liberal, she asked? Ginsberg's solution to the problem of violence she called a 'dance of life to death.' On the other hand, neither did she think much of Marcuse's idea of indoctrinating people in freedom, though she admitted that his contribution had been momentarily 'therapeutic'.

Joan, as befitted a North American, was much more positive about what the Congress had achieved. What she called the 'organised chaos or dissolution of the organisation of the Congress' as it evolved had moved her profoundly. Much less concerned than Jane with the vanities and standpoints of the individual speakers, she centred her analysis on groundlings like herself, either registrants or people who had initially been attracted to one event. She noted that some of the people who came to listen to Carmichael had stayed to listen to Marcuse. They had mingled and debated; and ultimately everybody had ended up 'meeting everybody else'. Which, in her view, was the whole point of the Congress in the first place.

She also emphasised that Carmichael's platform speeches had been less pro-violence than his critics suggested; that, in fact, what he had been asking for was not violence but autonomy for the black people of the United States within the context of brotherhood with black people everywhere. Yes, the so-called 'race riots' were violent. But they were nothing like the violence that the United States was inflicting on Vietnam. Perhaps the riots should be more violent. If the United States government was more preoccupied with violence at home, it would have less energy to devote to Vietnam and other foreign conflicts.

She ended by recalling the testimony of Thich Nhat Hahn on the first Monday evening. He had taught her that the Vietnam War was not supported by ordinary Vietnamese.

Fig 38. Come buy, come buy. Board with photographs for sale by John Haynes. 'Joan', with cigarette, on the left. By Ragna Karina Priddy. Courtesy Roger Priddy.

The anarchist Anne Marie Fearon, writing in *Freedom* on August 12, also emphasised the positive aspects of the Congress. Her main frame of reference, however, was the Roundhouse itself and the coincidence that Arnold Wesker from whom the IPS had hired the Roundhouse had finally raised enough money to buy the freehold just days after the Congress had started. She speculated that any use to which the building would now be put would make a 'grim and sad contrast' to the two weeks of the Congress, noting in particular the refreshing influence of the 'roustabouts'; how one of the youngsters had read his own poems to the audience as they had waited for the reappearance of Marcuse on Friday afternoon; how, on the final day they had paraded around the building with hollyhocks; and how they had made use of a 'huge swing' that a hippie had hung from the gallery.[25]

> Meanwhile the grown-ups also played. A pedal organ in one corner was in constant use. Impromptu poetry recitals were held. Poems were pinned up

on the wall, and were joined by a set of charcoal drawings. Someone discovered an old piano frame in the yard and began playing on it with two sticks; others joined in with metal pipes, milk crates, tin cans, and produced a mind-blowing sound. At odd moments people played flutes, banjos, recorders. Another time a middle-aged Dane announced that he felt like dancing; he danced; someone played a tambourine, others clapped or beat a rhythm on the hollow iron pillars.

Fearon's interpretation of the Congress's significance was, thus again, far more positive than Jane's. Like Joan, she was more interested in the activities of the ordinary participants than in those of the major speakers. The Congress had released a wealth of positive energy. It had provided an environment where people could repurpose rubbish and find new uses for domestic objects. The building itself had become a musical instrument. Interestingly, she said nothing about dialectics, violence, or liberation. The Congress had provided a lucky few with a two-week holiday from the routines of so-called responsible adulthood; and that, fundamentally, was why it mattered.

As for the larger, political, impact, it was the Black Power contingent that in the immediate term gained most from the Congress. For them, Carmichael's speeches were an enormous success, releasing spectacular yet often individually hazardous energies. For Malik, Carmichael's London-based acolyte number one, it led to a term of imprisonment following a speech he gave in Reading. For Roy Sawh and Ajoy Shankar Ghose it led to fines for inflammatory speeches at Speaker's Corner. All three were charged with contravening the Race Relations Act of 1965.[26]

Yet, in other respects, such as with the invigoration of the Universal Coloured People's Association (UCPA), much more constructive capital was made of it. Thus, when Obi Egbuna launched the party's Black Power manifesto in Upper Berkeley Street, London, on September 10, 1967, it was Carmichael's image and often his very words that dominated the proceedings, not least Carmichael's angry dismissal of white liberals and his advocacy of the concept of 'institutionalised racism.'[27]

At the same time, the Congress also fed into other, pre-existing, currents. By presenting a powerful example of what the politics of separatism and militancy could achieve, it also sent a strong message to radical women and to gays, though the latter, presumably, had their own heroes at the Congress: Allen Ginsberg and Paul Goodman.

So, finally, what can one say of the significance of the Congress? That it was, as David Cooper put it, the foundation event of the London Antiuniversity? Cooper put it that way in the introduction to the Penguin publication *The Dialectics of Liberation*, published towards the end of 1968.[28] That is, of course, true. But, as the previous paragraphs make clear, it is also much more than that.

Like any major event at which talking is a large part, the significance of the Congress lies not just in concrete actions and in the contemporary words of those who were there; it also resides in its meanings for today's audiences.

10. Too Much

For Berke, the year or so following the end of the Congress constituted another leap forward. All four organisers were busy as usual. For instance, during August, both Berke and Cooper attended the annual Korĉula Summer School on the Dalmatian coast, and, during October, they all presented papers at the Paris International Conference on Psychoses.[1] But Berke had primary responsibility for getting the recordings of the Congress onto long-playing records and for the quartet's next major enterprise: the London Antiuniversity.[2]

The Congress had helped to bring him out of Laing's shadow; and as his comments to the *Times* Diary column about the first volume of *Fire* suggest, he was clearly enjoying himself. Determined to give the magazine an extra push following its Congress debut, he told the paper it was the 'most beautiful and important magazine' of the decade. 'I think Mick Jagger would like it. I'd send him a copy, only I don't like him.'[3]

When the production of the records was briefly held up by a woman at the pressing plant objecting to Allen Ginsberg's swearing, it was thus further grist to an already hyperactive Berkeian mill. As was the threat of a prosecution for the Stokely Carmichael speeches under the Race Relations Act. If the Home Office was so concerned about the inflammatory content of Carmichael's speeches, Berke told a reporter from the *Hampstead and Highgate Express*, well, he would be pleased to send them the recording.[4]

That said, the production of the records, like the Congress itself, was naturally a group affair. John Haynes, who had taken on the role of official photographer for the Congress, provided the cover photographs, Jutta Werner contributed the design, while others with Kingsley Hall or Congress connections helped in the editing room or by liaising with the distributors.

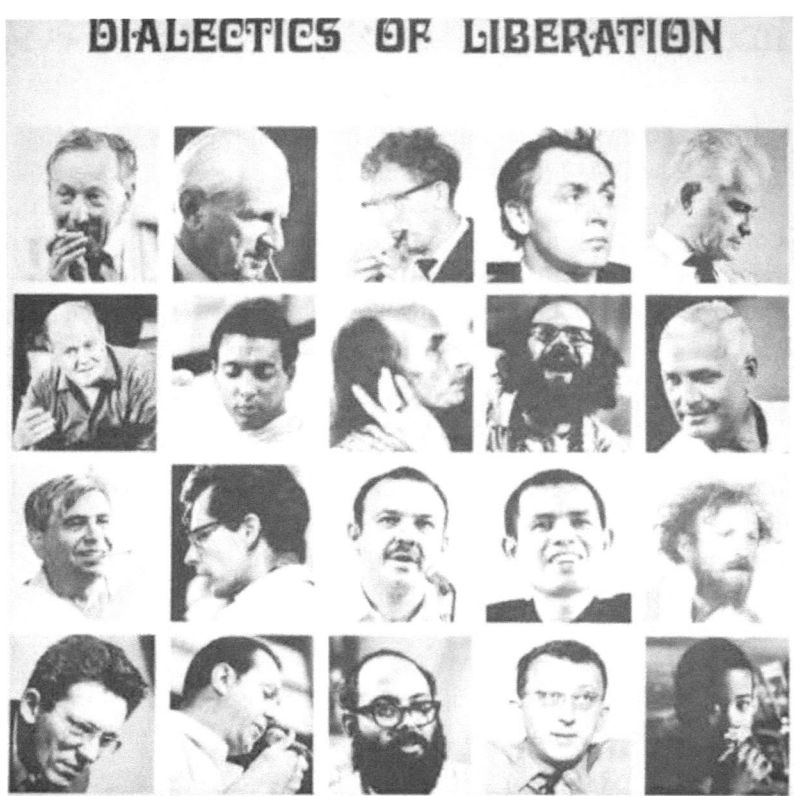

Fig 39. A reactionary's nightmare? Dialectics of Liberation album cover. From left to right: Gregory Bateson, Herbert Marcuse, Paul Goodman, R.D. Laing, Jules Henry, David Cooper, Stokely Carmichael, Julian Beck, Allen Ginsberg, Paul Sweezy, Lucien Goldmann, Francis Huxley, John Gerassi, Thich Nhat Hanh, Leon Redler, Gajo Petrović, Ross Speck, Joe Berke, Igor Hajek. Plus one of the younger participants. Photos by John Haynes, design by Jutta Werner. Private Collection.

Perhaps the oddest feature of the entire 23-LP set was the decision to include a photograph of a young black boy on the front cover, alongside headshots of Bateson, Goodman, Laing, Cooper, Sweezy and all the other major and not-so-major figures. But the simple explanation for that was that the youngster had turned up at the Marcuse event and Berke had been charmed by him.[5]

Anyway, in the end the production and release of the records took far longer than Berke or anyone else had estimated. The final

LP wasn't released until the summer of 1969, a good two years after the Congress had ended.

*

Just as there will probably always be some uncertainty over who came up with the idea of the Congress—Berke and Laing both claiming it as their idea and Redler stating that it emerged naturally out of the activities at Kingsley Hall—so too the question of who originated the Antiuniversity will also likely remain uncertain. Yet, as Berke was instrumental in getting the idea off the ground and as it reflected more his ideas than any of the other members of the IPS, it does seem fair to attribute it, once again, to him, especially as he had already tried to set up a free university in London.

It was Berke who wrote the first letter inviting people to participate in the project. This was sent out on the November 14, following an IPS committee meeting a week or so earlier; and it was Berke who put together the founding agenda. [6] That the first and then the subsequent meetings took place at his flat (in St George's Terrace, facing Primrose Hill) are also surely further clues to his pre-eminence, just as they might also indicate a lack of interest from Laing, who was moving in a direction away from politics *tout court* and towards a yet deeper engagement with spirituality.[7]

Once the bones of the project were agreed upon, events moved swiftly. By the end of the second meeting on December 7, an ad hoc committee was in place formed of Berke, Allen Krebs, David Cooper, Leon Redler, Juliet Mitchell, Morton Schatzman, the poet-publisher Stuart Montgomery and an Oxford student named Aubrey Raymond. And a location and an opening date were decided upon.

The Antiuniversity would meet in a property rented from the Bertrand Russell Peace Foundation at 49 Rivington Street, EC2, thus a stone's throw from Old Street in the East End. And the opening date would be on February 12.

Consistent with the ideas that had inspired the Congress, the organisers designed the Antiuniversity to more or less run itself. That said, as a large amount of money was involved, someone had to act as treasurer. This was Berke. Then there was also an 'organiser' (Krebs) and a secretary (initially Doris Meibach).

Fig 40. Why not give them a ring? Poster for the first term of the Antiuniversity of London, February 1968. Private Collection.

The 'faculty' such as it was, either recruited itself via informal networks or was recruited by the IPS and/or the committee members. By the end of January, over fifty individuals had pledged to deliver teaching sessions. A few of these were old friends of Berke, people like Calvin Hernton, John Keys and Alex Trocchi. Then there was Roy Battersby, Obi Egbuna, Francis Huxley and C.L.R. James and Russell Stetler of the Bertrand Russell Peace Foundation. Plus, of course, Laing, Cooper and Redler.

The first full faculty meeting took place in Rivington Street on Saturday, February 3. Predictably, it got off to an 'anti-start'. 'Within an hour', according to American poet Harold Norse, who covered the meeting for *International Times,* the building turned into a 'howling underground cell of clashing ideologies and aims.'[8] What went wrong he asked rhetorically? What went wrong was Berke's confession that he had accepted an invitation to appear with Stuart Montgomery and Michael Kustow on the BBC's *Late Night Line-Up* talk show. Trocchi was particularly peeved. What, collude with the hated establishment?

The catalogue which emerged out of this cacophony of competing dogmas was inevitably a potpourri, a half-formed object that functioned more as a work in progress than an accurate description of what would actually be on offer. Not surprisingly, bearing in mind Krebs involvement, it owed a good deal to FUNY. Indeed, the opening statement drew almost word for word from FUNY's Autumn 1965 catalogue: 'The Antiuniversity of London has been founded in response to the intellectual bankruptcy and spiritual emptiness of the educational establishment both in Britain and the rest of the Western world.'[9]

Some of the contributors went into unreasonable depth, providing egotistical, pompous, résumés which would not have been out of place in a conventional university. Others provided neither information about when their classes would meet nor anything about the content. Thus, under Harry Trevor, it simply says 'artist'. Still others, their countercultural affiliations on naked display, provided humorous or supercilious descriptions. Thus, Jeff Nuttall introduced his brief description with 'Jeff Nuttall is fat', while Jim Haynes offered 'dialogues about Relevant and Irrelevant Matters.'

*

Nonetheless, these problems apart, the opening day, having been trailed both in the official and in the unofficial media, was very well reported. Most surprising was an informative and by no means overly critical item on the BBC's early evening news programme. Presented by a suited Richard Whitmore, the item featured Krebs making a staged entry into the lounge, John Latham working on one of his book sculptures, and interviews with Krebs and Cooper.

Noting that the Antiuniversity neither demanded qualifications from its students nor awarded degrees, Whitmore asked Krebs what it was for? 'The whole question of what you get in general from education is a kind of moot point. Is it a diploma, a degree, a licence to practice, entree into the establishment, a secure middle-class future? This whole question may or may not have anything to do with what education is all about', responded Krebs, with a sneer on his face.[10]

Whitmore ended his item on a world-weary note: 'The battle cry against all establishment isn't new. So, for some it may seem too far to travel from the gleaming spires just to hear it all again.'

Yet, come they did. According to one journalist, by the end of the day no less than one-hundred-and-fifty people had paid the £8 registration fee, plus an additional 10 shillings for each of their chosen courses, even though 'anticheques were not accepted.'[11] Others agreed to pay in kind with goods or services.

Some of the registrants were, as Berke and Krebs hoped they would be, dropouts of one sort or another, such as working-class youngsters who had failed the 11+ or who had been broken by the system in some other way. But most were either university students or graduates, tired of conventional education's remorseless 'processing'.[12]

One of these was an American woman studying J.M.W. Turner for a Columbia PhD. She had heard 'by chance' that John Latham and Barry Flanagan were lecturing; another was 'a correctly dressed' management trainee, who signed up for the psychology courses. Then there was a social worker: 'I'd like to have qualified as a psychiatric social worker, but never did. There's a lot I could learn here that would be useful to me.' She signed up for Cooper's course.[13] There were even a number of genuine celebrities present, none perhaps more famous than P.L. Travers, the acerbic author of the Mary Poppins books.[14]

Naturally, not all the courses filled up. Those that did included Laing's and Cooper's offerings. Laing titled his course 'Psychology and Religion' and described it in the catalogue as an 'exposition of some descriptions of "inner" space in Greek, Christian and Egyptian mythologies'. Cooper lectured on politics and its connection with psychology, while Redler and Berke, not to be entirely outdone, offered courses on the 'politics of small groups' and 'Anti-Institutions' respectively.

By the time that journalist Richard Boston caught up with Berke's course it was already in its second term, truth, if truth were needed, that there is always a market somewhere for higher-educational courses with a snappy title. He recorded the following brief dialogue between Berke and one of the students. Berke: 'How can we discuss how we can discuss what we want to discuss?' Student: 'Maybe we don't need to discuss it.' 'In the subsequent discussion', remarks Boston, Berke 'himself said very little and after a while announced that he was not feeling well and was going home.' Nevertheless, Boston was impressed. 'This seemed a good example of a destructured class.'[15]

*

All that said, the Antiuniversity didn't just hold classes; it hosted other events, including study days and 'action research' out in the field. One of the best of these other events was a three-day conference titled 'The Digger Forum on Communal Living'. The conference, stemming from an article in hippie magazine *Oz*, took place at the end of April, and was designed to 'break new ground for the cultivation of the Digger dharma of love, freedom and sharing.' [16]

All sorts of groups came along: Welsh Quakers, Gypsies, Dominican monks, the Tribe of the Ancient Mushroom, the Hyde Park Diggers, the editorial committees of *IT*, *Oz* and *Hapt* magazines, even Berliners from the capital's commune movement.

Unfortunately, the Antiuniversity proved too small for the welcoming event, so the delegates, amounting to over one-hundred-and-forty people, adjourned to a nearby church hall, where Krebs got the event going by introducing Cooper and Berke as a 'very weird sort of kind' of psychiatrists.[17]

Cooper, in his speech, used some of the same terms of reference that he had used at the Congress; he spoke about the dialectic between the individual and the community. Berke then followed with a discourse about anti-communities and primitive Christianity. Both, however, misjudged the audience's appetite for intellectual content. Before he could end his speech, Berke was interrupted by a youth in a Mexican hat, gobbling 'like a turkey'. Soon, the whole room was in uproar. 'This is a bloody shambles,' somebody shouted.[18]

However, the following two days proved extremely productive. As a writer in issue 2 of *Gandalf's Garden* put it, 'The Forum has yielded a harvest of practical knowledge about various aspects of communal living and many of the participants have garnered a crop of valuable new contacts. The question arising from this is: What is the aftermath?'[19]

*

While the Antiuniversity's first few months were thus a (qualified) success — the rent and the faculty were paid, a 'commune' took care of the toilets and the lightbulbs and to some extent the relationship between teacher and student had been 'destructured' — by the end of May it had already lost some of its momentum.

Partly, this can be attributed to the foundational model itself — the founders never intended the Antiuniversity to become a permanent foundation.[20] But its fate was also tied to events outside the Antiuniversity, most notably *Les événements* in France, which saw the Sorbonne occupied, vicious street battles between police and students and a heightened, far more aggressive, ethos exported to England.

In early June, the Antiuniversity experienced a mini-revolution. The first commune moved out, a second, mostly German and Austrian, commune moved in, and a new anti-administration took over under Stuart Montgomery and the sound artist, Bob Cobbing. This too proved short-lived, however. Too many people wanted to lark about, too few people wanted to do the dirty work, Cobbing resigned and during early July the Antiuniversity fell into the hands of a third commune who rejected the notion of 'students' paying fees altogether and attempted to find a new way of funding it.

By this time, the property in Rivington Street resembled a 'Bowery flop-house', according to Roberta Elzey.[21] No one bothered to tidy up or to unblock the toilet. So, eventually the first organisers made the decision to return the building to the Bertrand Russell Peace Foundation.

Where this left the Antiuniversity as a body of teachers and students wasn't immediately obvious. Initially, meetings were held at the Arts Lab in Drury Lane and in parks, pubs and people's houses.

Meanwhile, Berke, Cooper, Redler, Morty Schatzman, Juliet Mitchell, Roberta Elzey, Roy Battersby and other first faculty members continued their involvement. There was also the addition of new voices, including the psychotherapist John Rowan and the Israeli artist and dissident Shimon Tzabar. Then a new fee structure was introduced, and a new co-ordinator named: Bill Mason, a long-standing friend of Redler.

As for Berke, he took a broadly philosophical view of the Antiuniversity's achievements. 'Our failure is our success. We have kept our integrity,' he told a feature writer in the *Observer* in September, 'We don't have a building any more, so we haven't been tied down to bureaucracy and administration. We haven't been assimilated into the liberal establishment.' At the same time, he continued to chaff at the conservatism of UK academics. 'They had [a free university] in Cambridge but it was just a little trip, just for fun at weekends. [Sir Edmund] Leach, the provost of Kings, thought it was great, so I asked him why he didn't drop being provost and come and be our provost in London.'[22]

*

While the Antiuniversity occupied most of Berke's anti-time, it wasn't the only one of his interests post the Congress. Another project he was involved in included a book of supposedly middle-class aphorisms called *Berke's Bourgeoisie*. But failing to find a publisher, he turned his attention to another book: *Counter Culture*. On its publication, this would be a follow up to the Cooper-edited *The Dialectics of Liberation*, which appeared from Penguin towards the end of November 1968.

The Dialectics of Liberation contained all of the morning speeches bar Speck's, Hajek's and Petrovic's. It was thus, as the contents list suggested, very closely linked to what was said from the platform at the Congress. Not that it was simply a transcript — far from it. Some of the speakers took the opportunity to repoint or in some cases to rewrite large sections of their speeches. But, inevitably, it already had a slightly backward feel to it.

Counter Culture, on the other hand, was far more contemporary. It was also a bigger beast, richer in design and much more ambitious in content. It, too, included some Congress material: for instance, Julian Beck's speech on the second Friday afternoon, plus Stokely Carmichael's Sunday the 23rd Black Power speech and a version of Berke's own 'The Possibilities of Revolutionary Change'. And then *inter alia* articles by Morton Schatzman ('Madness and Morals'), Peter Stansill ('New Experimental College'), Roberta Elzey ('Founding an Anti-University') and Berke himself ('Kommune 1 Visited' and 'The Free University of New York').

Elzey, who by now was Mrs Berke, following the couple's hippie wedding in the New Forest,[23] didn't just provide an account of the origins and progress of the Antiuniversity; she also provided a lot of practical and candid advice. Such as 'Mistakes Not to Make with Secretaries': 'Don't Recruit Her from Friends' ... 'Don't Underpay Her "for the Cause"' ... 'Don't Overwork Her' ... 'Don't Tolerate Inefficiency in the Guise of "Being Cool"' ... 'Don't Fuck Her Generally or Specifically'. And 'Your Co-ordinator Is Not God',[24] while Berke, in the second of his articles, revisited his pioneering free university days at FUNY.

Presumably he visited Kommune 1 in late 1968 or 1969. If so, it was his first visit to Germany and probably his last, even though he had several contacts there including former Kingsley Hall resident Heike Neumeister, Dieter Kunzelmann and Bernward Vesper, the latter of whom both attended the Congress. By all accounts it was a depressing and disillusioning visit — not that he said that, of course. That would have been to let the side down. The commune was a mess: shirts and underclothes strewn everywhere — in that sense it was like the final weeks at Rivington Street. Two television sets were on, their sound knobs turned to zero; while hippie favourite *Tanyet* blasted from the record player and some of the 'Kommunards' had public sex.

Although one wanted to talk to Berke, he did manage a few words with commune 'personality' Rainer Langhans about drugs. 'Rainer explained that the use of hash and other drugs had only begun recently. Six weeks prior the Kommune had been very down on pot and acid. Their view was that drugs were simply bourgeois tricks to keep the minds and energies of the kids away from the central task of bringing about political revolution.' 'I knew the argument', commented Berke mordantly, when he came to write up his article. It was the same argument that he had heard at Albert Einstein College in the early 1960s.[25]

*

By the time that *Counter Culture* was published (by Peter Owen, during the early Spring of 1970) Berke had entered his 30th year, and he was bourgeois himself. He had a son on the way and was living off a small legacy from his mother in a flat in West London rented from the Church of England. Sentences like 'The United States exists solely to create, develop, feed, encourage and participate in wars, anywhere in the world, all over the world' or 'THE STRUCTURE IS OURSELVES, THE REVOLUTION IS OURSELVES, THE REVOLUTION IS THE REVOLUTION' must therefore have sounded phoney even to him.[26] They certainly sounded phoney to others. Richard Holmes, in *The Times*, called the book a 'tampered oyster.' The 'statements of individual liberation ring grotesquely false' he added, though he appreciated Morton Schatzman's article and the articles on the free universities. Those, he said, were 'bitterly realistic.'[27] Andrew Rigby, writing in *Peace News*, was also harsh. Berke's rejig of his Congress speech was 'an insult to the intelligence of the reader.'[28] Both reviewers also pointed out the anomaly of the publisher charging 90 shillings, i.e., £4 10s, for a book that was ostensibly designed to help bring down Western capitalism.

When *The Guardian* sent along one of its star reporters, Terry Coleman, to interview Berke, he had a wonderful time exposing the American's many inconsistencies. But, even so, he liked him. Berke himself was one of the 'mildest-looking' men he had ever met; he had the air of a 'beneficent physician' and was kindly and humorous. Berke 'talked of anti-books, anti-hospitals, anti-universities', Coleman wrote. But when his wife came in with a tray of food, he said that he was 'not *against* sardines, or oranges, or even the Church of England.'[29]

*

Just as the early '70s marked a turning point in Berke's personal life, they also marked a turning point in Kingsley Hall, the 'experiment' that had in large part brought Berke to live in the UK in the first place. At the end of May 1970, Kingsley Hall closed. This was no sudden decision on Laing's part or that of anyone else in the Philadelphia Association. It had been signalled over a year earlier by the building's trustees; they had their own plans for the Hall, which did not include its continued use as an asylum.

The story of Kingsley Hall over the previous five years had encompassed all sorts of experiences: there had been ups-and-downs, twists-and-turns, comedy, melodrama and tragedy, some successes and some failures. Public, and particularly psychiatric, interest in the Hall was immense. But who was equipped to describe it? Laing started on an account but gave it up. It was too painful and perhaps, ultimately, too boring for him. Then Redler and Zeal had a go at a sort of anthology of residents' experiences and interviews. But that too foundered.

Nonetheless, some informed accounts by 'insiders' did appear. By Morton Schatzman, for instance, in his article in *Counter Culture*. This wasn't just an account of Kingsley Hall, mind. 'Madness and Morals' also looked at psychiatry's pre-history and at conventional mental hospitals. But the focus was on Kingsley Hall and, like Redler and Zeal, very much on what one might call the 'ordinary' residents' experiences.

One of these 'ordinary' residents was Mary Barnes, whose 'journey through madness' had continued to be one of Berke's own major preoccupations. For months after leaving Kingsley Hall, he had travelled back there three times a week for hourly sessions with Mary. Then three times had become twice. Then once. Until by the middle of 1968, Mary was travelling across London to see him.[30]

It was Schatzman who encouraged Mary to write about her experiences. Having moved into the Hall with his wife, Vivien, during January 1968, it was perhaps his way of establishing a kind of intimacy with her.

Berke built upon what Schatzman had done; and eventually these notes became the basis for Mary's part of Berke's next book, *Mary Barnes: Two Accounts of a Journey Through Madness*.

This, again, was another very different book for Berke, different to *Counter Culture* in style, different in content and very different in the circumstances in which it was written. For, following the closure of Kingsley Hall, Berke and Laing were not even on speaking terms. It was a falling out that had many causes, but the main one was probably Berke's decision to move out of Laing's orbit altogether and to set up his own asylum with Schatzman and several other people.

Although Berke didn't tell the whole truth about his relationship with Mary Barnes in his part of their 'journey through madness' book, what he did tell was moving and compelling. It was the story of an 'engaging, enraging, charismatic, baby, little girl and woman', her descent into 'madness' and her journey up again.[31] But, as befitted its subtitle: '*Two accounts*', it was also about him, his dreams and to a degree his mental suffering.

The book carried him almost full circle. If not quite back to his childhood, then back to the Albert Einstein College of Medicine and to his intuition that schizophrenia was not a medical illness. He wrote about his first mentor, John Thompson, and his second mentor, Laing, and about his close friends, people like Leon Redler and Morton Schatzman, and, of course, about Mary, the *'monster* of Kingsley Hall', a deeply disturbed yet nonetheless remarkable woman.³² What he didn't say, however, was anything about the Congress. It was a curious omission — or perhaps it was not, the Congress being tangential to Mary's life at Kingsley Hall, though she did exhibit at least one of her paintings there.³³ But, still, it was an opportunity missed. It would have been good to have Berke's impressions of Paul Goodman, of Jules Henry, and of Cooper and Laing as they moved amongst the participants.

11. The Infernal Nexus

Identity politics did not begin with the Congress. But it did galvanise it. Not only did it split black activists from white activists, but in the longer run, it played a role in splitting women from men and gay men from straights. In the first case, the impact of the Congress was direct and immediate. Multiracial organisations bled supporters. RAAS was reinvigorated. UCPA grew larger. Personal friendships were broken.[1] That's not to say that there were no other proximate factors, which also influenced these developments. There were, not least leading Conservative MP Duncan Sandys' call during the second week of the Congress for a complete ban on black immigration and his description of racially mixed children as 'misfits'.[2] But the impact of the Congress was profound. Carmichael came to England, seized the opportunities the Roundhouse offered him and conquered a good portion of Britain's black radicals. The Congress placed the politics of race and the politics of identity firmly on the agenda, with finally incalculable consequences for Britain's institutions.

One of the major speakers at the Congress who did not welcome the new focus on identity politics was Paul Goodman. For him, the Congress was a watershed moment. But in another and more subtle way. He was on the way out. Carmichael and Marcuse were on the way in.

By the beginning of 1968, radical young people in the UK had by and large lost patience with Goodman's practical and piecemeal anarchism. They were angry about education, angry about white rule in Rhodesia and South Africa and angrier still about Vietnam and other instances of American imperialism. And they certainly didn't want to waste time debating with so-called 'liberal whites' of the older generation like Paul Goodman.

One example of this new intolerance was the howling down of academics and democratically elected politicians on university campuses, another, strangely enough, was the Antiuniversity. On the one hand, the Antiuniversity was, as the first catalogue said, 'founded in response to the intellectual bankruptcy and spiritual emptiness of the educational establishment.' On the other, it set out to 'promote a position of social integrity and commitment.'³ Thus, amongst the predictable courses on mysticism, ways of 'turning-on' and avant-garde music and poetry, there were also courses on subjects like Black Power, the Sociology of Revolution, the Sociology of Guerrilla Warfare and the Sociology of World Revolution. These were not designed for teaching in the usual sense, which is to say to inform and to provoke individual thought and reflection — and sometimes action. They were designed to indoctrinate.

Not surprising then that Paul Goodman's name was not on the faculty list. Why should it have been? From his point of view, although the organisers of the Antiuniversity had got some of their thinking right, notably on the baleful role of the educational bureaucracy, they hadn't stood up for professionalism or for the integrity of the academic tradition.

In fact, Goodman didn't get on with most of the free universities of the sixties and early seventies. As he put it in his valedictory testament *New Reformation: Notes of a Neolithic Conservative*, of 1970:

> In *The Community of Scholars* I criticized present university administration and pointed out that a school of ten professionals and a hundred and fifty students — the equivalent of most medieval schools — could provide professional education better and more cheaply than what we now have. So I suggested that some professors secede and try it. Somehow this made me the father, or Dutch uncle, of the Free Universities, and since I am sympathetic to the Movement in general, I have had to take part also in the Free Universities. Their curriculum is the psychedelic experience, sensitivity training, the liberation of women, and Castro's Cuba, which are fine subjects but not the law, medicine, and engineering I had in mind.'⁴

Today, many of our conventional universities have adopted the worst possible educational mixture. They are highly bureaucratic *and* enablers of those who seek to indoctrinate. Much of the indoctrination is done in the name of (E)quality, (D)iversity and (I)nclusion or, less good-naturedly, decolonising the curriculum. Both phrases cover a range of practices for good as well as ill. But, overall, they are intellectually vacuous dogmas, patronising of their 'customer base', i.e., students, intolerant of those who disagree with their opinions and permeated with ad hominem judgments and racial and gender essentialism.

One of the reasons why Goodman called for a 'new reformation' was because he recognised that the '60s generation of young radicals had abandoned the long-standing Western belief in science, rationality, history, and professionalism. They had rejected the assertion that there was a 'nature of things' and they were 'doubtful that there was such a thing as simple truth.'[5]

'I had imagined the worldwide student protest had to do with changing political and moral institutions, and I was sympathetic to this,' he went on. 'But I now saw that we had to do with a religious crisis. Not only all institutions but all learning had been corrupted by the Whore of Babylon, and there was no salvation to be got from Works.'

It is not far from this standpoint, as described by Goodman, to decolonisers' assertions that today's Western universities are 'institutionally racist' and today's academic curricula 'disfigured' by whiteness.

Just like the '60s generation, the decolonisers, too, have lost their faith in truth, knowledge, and professionalism. They do not believe that students and academics get ahead because of their intellectual and moral qualities; they get ahead because they are male, heterosexual, and white or because they have been fortunate to find patrons amongst people who are themselves male, white, and heterosexual. Everything is a stitch up. Africa and Asia may have won their freedom long ago. But the Western empires remain, unchanged and inglorious, in our universities and in our heads. We must decolonise ourselves and our institutions.

What can be done about this unhappy situation? Where will it end up? Who can tell? If it is melodramatic to speak of a dawning dark age; it would be cowardly not to speak of the threat of one.

Appendix

The Institute of Phenomenological Studies produced a number of lists of 'invited participants' and/or major speakers at the Congress. Here is one of the first, dated 'June 28 [1967]'.

> United States: Paul Goodman, Herbert Marcuse, Gregory Bateson, Erving Goffman, Jules Henry, Joseph Campbell, Thomas Szasz, Allen Ginsberg, and Julian Beck.
> Great Britain: Elias Canetti, Isaac Deutscher, Marjorie Grene, Peter Brook, and P.M.S. Blackett.
> France: J.P. Sartre, Lucien Goldmann, Michel Foucault, Mircea Eliade, Joseph Gabel, and Francis Jeanson.
> Germany: Jakov Lind, Gunter Grass, Helmut Schelsky, and Werner Heisenberg.
> Belgium: Ernest Mandel.
> Poland: Adam Sharff.
> Mexico: Carlos Fuentes.

The following list is attached to a letter from Laing to Allen Ginsberg, dated July 9, 1966.

> Belgium: Ernest Mandel.
> France: Mircea Eliade, Michel Foucault, Joseph Gabel, Lucien Goldmann, Francis Jeanson, Claude Levi-Strauss, and Jean-Paul Sartre.
> Germany: Ernest Bloch, Gunther Grass, Werner von Heisenberg, Jacov Lind, Helmut Schelsky, and Carl Friedrich von Weizsäcker.
> Mexico: Carlos Fuentes.
> Poland: Adam Sharff.
> Great Britain: P.M.S. Blackett, Peter Brook, Elias Canetti, Isaac Deutscher, and Marjorie Grene.
> United States: Gregory Bateson, Julian Beck, Joseph Campbell, Allen Ginsberg, Erving Goffman, Paul Goodman, Jules Henry, Herbert Marcuse, and Thomas Szasz.

A flyer produced towards the end of 1966 contains this list:

> Gregory Bateson, David Cooper, Mircea Eliade, John Gerassi, Allen Ginsberg, Erving Goffman, Lucien Goldmann, Paul Goodman, Jules Henry, Ronald Laing, Jakov Lind, Ernest Mandel, Herbert Marcuse, and Paul Sweezy.

Here is a list with dates, contained in a letter from Berke to Jules Henry, dated December 30, 1966.

> Gregory Bateson (July 17), John Gerassi (July 18), Jules Henry (July 19), Erving Goffman (July 20), Paul Sweezy (July 21), Ernest Mandel (July 24), Mircea Eliade (July 25), Lucien Goldmann (July 26), Paul Goodman, July 27) and Herbert Marcuse (July 28).

Here is the list from Calvin Hernton's 'The Institute of Phenomenological Studies will make the move' article, published in *International Times*, January 16-29, 1967.

> 'Participants will include Gregory Bateson, Mircea Eliade, John Gerassi, Allen Ginsberg, Erving Goffmann, Lucien Goldman [sic], Paul Goodman, Jules Henry, Ernest Mandel, Herbert Marcuse, Paul Sweezy.'

The poster produced during the summer of 1967 contains the following list, with dates.

> R.D. Laing (July 15), Gregory Bateson (July 17), Stokely Carmichael (July 18), Jules Henry (July 19), Erving Goffman (July 20), Paul Sweezy (July 21) Allen Ginsberg, Stokely Carmichael, R.D. Laing 'and others' (July 22), Ernest Mandel (July 24), Paul Goodman (July 25), Lucien Goldmann (July 26), John Gerassi (July 27), Herbert Marcuse (July 28) and David Cooper (July 29)

NB. No mention was made of Carolee Schneemann's happening.

Here is the actual list of major speakers, again with dates.

> R.D. Laing (July 15), Gregory Bateson (July 17), Stokely Carmichael (July 18), Jules Henry (July 19), John Gerassi (July 20), Paul Sweezy (July 21), Stokely Carmichael, R.D. Laing, Allen Ginsberg, and Emmett Grogan (July 22), Stokely Carmichael (July 23), Ross Speck (July 24), Paul Goodman (July 25), Lucien Goldmann (July 26), Gajo Petrović and Igor Hajek (July 27), Herbert Marcuse (July 28) and David Cooper (July 29).

The event concluded with a happening by Carolee Schneemann and a set by The Social Deviants.

Notes

Introduction

1. Jeff Nuttall, *Bomb Culture*, 127.
2. R.D. Laing, "Massacre of the Innocents," 6.
3. Congress poster. Reproduced in *Peace News*, June 16, 1967.
4. Paul Goodman, *The Community of Scholars*, 74.
5. Ibid, 5.
6. Ibid, 63.
7. Ibid, 168. Italics in original.
8. Ibid, 166.
9. Ibid, 168.
10. Ibid, 130.
11. R.D. Laing, "Massacre of the Innocents," 6.
12. Susan Sherman, "Dialectics of Liberation, A Conference," *Ikon* 1, no.4 October 26, 1967.
13. Catalogue. *The Antiuniversity of London*. The quotations are from the preface. Unpaginated.
14. Richard Boston, "Anti-University," 702.
15. Most importantly, in Barnes and Berke, *Mary Barnes*, 83-94 and 225-284.
16. For the impact of these figures from a British 'security' point of view, see the very interesting folder in the UK National Archives, HO 325/104 available at https://www.documentcloud.org/documents/6200128-19680226-BP-HO-325-104-US-in-UK

Chapter 1

1. Martin Levy, unpublished interviews with Joe Berke. I published a revised version of some of the material from these interviews in Levy and Berke, "Martin Levy Interview with Joe Berke."
2. Ibid.
3. Ibid.
4. Ibid.
5. The words are inscribed on page 8 of Berke's copy of *The Legend*, in the Joseph Berke Papers.
6. Joe Berke to R.D. Laing, November 15, 1962, R.D. Laing Collection, GB 247 MS Laing GB666/1.
7. Demidjuk, *Joseph Berke: Expand a Man*, 27.
8. Barnes and Berke, *Mary Barnes*, 79. This and the following two quotations are from the first edition. The quotations which follow after those are from the 'revised' edition, published by Penguin Books in 1982.

9. Barnes and Berke, *Mary Barnes*, 80.
10. Ibid, 80-81.
11. Tytell, *The Living Theatre*, 173.
12. Joe Berke to R.D. Laing, November 15, 1962, R.D. Laing Collection, GB 247 MS Laing GB666/1.
13. Barnes and Berke, *Mary Barnes*, 87.
14. Naomi Esterson to Joe Berke, May 11, 1964, Joseph Berke Papers.
15. Martin Levy, unpublished interviews with Joe Berke.
16. Barnes and Berke, *Mary Barnes*, 89.
17. Ibid.
18. Joe Berke to R.D. Laing, [November 1963], R.D. Laing Collection, GB 247 MS Laing GB666/75.
19. Joe Berke to R.D. Laing, December 13, [1963], R.D. Laing Collection, GB 247 MS Laing GB666/7.
20. Joe Berke, "Universities," 11.
21. Joe Berke to R.D. Laing, December 13 [1963], R.D. Laing Collection, GB 247 MS Laing GB666/7.
22. Joe Berke to R.D. Laing, February 1 [1964], R.D. Laing Collection, GB 247 MS Laing GB666/11.
23. Laing wrote the lecture for an engagement at the Institute of Contemporary Arts, in Dover Street, part of its 'Aspects of Violence' series. The series accompanied the institute's 'Study for an Exhibition of Violence in Contemporary Art', which opened in February 1964 and ran to the end of March. See Joe Berke to R.D. Laing, December 13 [1963], R.D. Laing Collection, GB 247 MS Laing GB666/7.
24. Joe Berke to R.D. Laing, February 1 [1964], R.D. Laing Collection, GB 247 MS Laing GB666/11.
25. Ibid.
26. Ibid.
27. Ibid
28. Alexander Trocchi, *The Sigma Folio*, R.D. Laing Collection GB 247 MS Laing L408/2.
29. R.D. Laing to Joe Berke, undated, but July 8, 1964, Joseph Berke Papers.
30. Clancy Sigal to Alexander Trocchi, [c.June 1964], Alexander Trocchi Papers, Box 38, folder 8-9.
31. Alexander Trocchi, "Invisible Insurrection of a Million Minds," Campbell and Neil, *A Life*, 165. The document was first published in Edinburgh in 1962.
32. Ibid, 172.
33. Ibid.
34. Ibid, 176.
35. Joe Berke to R.D. Laing, October 15 [1964], R.D. Laing Collection, GB 247 MS Laing GB666/25.

36. R.D. Laing to Joe Berke, October 28, 1964, Laing Collection GB 247 MS Laing GB666/26.
37. Joe Berke to R.D. Laing, October 15 [1964], R.D. Laing Collection, GB 247 MS Laing GB666/25.
38. Joe Berke to R.D. Laing, [September 1964], R.D. Laing Collection, GB 247 MS Laing GB666/72.
39. Martin Levy, unpublished interviews with Joe Berke.
40. Ibid.
41. R.D. Laing to Joe Berke, October 28, 1964, R.D. Laing Collection, GB 247 MS Laing GB666/26.
42. Ibid.
43. Laing diary, R.D. Laing Collection, GB 247 MS Laing GB 247 MS Laing K22.
44. R.D. Laing to Joe Berke, October 28, 1964, R.D. Laing Collection, GB 247 MS Laing GB666/26,
45. Joe Berke to R.D. Laing, [November 1964], R.D. Laing Collection, GB 247 MS Laing GB666/76. Amongst many other possibilities, Berke was probably alluding to the time as a teenager when he was 'haunted by feelings of intense loneliness.' Martin Levy, unpublished interview with Joe Berke.
46. Martin Levy, unpublished interviews with Joe Berke.
47. Ibid.
48. R.D. Laing to Superintendent, Pilgrim's Bay State Hospital, London Island, New York, March 29, 1965, R.D. Laing Collection, GB 247 MS Laing GB666/29.
49. Joe Berke to R.D. Laing, [Spring 1965], Laing Collection, GB 247 MS Laing GB666/67.
50. Joe Berke to Alexander Trocchi, June 6, [1965], Alexander Trocchi Papers, Box 38, folder 10-11.
51. Joseph Berke, "The Free University of New York," *Peace News*, 6, quoting FUNY's first catalogue.
52. Ibid.
53. Joseph Berke, "The Free University of New York," in *Counter Culture*, 218.
54. Jeff Nuttall, *Bomb Culture*, 223.
55. Joe Berke to Alexander Trocchi, June 6, [1965], Alexander Trocchi Papers, Box 38, folder 10-11.
56. Coda Gallery, flyer. Joe Berke Papers.
57. Joe Berke to R.D. Laing, [Summer 1965], R.D. Laing Collection, GB 247 MS Laing GB666/81.
58. Ibid.

Chapter 2

1. Joe Berke to R.D. Laing, September 7, 1965, R.D. Laing Collection, GB 247 MS Laing GB666/83.
2. Oren and Hernton, '"The Enigmatic Career of Hernton's 'Scarecrow'," 615.
3. Joe Berke to R.D. Laing, September 7, 1965, R.D. Laing Collection, GB 247 MS Laing GB666/83.
4. Adrian Laing, *R.D. Laing*, 108.
5. Martin Levy, unpublished interviews with Joe Berke.
6. Joe Berke to R.D. Laing, [Summer 1965], R.D. Laing Collection, GB 247 MS Laing GB666/81.
7. Joe Berke to Carolee Schneemann, c. October 6, 1965, Carolee Schneemann Papers, Getty Research Institute, Series III, Box 35.
8. Ibid.
9. Martin Levy, interview with Morton Schatzman.
10. Joe Berke to Carolee Schneemann, c. October 6, 1965, Carolee Schneemann Papers, Getty Research Institute, Series III, Box 35.
11. Ibid.
12. Ibid.
13. Ibid.
14. Ibid.
15. Mullan, *Mad to be Normal*, 197.
16. Laing, *The Divided Self*, 11
17. Sigal, "Home Front," 8.
18. Martin Levy, unpublished interviews with Joe Berke.
19. Clancy Sigal, *Zone of the Interior*, 264.
20. Adrian Laing, *R.D. Laing*, 118.
21. Joseph Berke, "Zone of the Interior," 378.
22. Joe Berke to Gunther Weil, August 2, 1966, Joe Berke Papers.
23. Joe Berke to Carolee Schneemann, November 18, 1965, Carolee Schneemann Papers, Getty Research Institute, Series III, Box 35.
24. Ibid.
25. Joe Berke to Will Inman, c. October 6, 1965, Will Inman Papers, Box 1.
26. Joseph Berke, "The Free University of New York," *Peace News*, 7.
27. These 'others' included Pete Jenner of the LSE, the photographer John 'Hoppy' Hopkins, Felix de Mendelsohn, and the anti-nuclear activist George Clark. In the Spring of 1966, they set up the London Free School in Notting Hill. According to Hopkins, Berke who had a glancing association with the project, '*was* a berk.' 'I didn't get on with him very well.' Green, *Days in the Life*, 96.
28. Barnes and Berke, *Mary Barnes*, 228-29.
29. Ibid, 231-32.

30. See the letters from Roberta Elzey to Joe Berke, dated December 26, 1965, and January 8, 1966, in the Joseph Berke Papers.
31. That said, Laing, in conversation with Bob Mullan, gave a different reason for Berke's departure from full-time residence at Kingsley Hall. He said that it was at the request of John Layard, who found Berke 'absolutely insufferable.' See Mullan, *Mad to be Normal*, 198, for Laing's account, and Berke's "Trick or Treat" for his. There is probably truth in both.
32. Ibid, 274. The 'medical horror story' — perhaps with more than a nod to William Burroughs' fictional Dr. Benway.
33. Ibid.
34. Ibid.
35. For Berke's claim to have originated the Congress, see Martin Levy, unpublished interviews with Joe Berke. 'The Dialectics of Liberation was my idea. It came out of the wonderful influx of ideas and activities at Kingsley Hall and out of my interest in the Free University of New York and other things.' Compare, however, Laing's claim that the Congress was his idea. 'The Dialectics of Liberation was my idea which arose out of the turmoil of the '60s and my immediate network of that time.' Mullan, *Mad to be Normal*, 218. Leon Redler, in an interview with Jacky Ivimy, to some extent following both, also called it a natural outgrowth of the activities at Kingsley Hall.
36. For Laing's 'ambivalence' about the idea of holding a congress, see Martin Levy, interview with Paul Zeal.
37. See, for instance, Cooper's "Two Types of Rationality" and Laing's "Series and Nexus in the Family."
38. Laing and Cooper, *Reason and Violence*, 171-172.

Chapter 3

1. Barnes and Berke, *Mary Barnes*, 256.
2. Martin Levy, unpublished interview with Paul Zeal.
3. Noel Cobb, "Account of his Experiences at Kingsley Hall entitled Bedrock," R.D. Laing Collection GB 247 MS Laing L169/1, 2.
4. Ibid, 3.
5. Ibid.
6. Ibid, 9-10.
7. Abel, "Schizophrenia as a Way of Life," 8. Although the author gives the artist's name as 'Catherine', it is Mary Barnes who is described.
8. Joe Berke to Carolee Schneemann, October 4, 1966, Stiles, ed., *Correspondence Course*, 111.
9. *Daily Mirror*, July 24, 1967, 6.

10. Carolee Schneemann's 'Round House', her 'kinetic theater' piece for the congress.
11. Berke, "Auto de Fe," *Fire,* 1 (London: Fire, 1967), 2-3.
12. Martin Levy, unpublished interviews with Joe Berke.
13. Cooper, "The Institute of Phenomenological Studies," Allen Ginsberg Papers, Box 17.17. There were also two other members of the institute: John Heaton and Paul Senft. Both were friends of Laing. Neither of them, however, had much to do with the Congress. Cooper mentioned them on the final day as having other interests to occupy them. See the document appended to Joe Berke's letter to Will Inman, January 25, 1967, Box 1, Will Inman Papers, [number] and Joseph Berke Archive, PP/JB/IPS 1.1.12.
14. Laing, *The Politics of Experience,* 53. The chapter titled 'The Mystification of Experience' was itself revised from an intermediate version of the lecture, published in the *Journal of Existentialism*, volume 5, number 20, and in *Peace News*, July 22, 1965, pages 6-7.
15. David Cooper, "The Institute of Phenomenological Studies." Another version of this short document appeared on pages 22 and 23 of the first volume of *Fire* (London: Fire, 1967). There it has two titles. 'The Dialectics of Revolution' on the contents page, 'The Dialectics of Liberation' above the text.
16. Ibid.
17. Ibid.
18. Ibid.
19. Goodman, *Community of Scholars*, 97.
20. Martin Levy, unpublished interviews with Joe Berke.
21. Joe Berke to Allen Ginsberg, June 28, 1966, Allen Ginsberg Papers, Series 1 Correspondence Box 10, Folder 17.
22. Mullan, *Mad to be Normal,* 218.
23. Boston, "International Times," *New Society,* 637.
24. Joe Berke to Carolee Schneemann, December 25, 1966, Carolee Schneemann Papers, Getty Research Institute, Series III, Box 35. Berke's letter to Beck, also dated December 25, is in The Living Theatre Records at Yale.
25. Martin Levy, unpublished interviews with Joe Berke. 16 days, rather than the 14 days the Congress lasted, to take account of the time bringing in and removing the hundreds of chairs, etc.
26. Behind Pilkington's decision *not* to host the Congress was a scandalous situation involving Flora Papastavrou, her girlfriend 'Christine' and two other of Berke's friends named John and Linda Hofstetter. See the correspondence in the Joseph Berke Papers.
27. Noel Cobb, "Account of his Experiences at Kingsley Hall entitled Bedrock," 12.
28. P.H.S, "The Light of the Obscure," 8.

29. Laing, "Appearances and Disappearances," *Fire*, 1, 17. Other contributors to the magazine not mentioned in the text are Jutta Werner, who had trained as an illustrator, Kilton Stewart, Heike Neumeister and Jose Quinones, the latter being the psychiatric patient who had promised to introduce Berke to Afro-Cuban religious practices in 1964. Dodo von Greiff helped with the design. G. Spencer Brown, Noel Cobb, Patrick Schofield, David Jay, and Paul Zeal assisted Berke with editorial and business matters.
30. Laing, *"One-Dimensional Man"*. Cooper reviewed *Eros and Civilisation* in *New Left Review* 1, no.20 (Summer 1963).
31. Joe Berke to John Gerassi, December 8, 1966, Joseph Berke Archive, PP/JB/IPS 10.2.
32. Quoted by Calvin Hernton in a letter to Joe Berke, December 2, 1966, Joseph Berke Papers.
33. Hernton, "London: Eliade, Ginsberg, Goffman, Goodman, Laing, Marcuse," 4.
34. Ibid.
35. Ibid. For Captain Howard Levy, see Couture and Levy, "Levy: Why the US should Withdraw from Vietnam," 7.
36. Ibid.
37. Leon Redler to Julie Felix, February 17, 1967, Joseph Berke Archive, PP/JB/IPS 10.2.
38. Leon Redler to Stokely Carmichael, October 20, 1966, Joseph Berke Archive, PP/JB/IPS 10.2. Apparently, Carmichael didn't accept the invitation until May 1967. See Carmichael 'with Thelwell', *Ready for Revolution*, 572. NB. For convenience's sake, I have used 'Stokely Carmichael' throughout the text, even though Carmichael later changed his name to Kwame Ture.
39. Ibid.
40. For more on the book—*The Dialectics of Liberation*—and the series of records, see chapter 10. For the book alone, see Gavin Miller's article, "Psychiatric Penguins."
41. Joe Berke to Peter Wollen, November 29, 1966, Joseph Berke Archive, PP/JB/IPS 10.4.
42. Joe Berke to Jerzy Skolimowski, February 17, 1967, Joseph Berke Archive, PP/JB/IPS 10.4.
43. Congress flyer, attached to a letter from Joe Berke to Carolee Schneemann, December 25, 1966, Carolee Schneemann Papers, Getty Research Institute, Series III, Box 35.
44. M.H. Arnold to Joe Berke, [date], Joseph Berke Archive, PP/JB/IPS 10.6.
45. Pete Seeger to Leon Redler, February 6, 1967, Joseph Berke Archive, PP/JB/IPS 10.6.

46. Nigel Young to the Institute of Phenomenological Studies, May 25, 1967, Joseph Berke Archive, PP/JB/IPS 10.4. Young's point was a good one. It is interesting in this respect that one of the earliest lists of speakers for the Congress includes three nuclear physicists: Werner Heisenberg, Carl Friedrich von Weizsäcker and P.M.S. Blackett. See appendix.
47. B.L. Lewis to the Institute of Phenomenological Studies, April 26,1967, Joseph Berke Archive, PP/JB/IPS 10.6.
48. Barnard, "Seeds of Growth," 1 & 4.
49. Joe Berke to Paul Goodman, April 14, 1967, Joseph Berke Archive, PP/JB/IPS 10.2.
50. David Cooper, *Psychiatry and Anti-Psychiatry*, 124.
51. Laing, *The Politics of Experience*, 11 & 156.
52. Laing, "The Invention of Madness," 843.
53. Cooper, "Violence and Psychiatry," 8.
54. *In Two Minds* by David Mercer. Broadcast in the BBC's 'Wednesday Plays' series on March 1. Produced by Tony Garnett and directed by Ken Loach, the play was seen by 'almost ten million viewers.' Both Laing and Cooper received payment as 'chief technical advisers'. For further information about the play, including its reception, see Snelson, "From *In Two Minds* to MIND."
55. Adrian Laing, *R.D. Laing*, 130. Cf. however, Laing's support of the New Left *May Day Manifesto* of May 1967, a left humanist attack on Wilsonian socialism, which was co-edited by Raymond Williams, Stuart Hall, and E.P. Thompson. Laing is listed on page 45 of the pamphlet as a supporter of the 'political and educational campaign' which the manifesto inaugurated. Cooper's name, on the other hand, is absent.
56. Laing, "The Invention of Madness," 843.
57. See Stockley, "LSE: Free School in Summer?" 10-11. The pair took part in a discussion of 'tyranny', with *inter alia*, David Horovitz and Barbara Garson.
58. Adrian Laing, *R.D. Laing*, 130.
59. Mullan, *Mad to be Normal*, 195.
60. P.W., "International Congress Dialectics of Liberation," 10. The initials stand for Peter Willis, though it was apparently Bob Overy who, representing *Peace News*, attended the press conference.
61. Ibid.
62. For a list of some of the people who helped organise and/or run the Congress, see Berke, *Counter Culture*, 411-12. One important absence from the list is Harry Pincus, an American C.O. Pinus picked up Stokely Carmichael and George Ware from Heathrow Airport. See Prince, "'Do what the Afro-Americans are Doing,'" 523, and the British

Special Branch report in the UK National Archives, HO 325/104 available at https://www.documentcloud.org/documents/6200128-1968 0226-BP-HO-325-104-US-in-UK

Chapter 4.

1. Sinclair, *Kodak Mantra Diaries*, 'Roundhouse Morning' section. The book is unpaginated.
2. The major speakers who had arrived, that is. Herbert Marcuse, for one, would not arrive at the Congress until towards the end of the second full week.
3. Carolee Schneemann Papers, Getty Research Institute, Box 1, Folder 17.
4. Ibid.
5. See Susan Sontag's article on Goodman. 'I was told by mutual friends that he didn't really like women as people—though he made an exception for a few particular women, of course.' "On Paul Goodman," 274. Sontag adds, *inter alia*, that Goodman was one of her heroes.
6. Carolee Schneemann Papers, Getty Research Institute, Box 1, Folder 17.
7. For this and other quotations in this section, see Joseph Berke Archive, PP/JB/IPS 1.3.29.
8. For this and other quotations in this section, see Joseph Berke Archive, PP/JB/IPS 1.3.29, 1.3.41 and 1.3.43.
9. For this and other quotations in this section, see Joseph Berke Archive, PP/JB/IPS 1.3.29 and 1.4.21.
10. Barnard, "More Mystified than ever," 12.
11. Cooper, The Institute of Phenomenological Studies, Allen Ginsberg Papers, Box 17.17.
12. Barnard, Ibid. The purpose of the 'conductors' apparently was to prevent the seminars from falling into the hands of either 'hippies', or participants who were 'politically undisciplined'. See Jervis, "Dialettiche della Liberazione," 408.
13. Ibid.
14. Fearon, "Laing at the Roundhouse," unpaginated.
15. Miles, *Ginsberg*, 397.
16. "Allen Ginsberg and Steve Abrams at Legalise Pot Rally 1967."
17. "Day out for 'Flower People'," 1.
18. For this paragraph and the following three, see Carolee Schneemann Papers, Getty Research Institute, Box 1, Folder 17; Adrian Laing, *R.D. Laing*, 131; Clay, *R.D. Laing*, 144-45; Green, *Days in the Life*, 210, Morton Schatzman, "Trust me, I'm an Anti-Doctor," 68, and Martin Levy, unpublished interviews with Joe Berke. Needless to say of Laing's behaviour, sources conflict in some ways.
19. Martin Levy, unpublished interviews with Joe Berke.

20. Carolee Schneemann Papers, Getty Research Institute, Box 1, Folder 17.
21. [Fearon], "A Self-Governing congress," unpaginated.
22. Sinclair, *Kodak Mantra Diaries*, 'Bateson at the Roundhouse' section.
23. Ibid.
24. "Dialectuals' Masturbation."
25. Topic title from Bateson's synopsis printed in *Peace News*, July 28, 1967, 10.
26. For this and other quotations in this section, see Joseph Berke Archive, PP/JB/IPS 1.2.28 and 1.3.31.
27. For this and other quotations in this section, see Joseph Berke Archive, PP/JB/IPS 1.4.05.
28. For the further influence of Bateson's comments on Ginsberg see, for example, Ginsberg's remarks in Sinclair's *Kodak Mantra Diaries*, 'With Ginsberg' section. Miles mentioned the thesis in *International Times*, August 31-September 13, 8. '**Planet out of control**, abandon all nations, the planet drifts to random insect doom' (Burroughs). Bateson said at the Dialectics of Liberation congress, that within 15-30 years the amount of carbon monoxide[sic] given off by automobiles will have caused a layer round the Earth sufficient to raise the Earth's temperature by 15 degrees which will cause a melting of the ice-caps and a sea level rise of a 100 feet. ... **Save Earth Now!**' Presumably Miles received his information secondhand as the quotation shows he garbled it dreadfully. Bateson's comments inspired an intriguing correspondence with a scientist at the UK's Central Electricity Generating Board. Dr. Denis J.V. Murray wrote to him on the 16th of October 1967, 'At the Dialectics of Liberation congress here in July you mentioned the possibility that the continued burning of fossil fuels would increase the CO_2 content of the atmosphere resulting in increased heat absorption from the sun, the melting of the ice caps and an increase in sea level of the order of 300 feet. I was not very happy with this statement at the time and I see it has been reproduced in various journals.' In his reply to Wollard on the 23rd, Bateson admitted that he, too, was 'not entirely comfortable about the CO_2 story.' He went on, 'The story is certainly messy and I will not further propagate it unless I get further data.' For the full, very detailed, correspondence which the two men continued at least until February 1968, see Gregory Bateson Papers, Cor Box 7, Folder 307. Paul Zeal said that he was 'terrified and distressed' by Bateson's comments. See Martin Levy, unpublished interview with Paul Zeal.
29. For this and other quotations in this section, see Joseph Berke Archive, PP/JB/IPS 1.2.17 and 1.3.44.
30. There were two seminars timetabled to follow the panel discussion, one led by Bateson, picking up, again, on some of the observations

he'd made in his speech and one by Robert Priddy, one of the 'gammas.' Priddy's seminar, which was moderated, i.e., 'conducted' by Joseph Havens, a clinical psychologist from Amherst, Massachusetts, was about objectivity in the study of human relations. See Joseph Berke Archive, PB/JB/IPS 5.3. Unfortunately, neither seminar was recorded.
31. For this and other quotations in this section, see Joseph Berke Archive, PP/JB/IPS 1.3.32.
32. Mossman, "Love, Love, Love," 133.
33. For this and other unattributed quotations in this section, see the script of the programme in the BBC Written Archives Centre.
34. For more about the Vanderbilt event, which took place in April 1967, see Hendricks, "Stokely Carmichael and the 1967 IMPACT Convention."
35. For this incident, which was widely reported in the British press, see, for instance, the article by Eric Britter, "Looting Negroes Kill Policeman," 6. The policeman was named John Gleason. According to Britter, who based his account on local reports, he was beaten to death after shooting a twenty-two-year-old black man.
36. Reynolds, "Television," 5.

Chapter 5.

1. See Carmichael 'with Thelwell', *Ready for Revolution*, 505-511.
2. For instance, at the Cambridge Union in February 1965 where Baldwin debated with William F. Buckley Jr. on whether the 'American Dream' came at the 'expense of the American negro.' The BBC broadcast the debate. In fact, Baldwin was often on British television.
3. For this and all other quotations from Carmichael's speech in this section, see Joseph Berke Archive, PP/JB/IPS 1.4.10.
4. These are almost the same words Carmichael used in his "Toward Black Liberation" article, published in *The Massachusetts Review* in Autumn 1966. See p.643. He probably derived the term 'institutionalized racism' from his reading of Michael Harrington's *The Other Americans: Poverty in the United States*, of 1962. 'To belong to a racial minority is to be poor, but poor in a special way. The fear, the lack of self-confidence, the haunting, these have been described. But they, in turn, are the expressions of the most institutionalized poverty in the United States, the most vicious of the vicious circles. In a sense, the Negro is classically the "other" American, degraded and frustrated at every turn, and not just because of laws.' 'In the other America each group suffers from a psychological depression as well as from simple material want. And given the long history and the tremendous

institutionalized power of racism, this is particularly and terribly true of the Negro.' See pages 71-72 and 77. Carmichael quotes Harrington's book at the head of his "Who is Qualified?" article, first published in the *New Republic*, January 8, 1966. Although the phrase was quickly taken up by British black radicals, it did not gain major currency in the UK until it was used by Sir William Macpherson in reference to the police in *The Stephen Lawrence Inquiry*, of 1999.

5. The poem was first published in 1899. Carmichael misquotes. Kipling's words are 'half devil and half child.'
6. For Afrocentric interpretations of Western history more generally and their location in Western culture wars, see Howe, *Afrocentrism*.
7. Che Guevara, in his "Message to the Tricontinental" a conference held in Havana in January 1966. 'Hatred as an element of the struggle; a relentless hatred of the enemy, impelling us over and beyond the natural limitations that man is heir to and transforming him into an effective, violent, selective and cold killing machine. Our soldiers must be thus; a people without hatred cannot vanquish a brutal enemy.'
8. *If We Must Die*. First published in 1919. Carmichael knew a lot of poetry, and this was a favourite.
9. The lines are capitalised in the original. The poem appears in the June 1966 issue of the SNCC's newspaper *The Movement*, p.8.
10. Davis, *Autobiography*, 150.
11. Ibid.
12. For this and all other quotations from Carmichael in this section, see Joseph Berke Archive, PP/JB/IPS 1.4.10.
13. Rowbotham, *Threads through Time*, 145.
14. For Coon, see Hugill, "We are all the Children of '67," 18, and Sweetman, "Rosita Sweetman: As a Wife and Mother." Mitchell communicated her recollection of Carmichael's 'prone' remark to me via email. Ironically, Carmichael may have intended the remark humorously. See Peck, "'The only Position for Women in SNCC is Prone," for his first use of the expression, in 1964. Although Mitchell didn't stay for the entire Congress—she left for France after about a week—she credited the congress as a formative influence on the Women's Liberation Movement. See Mitchell, *Woman's Estate*, 43. 'The first whisperings of the Women's Liberation Movement in England were late in 1967; by 1968 it was a named and organized movement. Its earliest manifestations were from three distinct sources: American radical politics, psycho-cultural-political groups and, in 1968, the labour movement. Specifically, these were the American women in London working against the Vietnam war and for U.S. deserters (e.g., The Stoppit Committee), the grass-roots politics of Agitprop and the psycho-politics of the Dialectics of Liberation Congress and the Anti-University, and then the

strike of Ford women workers for equal pay.' It's worth adding to this that Mitchell knew all four organisers of the congress personally.
15. For this and all other quotations in this section, see Joseph Berke Archive, PP/JB/IPS 1.4.10.
16. Ali, "Demystifying Mr Carmichael," 108.
17. Ibid.
18. Ibid.
19. For all quotation in this and the following section, see Joseph Berke Archive, PP/JB/IPS 1.4.04.
20. Joyce, "Frank Joyce. October 17th, 2016."
21. *International Times*, No.17, July 26 to August 13, 1967, 21.
22. Jervis, "Dialettiche della Liberazione," 420.
23. Martin Levy, unpublished interview with Adam Saltiel. A year or so after the Congress, Berglund wrote to the IPS, asking if he could stay at Kingsley Hall during the summer of 1969. See Gregory Berglund to 'Dear Sir,' July 10, 1968. Joseph Berke Papers.

Chapter 6

1. Jessel, "Black Power Prophet," 10.
2. McKie, "Teachings,"5.
3. Henry, Culture against Man, 13.
4. Mullan, *Mad to be Normal*, 218. Actually, *Pathways to Madness* was not published until 1971. But the book builds upon some of the chapters in *Culture against Man*.
5. For the quotations in this section and the following one see the recordings in the Joe Berke Archive, PP/JB/IPS 1.4.13.
6. In the version of his speech published in Cooper-edited *The Dialectics of Liberation*, Henry added 'white' before 'American. See p.69.
7. Barnard, "A Little Less Mystified," 12.
8. R.D. Laing Collection, GB 247 MS Laing K28.
9. Although the article is unsigned, the style suggests Anne Marie Fearon, under whose name it appears in the bibliography.
10. "Doomsday 1967," 114.
11. Wells, "A Divine Joke," 41.
12. Peter Davis, unpublished interview with Roy Battersby.
13. For the quotations in this section, see the Joseph Berke Archive PP/JB/IPS 1.3.10 and 1.3.14.
14. Details from Chaney, *Runaway*, 235 - though Chaney changes the location of the event to Hampstead. According to Joe Berke, Goodman sexually harassed John Bateson. Which, if true, may have provided another reason for Bateson to remove him. See Martin Levy, unpublished interviews with Joe Berke.

15. Mullan, "Mad to be Normal," 217.
16. Petrović, "The Dialectics of Liberation," 608.
17. For these and other details of Gerassi's biography, see his interview with Tony Monchinski.
18. These are the first lines of Gerassi's book.
19. For the quotations in this section, see the recordings in the Joseph Berke Archive, PP/JB/IPS 1.4.16 S1 and 1.4.16 S2.
20. For all quotations in this section, see Joseph Berke Archive, PP/JB/IPS 1.1.14, 1.4.03, 1.4.16 S2 and 1.4.38.
21. Carolee Schneemann Papers, Getty Research Institute, Box 1, Folder 17.
22. Ibid.
23. The lecture turned out disastrously. As Horowitz writes in his memoir, *Radical Son,* p.136, 'I quickly realised I was over my head with these professional economists, but was partially saved my embarrassment by the fact that during my talk one of Laing's schizophrenic patients loped around our little circle like an ape, making loud simian noises.'
24. See, for instance, the Che Guevara article published in *New Left Review*, May-June 1967. The article is titled "Vietnam must not Stand Alone."
25. For all unattributed quotations in this and the following section, see Joseph Berke Archive, PP/JB/IPS 1.3.39 S1 and 1.3.40.
26. For the trial, see Porat, *Bitter Reckoning*, 154-166.
27. For the quotations in this and the following two sections, see Joseph Berke Archive, PP/JB/IPS 1.3.39 S2 and 1.3.40
28. McGlashan, "Mainspring of Black Power", 17, mentions Carmichael addressing a meeting in Brixton, as does Frank Collins, "Stokely Carmichael," 2, and other writers.
29. For the quotations in this section and the next that aren't in Peter Davis's *Anatomy of Violence* outtakes, see Joseph Berke Archive, PP/JB/IPS 1.1.18, 1.2.02 and 1.4.11.
30. Davis, *Anatomy of Violence* outtakes.
31. Ibid.
32. Ibid.
33. Ibid.
34. Zeal, *Paul's Journals*, 204
35. For the quotations in this and the following section, see Joseph Berke Archive, PP/JB/IPS 1.3.01,1.3.33 and 1.3.34.
36. Sinclair, *Kodak Mantra Diaries*, the 'Floating Garden to the Park' section.
37. For the quotations in this section not otherwise attributed, see Joseph Berke Archive, PP/JB/IPS 1.1.02 and 1.3.28.
38. Martin Levy, unpublished interview with Paul Zeal.

39. Davis, "How I Saved the Life." See also Davis's unpublished interview with Kolderup.

Chapter 7

1. Sinclair, *Kodak Mantra Diaries*, 'The Myth of Emmet[sic] Grogan is announced' section.
2. Joe Berke Archive, PP/JB/IPS 10.2.
3. That's the account Grogan gives in his early 70s memoir, *Ringolevio*, 484-485. And 'This book is true', he writes in an author's note. But *Ringolevio* isn't that sort of book. On the contrary, at least as far as bread-and-butter details like dates are concerned, it is sometimes wildly inaccurate. Nonetheless, it is an important source for the Congress and much of its content can be verified.
4. Ibid, 493.
5. National Archives, HO 376/154. The security brief is titled "'Black Power' in the United Kingdom" and dated August 11, 1970. *World in Action* was Granada Television's rival to the BBC's *Panorama*. Its programme about Carmichael was broadcast on August 7.
6. On the 19th Carmichael appeared at gatherings in Dalston and Notting Hill. Then (probably) on the 20th he addressed an audience at Brixton Town Hall. He also visited the West Indian Student Centre in Earls Court and the Africa Centre, in Covent Garden. For the workshop, see James, "The Caribbean Artists Movement," 219. For Carmichael's interview with Andrew Salkey, see Carmichael (with Thelwall), *Ready for Revolution*, 573. McGlashan's interview was carried in *The Observer* on July 25.
7. That said, one white person who Carmichael met at this time who certainly wasn't obscure was the anti-Apartheid activist Danny Schechter. Schechter's fellow activist Ronnie Kasrills remembers meeting Carmichael at Schechter's Islington bedsit. See Kasrills, "How Danny became the Postperson from Pluto," unpaginated. Incidentally, some of the anecdotes recorded of Carmichael at this time are touching. For example, at one meeting where he was addressing the question of 'white' accounts of West Indian history, he noticed a Jamaican lad crying. After the meeting, he spoke to him, and it turned out that the youngster was unemployed. 'If you ever need a strong right arm, you know where to find me,' he said. 'I won't be too busy to come.' See Collins, "Stokely Carmichael," 2. Another white person who Carmichael met was Bill Levy, at the time the assistant editor on *International Times*. A British Special Branch briefing reports Levy visiting the American embassy with Carmichael and making a recording of the conversation which took place there. UK National Archives, HO

325/104. See https://www.documentcloud.org/documents/6200128-19680226-BP-HO-325-104-US-in-UK

8. For the film crews, see Sinclair, *Kodak Mantra Diaries*, 'Open Forum Public Chaos' section.
9. Grogan, *Ringolevio*, 496. See also Hoffman, *Revolution for the Hell of it*, 53.
10. For this and all other unattributed quotations in this and the next four sections, see Joseph Berke Archive, PP/JB/IPS 1.4.28.
11. The conference, with delegates from as far afield as Bermuda and Nigeria, would go on to adopt over eighty resolutions, including one calling for the break-up of the United States into two halves: black and white. Other resolutions called for black youths to be trained in paramilitary warfare and for people to 'buy black'. See the article in *The Times*, July 24, 1967, 1.
12. Brecht's poem was published in German in 1937. Here are the final lines in the H.R. Hays translation:

    Alas, we
    Who wished to lay the foundations of kindness
    Could not ourselves be kind.

    But you, when at last it comes to pass
    That man can help his fellow man,
    Do no judge us
    Too harshly.

13. See Peter Coyote on the Digger ethos. 'A big key was Gregory Corso's poem, Power, where he said: "Power is standing on a street corner doing nothing." Because what we were about was autonomy, finding what authentic, autonomous impulses were. And then being responsive to them, and not making excuses, not waiting for the revolution.' Coyote, *Interview*.
14. Sinclair, ibid, 'Open Forum Public Chaos' section.
15. The story, which I haven't got room for here, is in chapter 6 of Laing's *Self and Others*. See also Adrian Laing, *R.D. Laing*, 37-38.
16. Whittuck, Andrew, *Interview*.
17. The 'angle', which Grogan does not reveal in *Ringolevio*, apparently financed Malik's 'operation' for over a year. See page 500.
18. Phillips, Mike and Trevor. *Windrush*, 238.
19. "Carmichael Report Is Ordered," 2.
20. Joseph Berke Archive, PP/JB/IPS 1.4.49.
21. For Carmichael's fear of assassination both in the United States and the UK, see Delano, "For Civil Rights Read Black Power," 9, and Ali. "Demystifying Mr Carmichael," 108.
22. Wilcox, "Stokely is a Guerrilla Fighter," 6.

23. For this and all other unattributed quotations in this and the following six sections, see Joseph Berke Archive, PP/JB/IPS 1.2.12, 1.3.25, 1.4.17 and 1.4.49.
24. Rowbotham, *Promise of a Dream*, 145.
25. For the information on Egbuna in this and the following two paragraphs, see John Wyver, "Earl Cameron and a Lost Play" and 'People's Minister of Information, JR,' "Looking at the Life of Freedom Fighter Obi Egbuna Sr."
26. The 'Sharpeville Massacre' had taken place on March 21, 1960.
27. For Carmichael's nickname, see, for example, Span. "The Undying Revolutionary."
28. Actually, Carmichael said the World Boxing Championship Commission. I have silently corrected him.
29. 'You Better Come on Home" is the title of a speech Carmichael gave at Morgan State College, Baltimore. It is reproduced in the SNCC's newspaper *The Movement*, June 1967, 4 & 9.
30. Zeal, *Paul's Journals*, 204.
31. See 'Ealing Man for Trial on Race Hate Charges', 7 and "Fined for "Race Hatred Speeches," 2. Alongside Sawh, three other men were charged: Alton Watson, Ajoy Ghose Shankar and Uyoruumu Ezekiel. The charges were related to offences at Speakers' Corner and Mahatma Gandhi Hall, Camden.
32. Rowbotham, *Promise of a Dream*, 145-146 and *Threads through Time*, 64.
33. For these and other quotations in this section, see Brook, *Tell me Lies*.
34. Sinclair, *Kodak Mantra Diaries*, 'Talking to McCartney' section.
35. McLachlan, "Cautious on Colour," 129.
36. House of Commons, Hansard, https://hansard.parliament.uk/commons/1967-07-26/debates/cd8acdfd-0d11-491b-a48b-fa660d3d731f/CommonsChamber
37. House of Commons, Hansard, https://hansard.parliament.uk/commons/1967-07-27/debates/326e1385-3dce-4e45-99ed-e37b7b2b9b7b/WrittenAnswers
38. McGlashan, "Michael X: New Leader may Take Over," 3.

Chapter 8

1. "The Law against Marijuana is Immoral in Principle and Unworkable in Practice," *The Times*, July 24, 1967, 9.
2. Cooper's popularisation of the term initially occurred via the title of his first book, *Psychiatry and Anti-Psychiatry*, of 1967, where he described it in the preface as antithetical to psychiatry in relation to the problem of schizophrenia. The book was widely reviewed, both in the popular and in the academic literature. Intriguingly, the term 'anti-

hospital' in relation to Villa 21 was already in use. See, for instance, Cooper, "The Anti-Hospital: An Experiment in Psychiatry," in *New Society*, March 1965. The phrase also appears in "Findings", again in *New Society*, January 1966, 19, the section titled "Some Results from the 'Anti-Hospital'".
3. Mullan, *Mad to be Normal*, 356.
4. Cooper, ed., *The Dialectics of Liberation*, 7.
5. Adrian Laing, R.D. Laing, 132.
5. See, for example, *Counter Culture*, 410, where Berke describes all four organisers of the Congress as anti-psychiatrists. He also defines the term. Anti-psychiatry: 'A term coined by David Cooper to denote the position of those who point out that it is not people who are *mad*, but the relations between them (in most highly organised form—Society) and seek to prevent the invalidation (via medico-psychiatric diagnoses) to fellow sufferers who happen to be exposing this—whether in the family, or institutions or the whole of society.'
6. Mullan, *Creative Destroyer*, 396.
7. Adrian Laing, R.D. Laing, 119.
8. Mullan, *Creative Destroyer*, 397.
9. For these and all other unattributed quotations in this and the following section, see Joseph Berke Archive, PP/JB/IPS 1.4.06.
10. For comparison, see Cooper's remarks at the end of his "Violence and Psychiatry" article, where he counsels 'mad' people to exercise discretion.
11. For the full letter, see *La Révolution Surréaliste*, 3 (April 18, 1925): 29. https://www.calameo.com/read/000695192d4621300a14f
12. Jervis was not the only Italian at the Congress. Others included Guido Neri and Renato Rozzi. See Jervis, "Dialettiche della Liberazione," 407.
13. Ibid, 407-08.
14. Eng, "Beyond Psychiatry," 472.
15. For Wilhelm Reich, see David Widgery's article, in *Preserving Disorder*. Widgery, who attended the Congress, describes 'the Marxist Reich of the interwar years' as the 'real patron saint' of the Congress', page 12.
16. At least July the 26th is the date on the manuscript. See R.D. Laing Collection, GB247 MS Laing A383. Presumably the seminar was a spin on Laing's 'What is Schizophrenia?'. This had appeared both as a lecture and as an article. For details, see Laing's *The Politics of Experience*, 9.
17. Cooper notes that several of his 'patients' were present on Monday. See the Joseph Berke Archive, PP/JB/IPS 1.4.06.
18. Joseph Berke Archive, PP/JB/IPS 5.3.
19. For Havens seminar and Congress seminars more generally, see the Joseph Berke Archive, PP/JB/IPS 5.3. The folder is titled 'Seminar Proposals That People Said They were Prepared to Give 1967.' Names

listed there include Surinder Suri, Roger Gottlieb, Martin Pawley and Richard Wiggs. People who *certainly* delivered seminars include Peter Wollen, Ben Brewster, Aage Rosendal Nielsen, Peter Cadogan, Frank Joyce and Danny Schechter. For the date and a summary of Schechter's seminar, which was said to have been one of the best, see Jervis, "Dialettiche della Liberazione," 417-418. Not all the seminars took place at the Roundhouse. Some of them were run on Primrose Hill or in pubs or cafes.
20. Barnard, "A Little Less Mystified," 12.
21. S[mall], M[artin], "Paul Goodman at the Roundhouse," unpaginated.
22. Ibid.
23. For this and the following quotations in this and the following section, see Joseph Berke Archive, PP/JB/IPS 1.1.16 and 1.1.17.
24. In fact, China already had atomic weapons. The conference took place at Veszprem, in Hungary. One of the British attendees was Robin Blackburn, a fact noted by Goodman during his speech.
25. Here, Goodman was picking up on Gerassi's remark during the panel discussion after Stokely Carmichael's speech on the previous Tuesday. Question is PG referring to the Tomkins Square Park hippie riot of June 1967, mention by Ginsberg in the Sunday Q&A.
26. A point Goodman made again in *New Reformation*, 123. Also, see my chapter eleven.
27. Barnard, "A Little Less Mystified," 12.
28. For this and other unattributed quotations in this section, se PP/JB/IPS 1.2.03 and 1.2.14.
29. The quotation, which the speaker translated word for word from the German edition of Marcuse's essay, can be found on page 84 of the 1969 edition of *A Critique of Pure Tolerance*.
30. Possibly this was Hans Metz. He was certainly in London for the congress. See Gladstone, "The Last of Provo," 18.
31. Allen Krebs to Joe Berke, January 16, 1967, Joseph Berke Papers.
32. Allen Krebs to Joe Berke, August 3, 1966 and October 28, 1966, Joseph Berke Papers.
33. The Internationalists were led by an Indian-born microbiologist named Hardial Bains. Almost immediately following the Congress, they hosted their own two-week 'Necessity for Change' conference in Regent's Park, London. One of the speakers was Paul Sweezy. Apparently, when participants objected to his presentation, Sweezy said he had arranged a tennis match, which if he left straight away he could just fit in before catching his flight back to the States. Daly, "Looking Back on Necessity for Change Conference."
34. Some of the Germans at the Congress had links to the Berlin commune movement, Dieter Kunzelmann for one, or to the Sozialistische

Deutsche Studentenbund, which sent a delegation. And all were deeply inspired by Stokely Carmichael's speeches. Returning to Germany after the Congress, Bernward Vesper wrote and published a pamphlet on black power and the riots-cum-rebellions. Like his girlfriend, the future Red Army Faction member Gudrun Ensslin, he despaired of the revolutionary potential of the working class and saw black people as a possible replacement.

35. For this and all other questions in this section, see Joe Berke Archive, PP/JB/IPS 1.3.24.
36. The Russians written to included Pyotr Kapitza, Yuri Karyakin and Ernst Neizvestny. See Joseph Berke Archive, PP/JB/IPS 10.2.
37. For this and all other quotations from Goldmann's speech, see Joseph Berke Archive, PP/JB/IPS 1.3.03.
38. Petrović mentions the paper in a letter to Berke, July 6, 1967. See Joseph Berke Archive, PP/JB/IPS 10.4. While Petrović was not the only member (or ex-member) of the board of *Praxis* to be invited to the Congress, he was the only one to accept the invitation.
39. For this and all other unattributed quotations from Petrović's speech, see PP/JB/IPS 1.4.12.
40. Marx used the phrase in a famous letter to Arnold Ruge in September 1843. It has been variously translated.
41. For the information in this paragraph, see Blažek, "The Deportation of the King of May," 46, and Miles, *Allen Ginsberg*, 367.
42. For this and all other unattributed quotations in this section, see PP/JB/IPS 1.4.12.
43. Sexual Offences Act 1967: 'An Act to Amend the Law of England and Wales relating to Homosexual Acts.'
44. In fact, sexual relations between men in Czechoslovakia were decriminalised in 1961. The act entered into force on January 1, 1962. See Seidl, "Decriminalization of Homosexual Acts," 186.
45. Widgery, "Goodbye Comrade M."
46. Ros Kane, via email to the author.
47. Goodman, "Memoirs of an Ancient Activist," 4.
48. For Joans's poems and further information about the Wednesday evening poetry session, see Joseph Berke Archive, PP/JB/IPS 1.4.39 and 1.4.40. Following the poetry, there was a film show about Cuba. The second poetry event took place on Thursday evening and included contributions by Allen Ginsberg, Susan Sherman and Ted Joans again. See Joseph Berke Archive, PP/JB/IPS 1.3.27.
49. For this event, including the following quotations, see Peter Davis's outtakes.
50. For this and all other unattributed quotations in this section, see Joseph Berke Archive, PP/JB/IPS 1.4.41. In 1968, a version of Ginsberg

speech, edited by Emmett Grogan, appeared in *The Digger Papers*. See the article by 'Eric', "Discovery #1 (In the Emmett Grogan Papers)".
51. Simon Vinkenoog to Joe Berke, April 4, 1967, in the Joseph Berke Archive PP/JB/IPS 10.4.
52. Canetti had in fact been invited to the Congress. See the appendix and the correspondence in Joseph Berke Archive, PP/JB/IPS 10.1.
53. These lines from Vinkenoog's speech are taken from the version published in *Freedom*, "Thoughts on Liberation," unpaginated. They do not appear on the recordings in the Joseph Berke Archive.

Chapter 9

1. Mullan, *Mad to be Normal*, 217. 'I met Marcuse in a friendly, affable, diplomatic way, but we never talked about anything. I never got on with him, we never clicked.'
2. Cockburn, "The Dialectics of Revolution."
3. *Eros and Civilization: A Philosophical Inquiry into Freud*, of 1955.
4. For this and all other quotations in this section, see Joseph Berke Archive, PP/JB/IPS 1.4.01 and 1.4.02.
5. Kellner, "Radical Politics, Marcuse, and the New Left," 13.
6. For this and all other quotations in this section, see Joseph Berke Archive, PP/JB/IPS 1.4.02.
7. For this and other quotations in this section, see Davis, *Anatomy of Violence* outtakes.
8. Barnard, "Disappointment, Enlightenment," 12.
9. Farren, *Give the Anarchist a Cigarette*, 103.
10. For this and all other unattributed quotations in this and the following section, see Joseph Berke Archive, PP/JB/IPS 1.1.12.
11. Presumably an artwork by artist John Latham. For Latham and Cooper in 1964, see Levy, "From 'Philadelphia-Sigma Subversion and Insurrection Center' to Kingsley Hall."
12. Barnard, "Disappointment, Enlightenment," 12.
13. The play, to which Cooper, Laing and Aaron Esterson had all generously contributed, drew much of its inspiration from Laing and Esterson's *Sanity, Madness and the Family*. See Snelson, "From *In Two Minds* to MIND."
14. Cooper's remark that the IPS didn't meet is not strictly true. There are references to meetings in the R.D. Laing Collection.
15. Grogan, *Ringolevio*, 503. For the timing of Grogan's speech, see Petrović, "The Dialectics of Liberation," 608, and R.G. Davis's letter to Joe Berke, August 1, 1967, which is in the Joseph Berke Papers. 'Dear Joe, I just had a call from Grogan who is in New York once again, and is trying to get the whole essential Haight-Ashbury scene to Europe.'

16. Ibid, 502.
17. For the court case, see Moyse, "The Price of Indecency" and "Round the Galleries," both unpaginated. For the IPS's discussions with Schneemann regarding her happening, see Carolee Schneemann Papers, Getty Research Institute. Box 1, Folder 17.
18. Ibid, Schneemann. Although Schneemann was always adamant that Berke was nothing but helpful, a few years later David Cooper apparently apologised on behalf of the full group. 'I always felt we owed you an apology... . But the disillusioning fact seems to have been that we didn't welcome a woman taking an equal space among ourselves, we distrusted a theatrical form, and we certainly didn't want a very young woman putting on a performance which incorporated our own words with a countering physicality.' For the attribution of the remarks to Cooper, See Harding, *Cutting Performances*, 204.
19. Schneemann Papers, Getty Research Institute. Box 1, Folder 17.
20. Davis, *Anatomy of Violence* outtakes.
21. Schneemann, *More than Meat Joy*, 152.
22. Schneemann, ibid.
23. Farren, ibid, 142.
24. For all of Jane and Joan's comments in this section, see Davis, *Anatomy of Violence* outtakes.
25. Fearon, "Adventure Playground for Grown-Ups," unpaginated.
26. For Malik's appearance in Reading and the court case that came out if it, see "Stokely is a Guerrilla Fighter—Black Muslim Michael X", 6; "Michael X: 'We can deal with Whitey if necessary'" 7'; and "Michael Appeal Dismissed," 1. For Sawh and Shankar, see "Ealing Man for Trial on Race Hate Charges", 7 and "Fined for "Race Hatred Speeches," 2.
27. Overy, "Black Power in Britain," 12.
28. Cooper, ed. *The Dialectics of Liberation*, 11.

Chapter 10

1. The Paris conference, organised by Maud Mannoni, took place at the Maison de la Chimie on the 21st and 22nd of October. Jacques Lacan gave the closing speech. Berke's paper, which he presented jointly with Redler, was based on their 'multigenerational' research into the families of schizophrenics. A report about the conference appeared in *Recherches*, No.8, December 1968.
2. During 1968 and for a few years afterwards the 'Antiuniversity' was spelled in a number of ways. Sometimes as one word, sometimes as two (with a space or a hyphen between 'Anti' and 'U/university') and sometimes with and sometimes without capital letters. I have spelled it here, as I have spelled it elsewhere in the book, on the grounds that

that is how Berke and most of the founders spelled it. But with the consequence that the reader will miss some nuances.
3. P.H.S. "The Light of the Obscure," 8.
4. [Isaaman], "Heathman's Diary."
5. Martin Levy, unpublished interviews with Joe Berke.
6. For the first letter and other letters and associated documents mentioned here and in the subsequent paragraphs, see Jakob Jakobsen's *Antiuniversity of London Tabloid*.
7. For Laing's move away from politics, see, *inter alia*, Adrian Laing, *R.D. Laing*, 134, and Peter Mezan, "After Freud and Laing". 'I guess I identified myself with the Left by being [at the Congress on the Dialectics of Liberation], but even at the time I made it clear that I really had no idea what could come of such an extraordinary conglomeration of people. Politically, I think I'm neutral really. I engage in no strictly *political* actions—except in the sense of following the Tao.'
8. Norse, Harold et al, "Three Views on the Anti-University," 6.
9. *The Antiuniversity of London* [Course catalogue], unpaginated.
10. BBC News. "Anti University of London opens Shoreditch."
11. Jones, "A Real Saving Thing," 213.
12. Elzey, "Founding an Anti-University," 231.
13. Jones, Ibid.
14. P.L. Travers to Joe Berke, October 6, 1968. Joseph Berke Papers. See also Levy, "Mary Poppins and the Anti-University."
15. Boston, "Anti-University," 702.
16. "Commune", in *Gandalf's Garden*, 2 (1968), 20. It would be interesting to learn how much this conference owed to Emmett Grogan.
17. Khan, "Digging for Victory," 7.
18. Ibid.
19. "Commune," Ibid.
20. Elzey, Ibid, 243. But see Cooper's remarks on page 11 of his introduction to the *Dialectics of Liberation*. He there describes the Antiuniversity as building on the success of the Congress and potentially taking an enduring form. '
21. Ibid.
22. "Successful Failure," 36.
23. Apparently, a service was performed by Leon Redler and Morton Schatzman. Guests included Redler's wife, Liz, Schatzman's wife, Vivien, and Calvin Hernton. Information from Leon Redler via email. Later, the couple 'remarried' on May 18, 1971 at St John's Wood Liberal Synagogue.
24. Elzey, Ibid, 236.
25. Berke, "Kommune I," 141.
26. Berke, The Creation of an Alternative Society," 16 and 18.

27. Holmes, "Just How Serious are You?" 14.
28. Rigby, "Living New Life-Styles," 11.
29. Coleman, "Far under the Culture Counter," 9.
30. Barnes and Berke, *Mary Barnes,* 359.
31. Ibid, 83.
32. Ibid, 172.
33. Barnes and Berke, *Mary Barnes,* 217.

Bibliography

Archives

Alexander Trocchi Papers, Department of Special Collections, Washington University, St. Louis, Missouri.

Allen Ginsberg Papers, Department of Special Collections, Stanford University.

BBC Written Archives Centre, Caversham Park, Reading.

Carolee Schneemann Papers, Department of Special Collections, Stanford University.

Carolee Schneemann Papers, Getty Research Institute, Los Angeles.

Gregory Bateson Papers, Department of Special Collections and Archives, University of California, Santa Cruz.

Joseph Berke Archive, 1960-2003, Planned Environment Therapy Trust (PETT) Archives and Special Collections, The Mulberry Bush, Toddington, Gloucestershire.

Joseph Berke Papers, Wellcome Collection, London. Uncatalogued. The papers were in Joseph Berke's own collection at the time I consulted them.

Jules Henry Papers, Department of Special Collections, Washington University Libraries.

Living Theatre Records, Beinecke Rare Book & Manuscript Library, Yale University.

The National Archives, Kew, Richmond, UK.

R.D. Laing Collection, Special Collections, University of Glasgow.

Will Inman Papers, Duke University, Durham, North Carolina.

Unpublished Interviews

Jacky Ivimy with, individually, Michael Horovitz, Jutta Laing and Leon Redler.

Martin Levy with, individually, Joe Berke, Morton Schatzman, Paul Zeal, Marjaleena Repo, Leon Redler and Adam Saltiel.

Peter Davis with, individually, Dag Kolderup and Roy Battersby.

Peter Davis and Jacky Ivimy with Gustav Metzger.

Unpublished Film

Peter Davis, *Anatomy of Violence* outtakes. Villon Films. www.villonfilms.com

Books, Articles, Films, TV Programmes and Websites

Amponsah, George (dir). *Black Power: A British Story of Resistance* – broadcast March 25, 2021. https://www.bbc.co.uk/iplayer/episode/m000tj50/black-power-a-british-story-of-resistance

Abel, Ruth. "Schizophrenia as a Way of Life," *The Guardian*, October 4, 1966.

Ali, Tariq. "Demystifying Mr Carmichael," *New Statesman*, July 28, 1967.

"Allen Ginsberg and Steve Abrams at Legalise Rally 1967." YouTube https://www.youtube.com/watch?v=AxOfFJfiMng

Angelo, Anne-Marie. "The Black Panthers in London, 1967-1972: A Diasporic Struggle Navigates the Black Atlantic." *Radical History Review* 103 (Winter 2009): 17-35.

The Antiuniversity of London [Course catalogue], London, 1968.

"Anti-Courses attract the Curious," *The Times*, February 13, 1968.

Arden, John. "Diggers Cultivate their Garden," *Peace News*, May 10, 1968.

Aronowitz, Stanley. "White Radicals and Black Revolt." *Liberation* 12, no.5 (August 1967): 11-13.

Barnard, Roger. "Anarchist Citizen and Man of Letters," *Peace News*, September 22, 1972.

---. "Disappointment, Enlightenment," *Peace News*, August 4, 1967.

---. "Goodman Observed," *New Society*, February 1, 1973

---. "A Little less Mystified," *Peace News*, July 28, 1967.

---. "Madness in the Age of Reason," *Peace News*, May 19, 1967.

---. "More Mystified than Ever," *Peace News*, July 21, 1967.

---. "Roger Barnard interviews Jules Henry," *Peace News*, August 4, 1967.

---. "Round House Dialectics," *New Society*, August 3, 1967.

---. "Seeds of Growth," *Peace News*, February 3, 1967.

Barnes, Mary and Joseph Berke. *Mary Barnes: Two Accounts of a Journey through Madness*. London: Penguin Books, 1982. First publication 1971 by MacKibbon & Kee.

Bateson, Mary Catherine. *With a Daughter's Eye: A Memoir of Margaret Mead and Gregory Bateson*. New York: William Morrow, 1984.

Bateson, Gregory. "Consciousness versus Nature." *Peace News*, July 28, 1967.

---. *Perceval's Narrative: A Patient's Account of his Psychosis 1830-1832*. London: The Hogarth Press, 1962.

BBC News. "Anti University of London opens Shoreditch" — broadcast February 12, 1968. YouTube video. https://www.youtube.com/watch?v=Kbi_KgBA7-c&t=15s

Berglund, Gregory. *The Third Bomb*. New Delhi: Jnanada Prakashan, 2009.

Berke, Joe. "Universities," *Peace News*, October 25, 1963.

Berke, Joseph, ed. *Counter Culture*. London: Peter Owen Ltd, 1969.

---, The Creation of an Alternative Society." In Berke, *Counter Culture*, 12-34.

---. "The Free University of New York." in Berke, *Counter Culture*, 212-27.

---. "The Free University of New York." *Peace News*, October 29, 1965.

---. "Kommune 1 Visited." in Berke, *Counter Culture*, 138-42.

---. "R.D. Laing." *British Journal of Psychotherapy* 7, no.2 (1990): 175-77.

---. "Zone of the Interior." *Existential Analysis: Journal of the Society for Existential Analysis* 18, no.2 (2007): 377-78.

Berke, Joseph H. "Auto de Fe." *Fire* 1 (1967): 2-3.

Berke, Joseph H. "Trick or Treat: The Divided Self of R.D. Laing." *Janus Head* 4, no.1 (2001): http://janushead.org/wp-content/uploads/2020/07/Joseph-H.-Berke.pdf

Berke, Joseph and Calvin C. Hernton. *The Cannabis Experiment: An Interpretative Study of the Effects of Marijuana and Hashish*. London: Quartet Books. First publication 1974 by Peter Owen Limited.

"Bitter Attack on Whites," *The Times*, July 25, 1967.

Blass, Thomas. "The Roots of Stanley Milgram's Obedience Experiments and their Relevance to the Holocaust." *Analyse & Kritik* 20 (1998): 47-53.

Blažek, Petr. "The Deportation of the King of May: Allen Ginsberg and the State Security." In *Behind the Iron Curtain. English Language Review* 2 (2012): 34-47.

"The Bomb inside Us," *Peace News*, August 28, 1964.

Boston, Richard. "Anti-University," *New Society*, May 16, 1968.

---. "International Times," *New Society*, October 27, 1966.

"British Ban on Stokely Carmichael," *The Guardian*, July 28, 1967.

Bourne, Tom. "Herbert Marcuse: Grandfather of the New Left." *Change* 11, no.6 (September 1979): 37-38, 64.

Britter, Eric. "Looting Negroes Kill Policeman," *The Times*, July 17, 1967.

Brook, Peter (dir). *Tell me Lies*, 1968. https://rarefilmm.com/2021/09/tell-me-lies-1968/

Buchanan, Tom. *East Wind: China and the British Left, 1925-1976*. Oxford University Press, 2012.

Bunce, R.E.R. and Paul Field. "Obi Ebguna, C.L.R. James and the Birth of Black Power in Britain: Black Radicalism in Britain 1967-72." *Twentieth Century British History* 22, no.3 (2011): 391-414.

Bunce, Robin and Paul Field. *Darcus Howe: A Political Biography*. London: Bloomsbury, 2014.

Burgess, Anthony, "Television," *The Listener*, January 12, 1967.

Campbell, Allan and Niel, Tim. *A Life in Pieces: Reflections on Alexander Trocchi*. Edinburgh: Rebel Inc., 1997.

Carmichael, Stokely. "APM Stokely Carmichael Speech at University of California, Berkeley." YouTube video, recording of a speech delivered on October 29, 1966, posted by American Public Media, https://www.youtube.com/watch?v=ifH5X9dYzG8.

---. "Black Liberation." *The Massachusetts Review* 7, no.4 (Autumn 1966): 639-51.

---. "Who is Qualified?" *New Republic*, January 8, 1966, 20-22.

---. "You better come on Home," *The Movement*, June 1967.

Carmichael, Stokely and Charles V. Hamilton. *Black Power: The Politics of Liberation in America*. Harmondsworth: Penguin Books, 1969. First published 1967 by Random House.

Carmichael, Stokely and Ekwueme Michael Thelwall. *Ready for Revolution: The Life and Struggles of Stokely Carmichael (Kwame Ture)*. New York: Scribner, 2005.

"Carmichael Report is Ordered," *The Times*, July 25, 1967.

Caute, David. *Sixty-Eight: The Year of the Barricades*. London: Grafton Books, 1988.

Chaney, Anthony. *Runaway: Gregory Bateson, the Double Bind, and the Rise of Ecological Consciousness*. Chapel Hill: The University of North Carolina Press, 2017.

Chapman, Adrian. "Dwelling in Strangeness: Accounts of the Kingsley Hall Community, London (1965-1970), Established by R.D. Laing." *Journal of Medical Humanities* 42 (2021): 471-94.

Clay, John. *R.D. Laing: A Divided Self*. London: Hodder & Stoughton, 1996.

Cockburn, Alexander. "The Dialectics of Revolution ... Ugh, Recycling." *The Nation*, November 29, 2007. https://www.thenation.com/article/archive/dialectics-revolution-uh-recycling/

Coleman, Terry. "Far Under the Culture Counter," *The Guardian*, April 11, 1970.

Collins, Frank. "Stokely Carmichael: Black Power and Racial Violence in Britain," *Socialist Leader*, July 29, 1967.

Commoner, Barry. *Science and Survival*. New York: The Viking Press, 1966.

"Commune," *Gandalf's Garden*, 2 (1968).

Cooper, David. "The Anti-Hospital: An Experiment in Psychiatry," *New Society*, March 11, 1965.

---, ed. *The Dialectics of Liberation*. Harmondsworth: Penguin Books, 1968.

---. *Psychiatry and Anti-Psychiatry*. London: Paladin, 1970. First published 1967 by Tavistock Publications.

---. "Two Types of Rationality." *New Left Review* 1, no.29 (January-February 1965).

---. "Violence and Psychiatry," *Peace News*, May 19, 1967.

---. "Violence in Psychiatry." *Views* 8 (Summer 1965): 18-25.

Couture, Lise and Howard Levy. "Levy: Why the US should Withdraw from Vietnam," *Peace News*, July 14, 1967.

Coyote, Peter. *Interview by Etan Ben-Ali*. The Digger Archives. https://www.diggers.org/oralhistory/peter_interview.html

Crossley, Nick. *Contesting Psychiatry: Social Movements in Mental Health*. London: Routledge, 2005.

Culk, Jan. "Igor Hajek," *The Independent*, April 27, 1995.

Daly, Richard. "Looking Back on Necessity for Change Conference." *TML Weekly Information Project*, no.41, December 23, 2017. https://cpcml.ca/Tmlw2017/W47041.HTM

Davies, Mererid Puw. "'Burn!, Baby! Burn!': Paris, Watts, Brussels, Berlin and Vietnam in the Work of Kommune I, 1967." *Forum for Modern Language Studies* 54, no.2 (2018): 136-56.

Davis, Angela. *An Autobiography*. London: Hutchinson and Company, 1975.

Davis, Angela Y. "Marcuse's Legacies." In *Marcuse: A Critical Reader*. Edited by John Arbromeit and W. Mark Cobb, 43-49. London: Routledge, 2003.

Davis, Peter (dir). *Anatomy of Violence*, 1967.

Davis, Peter. "How I saved the Life of Allen Ginsberg … Well, Probably … Well, Maybe." Roundhouse: Celebrating Fifty Years. https://50.roundhouse.org.uk/content-items/saved-life-allen-ginsberg-well-probably-well-maybe

"Day out for 'Flower People'." *Birmingham Daily Post*, July 17, 1967.

Delano, Tony. "For Civil Rights Read Black Power," *Daily Mirror*, June 15, 1967.

Demidjuk, Stanislav. "Joseph Berke: Expand a Man," *Friends*, May 15, 1970.

Deutscher, Isaac. "On the Arab-Israeli War." *New Left Review* 1, no.44 (July-August 1967): 30-46.

"Dialectuals' Masturbation." *International Times*, no.17, July 28 - August 13, 1967.

"Doomsday 1967." *Nature* 213, no.5072, (January 14, 1967).

"Ealing Man for Trial on Race Hate Charges." *County Times and Gazette*, October 27, 1967.

Egbuna, Obi. *Destroy this Temple: The Voice of Black Power in Britain*. London: MacGibbon & Kee, 1971.

Ellis, Sylvia A. "Promoting Solidarity at Home and Abroad: The Goals and Tactics of the Anti-Vietnam War Movement in Britain." *European Review of History: Revue Européene d'Histoire* 21, no.4 (2014): 557-576.

Elzey, Roberta. "Founding an Anti-University." in Berke, *Counter Culture*, 229-48.

Eng, Erling. "Beyond Psychiatry." *The Hudson Review* 20, no.3 (Autumn 1967): 469-72.

Eribon, Didier. *Michel Foucault*. London: Faber & Faber, 1992.

Eric. "Discovery #1 (In the Emmett Grogan Papers)." *Digger Feed: Dinosaurs are Dancing* (September 5, 2017). https://diggerfeed.org/2017/09/05/discovery-1-in-the-emmett-grogan-papers/

Esterson, A., D.G. Cooper and R.D. Laing. "Results of Family-Orientated Therapy with Hospitalized Schizophrenics." *British Medical Journal*, September 18, 1965.

Fanon, Frantz. *Black Skin, White Masks*. Translated by Richard Philcox. London: Penguin Books, 2021. First English publication 1967 by Grove Press.

Fanon, Frantz. *The Wretched of the Earth*. Translated by Constance Harrington. London: Penguin Books, 2001. First English publication 1965 by MacGibbon & Kee.

Farren. Mick. *Give the Anarchist a Cigarette*. London: Pimlico, 2002.

Fearon, A.M. "Laing at the Roundhouse," *Freedom*, July 22, 1967.

Fearon, Anne Marie. "Adventure Playground for Grown-Ups," *Freedom*, August 12, 1967.

[Fearon, Anne Marie] "A Self-Governing congress," *Freedom*, July 29, 1967.

"Findings," *New Society*, January 12, 1966.

"Fined for 'Race Hatred' Speeches." *Marylebone Mercury*, December 15, 1967.

Foster, John Bellamy. "The Commitment of an Intellectual: Paul M. Sweezy (1910-2004)." *Monthly Review*, 56, no.5 (October 2004): 5-39.

Foucault, Michel. *Madness and Civilization: A History of Insanity in the Age of Reason*. Translated by Richard Howard. London: Routledge, 2001. First English publication 1967 by Tavistock Publications.

Fowler, Norman. "Stokely Carmichael Recordings for Sale," *The Times*, August 5, 1967.

Fraser, Ronald. *1968: A Student Generation in Revolt*. New York: Pantheon Books, 1988.

Fryer, Peter. "A Map of the Underground: The Flower Power Structure & London Scene." *Encounter* 29, no.4 (October 1967): 4-20.

Gale, David. "Far Out," *The Guardian,* September 8, 2001.

Gelber, Jack. "Julian Beck, Businessman." *The Drama Review* 30, no.2 (Summer 1986): 6-29.

Gerassi, John. "Sane, Civil Right and Politics." *Liberation* 11, no. 4 (July 1966): 44-47.

Gerassi, John and Tony Monchinski. "Living History: Talking with Tito." *Cultural Logic: A journal of Marxist Theory & Practice* 8 (2001). https://ojs.library.ubc.ca/index.php/clogic/article/view/191964

Ginsberg, Allen. *The Fall of America Journals 1965-1971*. Edited by Micheal Schumacher. Minneapolis: University of Minnesota Press, 2020.

G[ladstone], G[uy]. "A Case for Provocation," *Freedom*, May 27, 1967.

Gladstone, Guy. "The Last of Provo?" *Resistance* 4, no.3 (September/October 1967).

"Goodman to lead Massive Anti-Draft Movement?" *Peace News*, April 21, 1967.

Goodman, Paul. *The Community of Scholars*. New York: Random House, 1962.

---. "Memoirs of an Ancient Activist," *WIN*, November 15, 1969.

---. *New Reformation: Notes of a Neolithic Conservative*. Oakland: PM Press, 2010. First published 1970 by Random House.

---. *People or Personnel: Decentralizing and the Mixed Systems and Like a Conquered Province: The Moral Ambiguity of America*. New York: Vintage Books, 1968. *People or Personnel* first publication 1965, *Like a Conquered Province* first publication 1967.

Goodman, Paul and Roger Barnard, Bob Overy and Colin Ward. "Utopian means they don't want to do it!" *Anarchy* 85 (March 1968): 87-89. An interview with Paul Goodman.

Green, Jonathan. *Days in the Life: Voices from the English Underground 1961-1971*. London: Heinemann, 1989.

Grogan, Emmett. *Ringolevio: A Life played for Keeps*. St. Albans: Panther Books, 1974. First published 1972 by Little, Brown and Company.

Guevara, Ernesto 'Che'. "Message to the Tricontinental." *Marxists Internet Archive*. https://www.marxists.org/archive/guevara/1967/04/16.htm

Harding, James M. *Cutting Performances: Collage Events. Feminist Artists, and the American Avant-Garde*. Michigan: University of Michigan Press, 2012.

Harrington, Michael. *The Other America: Poverty in the United States*. New York: Macmillan, 1962.

Harris, Dominic. *The Residents: Stories of Kingsley Hall, East London, 1965-1970 and the Experimental Community of R.D. Laing*. Dominic Harris, 2012.

Haynes, Jane. *Who is it that can tell me who I am?* London: Constable, 2009.

Heineman Jr., Ben W. "Black Power: The Civil Rights Dilemma," *New Society*, January 26, 1967.

Hendricks, Jennifer. "Stokely Carmichael and the 1967 IMPACT Convention: Black Power, White Fear and the Conservative South." *Tennessee Historical Quarterly* 63, no.4 (Winter 2004): 284-304.

Henry, Jules. *Culture against Man*. Harmondsworth: Penguin, 1972. First English publication 1966 by Tavistock Publications.

Hernton, Calvin. "London: Eliade, Ginsberg, Goffman, Goodman, Laing, Marcuse" *International Times*, January 16-29, 1967.

---. *Scarecrow*. New York: Doubleday, 1974.

---. "Umbra: A Personal Recounting—a Lower East Side Cultural Group of the 1960's—Lower East Side Retrospective." *African American Review* 27, no.4 (Winter 1993): 579-84.

Hernton, Calvin C. *Sex and Racism*. St. Albans: Paladin, 1970. First publication as *Sex and Racism in America* 1965 by Doubleday.

Hill, John. "From *Five Women* to *Leeds United!*: Roy Battersby and the Politics of 'Radical' Television Drama." *Journal of British Cinema and Television* 10, no.1 (2013): 130-50.

Hinckle, Warren. "The Social History of the Hippies, *Ramparts* 5, no.7 (March 1967): 5-26.

Hoffman, Abbie. *Revolution for the Hell of it*. New York: The Dial Press, 1968.

Höhn, Maria and Martin Klimke, *A Breath of Freedom: The Civil Rights Struggle, African-American GIs, and Germany*. London: Palgrave Macmillan, 2010.

Holmes, Richard. "Just How Serious are You?" *The Times*, March 28, 1970.

Horowitz, David. *Radical Son: A Generational Odyssey*. Simon and Schuster, 1998.

Howarth-Williams, Martin. *R.D. Laing: His Work and its Relevance for Sociology*. London: Routledge and Kegan Paul, 1977.

Howe, Stephen. *Afrocentrism: Mythical Pasts and Imaged Homes*. London: Verso, 1998.

[Isaaman, Gerald], "Heathman's Diary," *The Hampstead and Highgate Express*, August 4, 1967.

Jackson, Kevin. *The Verbals: Kevin Jackson in Conversation with Iain Sinclair*. Tonbridge: Worple Press, 2003.

Jakobsen, Jakob. The Antihistory Project, 2014 -. https://antihistory.org/

Jakobsen, Jakob, ed. *Antiuniversity of London Tabloid, 2012*. https://monoskop.org/File:Antiuniversity_of_London_Antihistory_Tabloid_2012.pdf

Jakobsen, Jakob, ed. *New Experimental College Tabloid, 2014*. http://files.antihistory.org/NEC_Tabloid.2014.pdf

James, C.L.R. "Black Power." *Marxists Internet Archive*. https://www.marxists.org/archive/james-clr/works/1967/black-power.htm

James, Louis. "The Caribbean Artists Movement." In *West Indian Intellectuals in Britain*. Edited by Bill Schwarz, 209-27. Manchester University Press, 2003.

Jenner, Peter. "The London Free School." *Resurgence* 1, no.2 (July-August 1966).

Jervis, Giovanni. "Il congresso di Londra: 'Dialettiche della Liberaziona,'" *Quaderni Piacentini* 32 (October 1967): 405-20.

Jessel, Stephen. "Black Power Prophet," *The Times*, July 19, 1967.

Jones, Mervyn. "A Real Saving Thing," *New Statesman*, February 16, 1968.

Joyce, Frank. "Frank Joyce. October 17th 2016." Detroit: Detroit Historical Society, 2017. Interview with William Winkel. https://detroit1967.detroithistorical.org/items/show/497

Kasrills, Ronnie. "How Danny became the Postperson from Pluto," *ColdType*, No.96 (April 2015). https://projects.kora.matrix.msu.edu/files/210-808-4099/DanTribute48pagenewopt.pdf

Kellner, Douglas. "Radical Politics, Marcuse, and the New Left." In *Collected Papers of Herbert Marcuse*, Vol.3, The New Left and the 1960s. Edited by Douglas Kellner. London: Routledge, 2005.

Kermode, Frank. "Antiuniversity," *The Listener*, February 29, 1968.

Khan, Naseem. "Digging for Victory," *The Guardian*, April 29, 1968.

Kopecký, Petr. "Czeching the Beat, beating the Czech: Ginsberg and Ferlinghetti in Czechia." *The Sixties: A Journal of History, Politics and Culture*, no.1 (June 2010): 97-103.

Kramer, Jane. *Allen Ginsberg in America*. New York: Vintage Books, 1970.

Krebs, Allen. *The University*. Boston: New England Free Press, 1968. First published Summer 1967 in *Treason!*.

Kustow, Michael. *In Search of Jerusalem*. London: Oberon Books, 2009.

---. *Peter Brook: A Biography*. London: Bloomsbury, 2005.

Laing, Adrian. *R.D. Laing: A Life*. Stroud: Sutton Publishing, 2006.

Laing, R.D. "Appearances and Disappearances." *Fire* 1 (1967): 17-19.

---. *The Divided Self*. Harmondsworth: Penguin Books, 1965. First published 1960 by Tavistock Publications.

---. "The Invention of Madness," *New Statesman,* June 16, 1967.

---. "Massacre of the Innocents," *Peace News*, January 22, 1965.

---. "One Dimensional Man." *New Left Review,* 1, no.26 (July-August 1964).

---. *The Politics of Experience and The Bird of Paradise*. Harmondsworth: Penguin Books, 1967.

—, *Self and Others*. Harmondsworth: Penguin Books. First published 1961 by Tavistock Publications.

—, "Series and Nexus in the Family." *New Left Review*, 1, no.15 (May-June 1962).

Laing, R.D. and D.G. Cooper. *Reason and Violence: A Decade of Sartre's Philosophy 1950-1960*. London: Tavistock Publications, 1964.

Laing, R.D. and A. Esterson. *Sanity, Madness and the Family: Families of Schizophrenics*. London: Tavistock Publications, 1964.

Levy, Martin. "Free and Easy?" *Times Higher Education*, November 12-18, 2015.

---. "From 'Philadelphia-Sigma Subversion and Insurrection Center' to Kingsley Hall: Exploring the Laing-Trocchi-Berke Connection." *Beatdom*, March 21, 2020. https://www.beatdom.com/philadelphia-sigma-subversion/

---. "Mary Poppins and the Anti-University." WONKHE, February 15, 2019. https://wonkhe.com/blogs/mary-poppins-and-the-anti-versity/

---. "Wooden Huts Anyone? Paul Goodman's *The Community of Scholars* after (more than) Fifty Years." Self and Society 44, no.4 (December 2016): 339-45.

Levy, Martin and Joe Berke. "Martin Levy Interview with Joe Berke." *Self & Society* 45, nos.3-4 (October-December 2017): 298-320. This is an edited-for-publication version of my interviews with Joe Berke.

Lucie-Smith, Edward. "The Image of Violence," *The Times*, February 25, 1964.

Macintyre, Alasdair. "Fallen among Fantasies." *New Society*, December 12, 1968.

Malchow, H.L. *Special Relations: The Americanization of Britain?* Stanford: Stanford University Press, 2011.

Marcuse, Herbert. "Some General Comments on Lucien Goldmann." In *Cultural Creation in Modern Society*. By Lucien Goldmann, 126-28. Translated by Bart Grahl. Oxford: Basil Blackwell, 1977.

---. "Repressive Tolerance." In *A Critique of Pure Tolerance*. By Robert Paul Wolff, Barrington Moore Jr. and Herbert Marcuse. Boston: Beacon Press, 1969. The book first published in 1965.

"Marx as a Brilliant Guy," *The Times*, January 5, 1968.

Marwick, Arthur. *The Sixties: Cultural Revolution in Britain, France, Italy and the United States, c.1958-c.1974*. Oxford University Press, 1998.

McKie, David. "Teachings of Black Power Apostle," *The Guardian*, July 19, 1967.

McGlashan, Colin. "Black Power Leader Leaves Mark on Britain," *The Observer*, August 6, 1967.

McGlashan, Colin. "Mainspring of Black Power: Colin McGlashan talks to Stokely Carmichael," *The Observer*, July 23, 1967.

McGlashan, Colin. "Michael X: New Leader may Take Over," *The Observer*, August 13, 1967.

McLachlan, Donald. "Cautious on Colour," *The Spectator*, August 4, 1967.

Mezan, Peter. "After Freud and Jung, now comes R.D. Laing." *Esquire*, January 1, 1972. https://classic.esquire.com/article/1972/1/1/after-freud-and-jung-now-comes-rd-laing

"Michael X Appeal Dismissed," *Reading Evening Post*, December 21, 1967.

"Michael X: 'We can deal with Whitey if necessary,'" *Reading Evening Post*, July 25, 1967.

Miles, Barry. *Ginsberg: A Biography*. New York: HarperCollins, 1990.

Miles, Barry. "Miles." *International Times*, no.18, August 31-September 13, 1967.

Miller, Gavin. "Psychiatric Penguins: Writing on Psychiatry for Penguin Books, c.1950-1980." *History of the Human Sciences* 28, no.4 (2015): 76-101.

Mitchell, Juliet. "Looking Back at Women's Estate." Verso Blog, February 3, 2015. https://www.versobooks.com/en-gb/blogs/news/1836-juliet-mitchell-looking-back-at-woman-s-estate

Mitchell, Juliet. *Women's Estate*. Harmondsworth: Penguin Books, 1971.

Mossman, James. "Love, Love, Love," *The Listener*, August 3, 1967.

Moyse, Arthur. "The Price of Indecency," *Freedom*, July 29, 1967.

Moyse, Arthur. "Round the Galleries," *Freedom*, February 25, 1967.

Mullan, Bob. *Mad to be Normal: Conversations with R.D. Laing*. London: Free Association Books, 1995.

Mullan, Bob, ed. *R.D. Laing: Creative Destroyer*. London: Casell, 1997.

Nhat Hanh, Thich. *Vietnam: The Lotus in the Sea of Fire*. London: SCM Press, 1967.

Norse, Harold. *Memoirs of a Bastard Angel*. London: Bloomsbury, 1990.

Norse, Harold, Alexander Trocchi and Robert Tasher. "Three Views on the Anti-University," *International Times*, February 16-29, 1968.

Nuttall, Jeff. *Bomb Culture*. London: Paladin, 1970. First published 1968 by MacGibbon & Kee.

Oakley, Chris. "Dangerous Liaisons: The Rivalrous Resemblance of David Cooper and R.D. Laing." *Free Associations* 4, part 2 (1993): 277-93.

Oren, Michel and Calvin Hernton. "The Enigmatic Career of Hernton's 'Scarecrow'." *Callaloo* 29, no.2 (Spring 2006): 608-18.

Overy, Bob. "Black Power in Britain," *Peace News*, September 15, 1967.

P.H.S. "The Light of the Obscure," *The Times*, August 8, 1967.

Peck, Sabina. "'The Only Position for Women in SNCC is Prone': Stokely Carmichael and the Perceived Patriarchy of Civil Rights Organizations in America." *History in the Making* 1, no.1 (Summer/Autumn 2012): 29-35.

The People's Minister of Information JR. "Looking at the life of Freedom Fighter Obi Egbuna Sr." *San Francisco Bay View* (March 10, 2014). https://sfbayview.com/2014/03/looking-at-the-life-of-freedom-fighter-obi-egbuna-sr/

Petrović, Gajo. "The Dialectics of Liberation." *Praxis: Revue Philosophique Edition Internationale* 3, no.4 (1967): 606-13.

Phillips, Mike and Trevor Phillips. *Windrush: The Irresistible Rise of Multi-Racial Britain*. London: HarperCollins, 1998.

Pickering, Andrew. *The Cybernetic Brain: Sketches of another Future*. Chicago: The University of Chicago Press, 2011.

Porat, Dan. *Bitter Reckoning: Israel tries Holocaust Survivors as Nazi Collaborators*. Massachusetts: Harvard University Press.

Prince, Simon. "'Do what the Afro-Americans are Doing': Black Power and the Start of the Northern Ireland Troubles." *Journal of Contemporary History* 50, no.3 (2015): 516-35.

R. "Angry Arts," *Freedom*, July 8, 1967.

Reynolds, Stanley. "Television," *The Guardian*, July 18, 1967.

Rigby, Andrew. "Living New Life-Styles," *Peace News*, May 1, 1970.

Robinson, Lucy. *Gay Men and the Left in Post-War Britain*. Manchester University Press, 2008.

Robinson, Lucy. "Three Revolutionary Years: The Impact of the Counter Culture on the Development of the Gay Liberation Movement in Britain." *Cultural and Social History* 3 (2006): 445-71.

Rossabi, Andrew. "'Anti-Psychiatry': An Interview with Dr Joseph Berke." In *Laing and Anti-Psychiatry*. Edited by Robert Boyers, 273-86. New York: Harper and Row Publishers, 1971.

Roszak, Theodore. *The Making of a Counter Culture: Reflections on the Technocratic Society and its Youthful Opposition*. London: Faber and Faber, 1970.

Rowbotham, Sheila. *A Century of Women: The History of Women in Britain and the United States*. New York: Viking, 1997.

---. *Promise of a Dream: Remembering the Sixties*. London: Allen Lane, 2000.

---. *Threads through Time: Writings on History and Autobiography*. London: Penguin Books, 1999.

Sale, Kirkpatrick. *SDS*. New York: Random House, 1973.

Sayre, Nora. "Free University," *New Statesman*, April 1, 1966.

Schatzman, Morton. "Madness and Morals." in Berke, *Counter Culture*, 288-313.

Schatzman, Morton. "Trust me, I'm an Anti-Doctor," *The Observer*, July 7, 1996.

Schneemann, Carolee. *More than Meat Joy: Performance Works and Selected Writings*. Edited by Bruce R. McPherson. New York, McPherson and Company, 1998.

Seidl, Jan. "Decriminalization of Homosexual Acts in Czechoslovakia in 1961." In *Queer Stories of Europe*. Edited by Kārlis Vērdiņš and Jānis Ozoliņš, 174-194. Cambridge: Cambridge Scholars, 2016.

Sherman, Susan. *America's Child: A Woman's Journey through the Radical Sixties*. Evanston: Northwestern University Press, 2007.

Sherman, Susan. "Dialectics of Liberation. A Conference." *Ikon* 1, no.4 (1967): 4-7.

Sigal, Clancy. "Home Front: Anyone for a Game of Psycho-Cowboys?" *The Guardian: Weekend*, January 28, 1995.

Sigal, Clancy, *Zone of the Interior*. Hebden Bridge: Pomona, 2005. First published 1976 by Crowell.

Sinclair, Iain. *The Kodak Mantra Diaries October 1966 to June 1971*. London: Albion Village Press, 1971.

Sinclair, Iain and Robert Klinkert (dir) *Ah! Sunflower*. London: The Picture Press, 2007.

S[mall], M[artin]. "Paul Goodman at the Roundhouse," *Freedom*, August 26, 1967.

Smith, J. and André Moncourt. *Red Army Faction: A Documentary History – Volume I: Projectiles for the People*. Oakland: PM Press, 2009.

Snelson, Tim. "From *In Two Minds* to MIND: The Circulation of 'Anti-Psychiatry' in British Film and Television during the long 1960s," *History of the Human Sciences* 34, no.5, 53-81.

Sontag, Susan. "On Paul Goodman." In *Growing Up Absurd*. By Paul Goodman. Forward by Cary Nelson Blake, 273-279. New York: New York Review Books, 2012. Sontag's essay first published 1972 in *New York Review of Books*.

Span. Paula. "The Undying Revolutionary: As Stokely Carmichael, he Fought for Black Power. Now Kwame Ture's Fighting for his Life," *The Washington Post*, April 8, 1998. https://www.washingtonpost.com/archive/lifestyle/1998/04/08/the-undying-revolutionary-as-stokely-carmichael-he-fought-for-black-power-now-kwame-tures-fighting-for-his-life/4adb14ec-0db8-4668-8af6-84f877b3c61a/

Spencer, Catherine. *Beyond the Happening: Performance Art and the Politics of Communication*. Manchester: Manchester University Press, 2020.

Springer, W. Bruce. "A Black Carnival in the Park: Hippies, Housewives, Husbands join in an Ungainly Alliance," *The Crimson*, April 20, 1967.

Staub, Michael E. *Madness is Civilization: When the Diagnosis was Social, 1948-1980*. Chicago: The University of Chicago Press, 2011.

Steiner, George. "On Paul Goodman," *Commentary*, January 8, 1963.

Stiles, Kristine, ed. *Correspondence Course: An Epistolary History of Carolee Schneemann and her Circle*. Durham: North Carolina, 2010.

Stockley, Nancy. "LSE: Free School in Summer?" *Peace News*, June 9, 1967.

"Stokely is a Guerrilla Fighter — Black Muslim Michael X," *Reading Evening Post*, July 24, 1967.

"Successful Failure," *The Observer: Review*, September 29, 1968.

Sweetman, Rosita. "Rosita Sweetman: As a Wife and Mother I Learned Feminism all over," *The Irish Times*, August 26, 2020. https://www.irishtimes.com/culture/books/rosita-sweetman-as-a-wife-and-mother-i-learned-feminism-all-over-1.4338608

Thomas, Nick. *Protest Movements in 1960s West Germany: A Social History of Dissent and Democracy*. Oxford: Berg, 2003.

Tomlinson, B.R. "What was the Third World?" *Journal of Contemporary History* 38, no.2 (2003): 307-21.

Tytell, John. *The Living Theatre: Art, Exile and Outrage*. New York: Grove Press, 1995.

"University of North Ken," *New Society*, March 17, 1966.

Vinkenoog, Simon. "Thoughts on Liberation," *Freedom*, August 26, 1967.

Vries, Bernhard de. "The Amsterdam Provos." *Resurgence*, 1, no.2 (July-August 1966): 14-15.

Wall, Oisin. "Basaglia and the British Anti-Psychiatrists, 1960-1970." In *Basaglia's International Legacy: From Asylum to Community*. Edited by Tom Burns and John Foot, 23-42. Oxford University Press, 2020.

Wall, Oisin. *The British Anti-Psychiatrists: From Institutional Psychiatry to the Counter-Culture, 1960-1971*. New York: Routledge, 2017.

Wallerstein, Immanuel. "Reading Fanon in the 21st Century." *New Left Review* 57 (May-June 2009): 117-25.

Walzer, Michael. *The Company of Critics: Social Criticism and Political Commitment in the Twentieth Century*. New York: Basic Books, 1988.

Ward, Colin. "Remembering Paul Goodman," *Freedom*, September 16, 1972.

Waters, Rob. "Black Power on the Telly: America, Television, and Race in 1960s and 1970s Britain." Journal of British Studies 54, no.4 (October 2015): 947-70.

---. "Integration or Black Power!" *The Political Quarterly* 89, no.3 (July-September 2018): 409-15.

---. *Thinking Black: Britain, 1964-1985*. Oakland: University of California Press, 2019.

Weequahic High School. *The Legend: January 1957*, Newark: Weequahic High School, 1957.

Weindling, Paul J. *John W. Thompson: Psychiatrist in the Shadow of the Holocaust*. Rochester: University of Rochester Press, 2010.

Wells, John. "A Divine Joke," *Spectator*, January 13, 1967.

"What Next?" *New Society*, July 27, 1967.

Whitehead, Peter (dir) *Wholly Communion*, 1965. YouTube video. https://www.youtube.com/watch?v=QIRWSlDR9KI&t=587s

Whittuck, Andrew. *Interview by Journalist John May*. Star Brewery Gallery Lewes. https://www.starbrewerygallery.com/andrew-whittuck

Widgery, David. "Goodbye Comrade M." *Marxists Internet Archive*. https://www.marxists.org/archive/widgery/1979/09/marcuse.htm. Widgery's article, an obituary of Marcuse, first published in September 1979.

Widgery, David. *Preserving Disorder: Selected Essays 1968-88*. London: Pluto Press, 1989. Widgery's "The Dialectics of Liberation" essay in this collection first published 1987 by *New Society*.

Wilcox, David. "Stokely is a Guerrilla Fighter: Black Muslim Michael X," *Reading Evening Post*, July 24, 1967.

Wild, Rosalind Eleanor. "Black was the Colour of our Fight: Black Power in Britain, 1955-1976." PhD. thesis, University of Sheffield, 2008. https://ethos.bl.uk/OrderDetails.do?did=2&uin=uk.bl.ethos.489059

W[illis], P[eter]. "International Congress Dialectics of Liberation," *Peace News*, June 16, 1967.

Wyver, John. "Earl Cameron and a Lost Play." (July 6, 2020) *Illuminations*. https://www.illuminationsmedia.co.uk/earl-cameron-and-a-lost-play/

Zeal, Paul. *Paul's Journals*. Taunton: Paul Zeal, 2006.

Index

Abel, Ruth 56-57
Abernathy, Ralph 107
Abrams, Steve 13-14, 88, 281
Addonizio, Hugh J. 115
Albert Einstein College of Medicine 20-24, 27, 30, 68, 263, 266
Ali, Muhammad 187
Ali, Tariq 116, 155, 178, 183, 199
Althusser, Louis 224
Amis, Kingsley 196
Annesley, David 56
Anti-psychiatry 10, 11, 17, 33, 60, 64, 72, 73, 81, 174, 199-200, 207, 249, 290, 294-295
Antiuniversity 13, 252, 253, 255-262, 267-268
Arnold, M.H. 71
Arrhenius, Svante 97
Artaud, Antonin 36, 73, 205, 206, 247
Awdykowicz, Stepha 131-132
Baez, Joan 67-68
Baldwin, James 107, 283
Bamford, Chris 91
Bamford, Geoffrey 91, 165
Baran, Paul 151
Barchilon, Jose 22
Barker, Paul 75
Barlow, Nora 131
Barnard, Roger 71, 87-88, 125, 207, 213, 241, 243-244
Barnes, Mary 28-29, 31, 46, 49-50, 51, 55-57, 207, 265-266
Barnes, Mary and Berke, Joe
  *Mary Barnes
    Two Accounts of a Journey
    Through Madness* 265-266
Basaglia, Franco 205
Bateson, Gregory 12, 26, 27, 74, 80, 85, 90-100, 125, 126, 127, 128-130, 131, 132, 200, 201, 205, 228, 254, 271-272, 282
Bateson, John 80, 130-131, 228, 285
Bateson, Lois 80
Battersby, Roy 13, 69, 75, 127-128, 145-146, 150, 154, 256, 261
Beatles 199, 248
Beavoir, Simone de 247
Beck, Julian 14, 23, 60, 61, 155, 156, 158-160, 262, 271-272
Beneš, Jan 228
Ben-Gurion, David 125
Benjamin, Walter 65, 223
Berg, Alban 132
Berglund, Gregory 116-7, 120, 285
Berio, Luciano 229
Berke, Joe 7, 10, 13-14, 15, 17-41, 43-53, 55-71, 75, 77-78, 88, 90, 91, 117, 120, 122, 146, 151, 155, 157, 160, 165, 183, 199, 200, 206-207, 215, 216, 218, 219-222, 229, 233, 240, 253-266, 272, 275, 276, 277, 278, 279, 285, 290, 294- 295
Berke, Joe (ed)
  Counter Culture 261-264, 265, 290
Berke, Joseph 18
Berke, Roberta, *see under* Elzey, Roberta
Berke, Rose 17-18, 20, 56, 263
Bertrand Russell Peace Foundation 13, 143, 255, 256, 261
Bhagavad Gita 86, 174
Black Mountain College 10, 34, 36
Black Power 12, 13, 107, 109-112, 147, 162, 168, 177, 181-

195, 201, 211, 222, 229, 245, 251, 262, 268
Blackburn, Robin 67, 155, 291
Blackett, P.M.S. 271, 280
Blake, William 92
Bloch, Ernest 60, 271
Boas, Franz 121
Boggs, Grace Lee 229
Boston, Richard 61, 75, 259
Boyd, Joe 13
Bragaw Avenue School 18
Braithwaite, Edward 166, 180, 229
Braithwaite, Rudy 180
Braun, Eva 231
Brecht, Bertolt 65, 168-169, 288
Breton, André 206
Briskin, Sid 26, 28, 37, 45, 199, 206
Brixton Town Hall 149, 287
Brook, Peter 60, 196, 199, 271
Brownlow, Kevin 177
Buber, Martin 143, 208
Burroughs, William S. 30, 33, 35, 71, 165, 167, 176, 231, 277, 282
Cadogan, Peter 68, 119, 156, 207, 219
Cage, John 229
Campbell, Joseph 271
Camus, Albert 48
Canetti, Elias 233, 271, 293
Cannabis, *see under* Marijuana
Cardew, Cornelius 13
Caribbean Artists Movement (CAM) 229
Carmichael, Stokely 7, 12, 68-69, 74, 78-79, 81, 88-90, 103-105, 107-119, 121, 124-126, 130, 138, 148-149, 162, 165-169, 171-191, 193- 199, 201, 205, 206, 208, 209-210, 211, 213, 220, 221, 224, 228, 229, 235, 237, 238, 242, 249, 251, 253, 254, 262, 267, 272, 279-280, 283-284, 286, 287, 288, 289, 292
Carson, Rachel 91, 129
Cassady, Neil 30, 162
Castoriadis, Cornelius 229
Castro, Fidel 132-133, 148
Chamberlain, Thomas 97
Chelsea School of Art 63
China 84, 102, 104, 109, 113, 148, 149, 154, 194, 208-209, 228, 291
Chtcheglo, Ivan 33
Churchill, Ben 69-70, 127
Clifton, Richard 72
Climate change 97-98, 127, 231, 282
Cobb, Noel 56, 63, 279
Cobbing, Bob 260
Cockburn, Alexander 69
Coleman, Terry 264
Coleridge, Samuel Taylor 130
Coltrane, John 117
Columbus, Christopher 109
Committee of 100 68
Commoner, Barry 97, 129
Coon, Caroline 89, 114
Cooper, David 13, 14, 17, 26, 37, 41, 47, 52-53, 58-60, 63, 65-68, 70, 72-74, 80-81, 82, 87, 90, 117, 118, 147, 165, 166, 167, 174-175, 180, 183, 190, 199, 200, 201, 203-205, 206, 224, 226, 229, 232, 235, 242-244, 245, 252, 253, 255, 258, 259, 260, 261, 266, 271- 272, 278, 280, 290, 293, 294
  Psychiatry and Anti-Psychiatry 72, 73, 289
Cooper, David (ed)
  The Dialectics of Liberation 14, 69, 200, 252, 262, 285
Cooper, Simone 203
Corso, Gregory 30, 169, 288
Crossman, Richard 103

Cuba 12, 38-39, 69, 84, 124, 132-133, 137, 138, 141, 145, 148, 154, 191, 193, 197, 209, 210, 212, 229, 268, 292
Cunnold, Joan 26, 46
Davis, Angela 112-113, 116, 166, 167
Davis, Peter 70, 154-155, 162-163, 166, 248
Davy, Antonia 62
Day, Robin 103
Debord, Guy 33
Deming, Quentin 68
Desnoes, Edmundo 183, 191
Destruction in Art Symposium (DIAS) 57, 58, 245
Detroit, MI 119
Deutscher, Isaac 60, 271
Dhondy, Farrukh 166
Diggers 165, 171, 181, 219, 237, 259
Dingleton Hospital 24, 50, 56
Diop, Cheikh Anta 110
Dixon, Brian 108
Driberg, Tom 196
Du Bois, W.E.B. 117
Dwoskin, Steven 142
Dye, Diane 62
Dylan, Bob 24
Eastern Pennsylvnia Psychiatric Research Institute (EPPI) 200
Eaton, Arthur 41
Egbuna, Obi 13, 88, 166, 181, 183, 184-186, 191, 251, 256
Eichmann, Adolf 145
Eisenhower, Dwight D. 125
Eliade, Mircea 65, 271272
Elliott, Philip 72
Elzey, Roberta 48-49, 50-51, 63, 261, 262-263
Emerson College 30
Eng, Erling 98-100, 126, 128, 206
Ennslin, Gudrin 183, 292
Epstein, Philip 183, 191

Esterson, Aaron 25, 26, 27, 28, 47, 51, 55-56, 199, 293
Esterson, Julian 28
Esterson, Naomi 28
Exploding Galaxy commune 245
Fainlight, Harry 48, 233
Fainlight, Ruth 46
Faisal II, King 144
Faludy, Georgy 37
Fancher, Edwin 165
Fanon, Frantz 79, 108, 109, 117, 187, 205, 206
Farren, Mick 242
Fearon, Anne Marie 88, 90, 207, 250-251
Felix, Julie 67-68
Fisk University 104
Flanagan, Barry 13, 258
Flower Power 89, 114, 170, 171, 201, 232
Ford, Peter 207
Foucault, Michel 73, 202, 206, 271
  Madness and Civilization 73
Fourier, Charles 238
Free Speech Movement 215
Free University of New York (FUNY) 11, 38-40, 47, 49, 65, 87, 146, 216, 217, 218, 257, 262-263
Free University of West Berlin 193, 217, 219
Freud, Sigmund 22, 30
Friedland, Robert 17-18
Friedland, Susan 17-18
Fromm, Erich 205
Froshaug, Judy 75
Fuentes, Carlos 60, 271
Fugs 32, 242
Fuller, Buckminster 233
Gabel, Joseph 206, 271
Galbraith, J.K. 155
Gandhi, Mahatma 44, 148, 208

Garvey, Marcus 117, 148
Garvey, Mary 46, 47
Geesin, Ron 142
Gerassi, Fernando 65, 131, 132
Gerassi, John 65-66, 75, 103-104, 107, 113, 115, 117-118, 119, 124, 131-141, 142, 151, 154, 170, 182, 201, 208, 210, 211, 223, 224, 229, 237, 271-272
Gervasi, Sean 141, 151-152, 155, 156, 157, 158
Ghose, Ajoy Shankar 172, 175, 181, 193, 251, 289
Ginsberg, Allen 12, 14, 20, 23, 30, 33, 35, 36, 43, 60, 77, 81, 88-89, 91, 98, 103-105, 107, 114, 128, 130, 131, 157, 158, 161-163, 165, 166, 167, 168, 171-177, 178, 180, 183, 187, 197, 207, 219, 226-227, 228, 229, 231-232, 233, 249, 252, 253, 271-272, 278, 282, 292-93
  Howl 23, 33, 35, 48
Girodias, Maurice 48
Global warming *see under* Climate change
Goffman, Erving 60, 65, 70, 74, 98, 157, 200, 206, 223, 271-272
Goldberg, Lesley 91
Goldberg, Richard 91
Goldmann, Lucien 60, 65, 75, 222-224, 271-272
Goodman, Paul 9-12, 24, 30-31, 36, 38, 59, 60, 65, 71, 75, 79, 91, 98-100, 103-105, 119, 122, 126, 128, 130-131, 133, 138-141, 151, 207-216, 217, 220, 224, 227, 228, 232, 235, 238, 252, 254, 266, 267-269, 271-272, 281, 285, 291
  The Community of Scholars 9-10, 30-31, 38, 122, 212, 268
Grady, Panna 63, 75, 161, 165-166, 167, 196, 197, 207

Grass, Gunter 271
Greene, James 207
Greenhouse effect *see under* Climate change
Greer, Maretta 161, 162
Gregory, Dick 68
Grene, Marjorie 60, 271
Gritten, John 108
Grogan, Emmett 165-166, 167, 168, 169, 171- 173, 180, 242, 245, 272, 293, 295
Gruenwald, Malkiel 145- 146
Guerrilla warfare 81, 83, 86, 104, 139, 268
Guevara, Che 110, 137, 138, 139, 143, 232, 284, 286
Hahnemann Medical College 201
Hajek, Igor 223, 226-228, 262, 272
Hamilton, Vickie 207
Havens, Joseph 207, 283, 290
Haynes, Jane 62
Haynes, Jim 13, 257
Haynes, John 62, 253
Hegel, Georg Wilhelm Friedrich 170
Heidegger, Martin 60, 131
Heisenberg, Werner 271, 280
Henderson Hospital 24
Henry, Jules 13, 31, 48, 65, 74, 121-126, 131, 140, 149, 170, 201, 205, 208, 220, 254, 266, 271-272, 285
  Culture against Man 31, 122
Hernton, Calvin 43, 48, 57, 66-67, 71, 256, 272, 295
Hesse, Herman 10, 23, 31, 36
Hillel, Rabbi 197
Hippies 114, 137, 162, 165, 167, 171, 173, 189, 201, 202, 211, 221, 222, 227, 237, 250
Hiro, Dilip 166
Hiroshima 186

Hitler, Adolf 82, 231, 245
Ho Chi Minh 154
Hodges, Mike 75
Hogg, Quentin 198
Holder, Ram John 192
Hollingshead, Michael 14, 35, 40-41
Holmes, Jeremy 90, 206
Holmes, Richard 263
Homosexuality 12, 30, 105, 131, 172, 227, 228, 252, 267, 292
Hopkins, John 199, 276
Horne, Frances 63
Horowitz, David 142-147, 280, 286
Horowitz, Irving 136-137, 142
Howard University 184
Howe, Darcus 112, 166
Hughes, Ted 27-28
Huncke, Herbert 30
Huntley, Jessica 112, 166
Hussein, King 144, 145
Husserl, Edmund 131
Huxley, Aldous 92, 239
Huxley, Francis 13, 67, 98-100, 126, 128, 130, 157, 199, 256
Inman, Will 32
Institute for the Study of Non-Violence 68
Institute of Phenomenological Studies (IPS) 58-62, 66-67, 68, 70, 74-75, 78, 80, 81, 87, 89, 100, 165, 174, 175, 181, 200, 206, 218, 220, 238, 240, 244, 245-246, 250, 255, 256, 271-272, 278
Institutionalised racism 108-109, 119, 189, 251, 269, 283-284
Internationalists 219
Jackson, Don 26
Jacobi Hospital 21
Jagger, Mick 253
James, C.L.R. 112, 117, 139, 142, 147-149, 150, 151, 158, 182, 229, 256
Jeanson, Francis 271
Jenkins, Roy 198
Jervis, Giovanni 205-206, 238, 290
Jessel, Stephen 108, 121
Joans, Ted 229, 292
Johnson, Lyndon B. 95, 139, 167
Johnson, Nicholas 72
Johnson, Paul 71
Jones, Evan 229
Jones, LeRoi 162
Jones, Mark 196-197
Jones, Maxwell 24, 56
Joyce, Frank 119, 154, 291
Kastner, Rudolf 145-146
Keen, Graham 49
Kennedy, John F. 29
Kennedy, Robert 132
Kerouac, Jack 30
Kerr, Clark 215
Kesey, Ken 162-163
Keys, John 32, 43, 48, 256
Khalifa, Stefan 166, 180
King, Martin Luther 101, 107, 113, 193
Kingsley Hall 7, 11, 28, 37, 38, 41, 43-52, 55-57, 62-65, 66, 71, 74, 76, 143, 162, 207, 221, 245, 248, 253, 255, 262, 264- 265, 277, 278, 285
Kipling, Rudyard 109, 284
Klinkert, Robert 70, 77, 91
Koch, Johannes 183
Kolderup, Dag 162- 163
Kommune I 245, 262-263
Korčula Summer School 253
Korngold, Murray 205
Krebs, Allen 38-39, 146, 218, 255-258
Krebs, Sharon 38
Kuby, Gabriele 219

Kunzelmann, Dieter 183, 262, 291
Kupferberg, Tuli 36
Kustow, Michael 142, 158, 159, 196, 257
Ky, Nguyen Cao 102
La Rose, John 166, 183, 191, 229
Lacan, Jacques 206, 207, 294
Laing, Adrian 28, 73, 74
Laing, Anne 28, 46
Laing, Fiona 28
Laing, Jutta *see under* Werner, Jutta
Laing, Karen 28
Laing, Paul 28
Laing, R.D. 10-11, 13, 14, 17, 20, 21, 22, 23, 24-29, 30, 31-32, 33, 35-41, 43, 45-53, 55-58, 60-68, 70, 72-76, 78, 79, 80, 81, 82-87, 90-91, 92, 93, 98, 100, 102, 103, 108, 121, 122, 125, 126, 128, 130, 131, 140, 142, 143, 147, 149, 150, 158, 165-171, 173-174, 182, 199, 200-201, 202, 203, 205, 206, 213, 214, 218, 220, 244, 245, 253, 255, 256, 259, 264, 265, 266, 271-272, 274, 277, 280, 290, 293, 295
  Self and Others 25, 288
  The Divided Self 20, 22, 25, 31, 56, 62, 151
  The Politics of Experience and The Bird of Paradise 11, 35, 72
Laing, R.D. and Cooper, D.G. *Reason and Violence* 52, 65
Laing, Susan 28
Lamarck, Jean-Baptiste 92
Lamm, Stefan 154
Langham Clinic 49
Langhans, Rainer 263
Late Night Line-Up 257
Latham, Barbara 142
Latham, John 142, 258, 293

Latin America 60, 65, 81, 115, 116, 132, 133-137, 139-141, 147, 148, 152-153, 182, 189, 209
Lavrin, Beba 33
Layard, John 46, 47, 277
Leary, Timothy 24, 33, 35, 40-41, 43
Legalise Pot Rally 88-89, 199
Lenin, Vladimir 144, 148
Lester, Muriel 74
Levi-Strauss, Claude 271
Levy, Bill 13, 287
Levy, Howard 66-67
Lewis, B.L. 71
Lind, Jacov 60, 271
Liss, Jerome 24
Litzky, Hannah 20
Living Theatre 61, 155, 159-160
London School of Economics (LSE) 73, 78, 132
Long Island College Hospital 31
Long, Worth 31, 112
Luxemburg, Rosa 144
Lysergic Acid Diethalamide (LSD) 28, 32, 35, 40-41, 43, 47, 55, 66, 91, 96, 131, 140, 163, 171, 174, 201, 204, 212, 228, 232
Mackay, John 207
Mai, Nhat Chi 101
Malcolm X 66, 107, 113, 116, 117, 183, 184, 187, 209
Malik, Michael Abdul 75, 88, 91, 112, 113, 117, 166, 167, 180-181, 182-184, 185, 189, 191, 198, 199, 251, 288
Malina, Judith 23
Mandel, Ernest 60, 65, 75, 271-272
Mannoni, Maud 206, 294
Mao Tse-tung 113, 148, 154, 155, 167, 175, 194, 222, 227

Maoism 154-155, 208, 216, 228
Marcuse, Herbert 12, 64-65, 75, 91, 112, 132, 150, 151, 212, 217, 222, 223, 235-242, 243, 248, 249, 250, 267, 271-272, 293
  Eros and Civilization 65, 222, 236, 239
  One-Dimensional Man 65, 150, 236
Marcuse, Inge 235
Marijuana 14, 32, 56, 57, 89, 131, 172, 198
Marx, Karl 11, 23, 96, 111, 112, 143, 170, 206, 215, 218, 225, 238, 292
Maschler, Tom 75
Mason, Bill 261
McCann, Eamonn 183
McCarthy, Joseph 46
McCartney, Paul 89
McClure, Michael 33
McGlashan, Colin 166
McKay, Claude 111
McKie, David 108, 121
McLuhan, Marshall 60, 202, 233
McNamara, Robert 124, 139
Meibach, Doris 256
Mellon, Jim 38
Melly, George 199
Mental Health Act 1959 203
Mercer, David 13, 244, 280
Metzger, Gustav 57, 229-231, 245
Metzner, Ralph 40
Michael X *see under* Malik, Michael Abdul
Michaelson, Jean 248
Milgram, Stanley 85, 299
Mill, John Stuart 111
Miller, Jonathan 199
Mills, C. Wright 125
Minkowski, Eugène 206
Minneapolis, MN 168

Mishra, Rammurti 40
Mitchell, Adrian 48
Mitchell, Juliet 13, 114, 255, 261
Mohammed, Elijah 184
Moliere 224
Mollo, Andrew 177
Montgomery, Stuart 255, 257, 260
Moore, Jack Henry 13
Mossman, James 103- 105
Mullan, Bob 74, 200, 277
Mussolini, Benito 146
Nagasaki 186
National Conference on Black Power 168
Neumeister, Heike 262, 279
New Experimental College 12, 36, 216, 217, 221, 262
Newark, NJ 11, 17-20, 104, 113, 114, 115, 116, 168, 171, 177, 178, 184, 186
Nhat Hanh, Thich 12, 101- 102, 250
Nietzsche, Friedrich 11, 86, 186, 238
Nkrumah, Kwame 148, 185
Non-violence 12, 68, 107, 110, 114, 118, 140, 173, 178, 192, 207
Norse, Harold 257
Nuclear weapons 23-24, 57-58, 68, 93, 97, 102, 114, 117, 119, 120, 141, 194, 202, 208-209, 222
Nuttall, Jeff 9, 40, 46, 49, 257
Nyack, NY 168
Nyerere, Julius 209
Odinga, Jaramogi Oginga 186
Ohnesorg, Benno 219
Ono, Yoko 61
Organisation of Latin American Solidarity (OLAS) 141, 182
Orlovsky, Peter 35
Ové, Horace 166, 180
Overy, Bob 75, 280

Padmore, George 117, 147
Panorama 102-104, 107, 166, 180, 187, 214, 228, 287
Papastavrou, Flora 37, 278
Paris International Conference on Psychoses 253
People against Racism (PAR) 119
Petrović, Gajo 222-223, 224-226, 227-228, 262, 272, 286, 292
Philadelphia Association (PA) 37, 40, 221, 264
Phillipson, Herbert 26
Picasso, Pablo 131
Pilkington, Stephen 62, 278
Pink Floyd 61
Plainfield, NJ 104
Plath, Sylvia 27-28
Polanski, Roman 69
Polo, Marco 109
Praxis school 224-226, 292
Provo 12, 202, 216, 217-218, 237
Pythagoras 110
Quinonis, Joe 31-32, 38
Racial Adjustment Action Society (RAAS) 181, 198, 267
Raleigh, Sir Walter 109
Rawick, George 116, 117, 118, 139
Raymond, Aubrey 255
Redler, Leon 13, 14, 16, 24, 30, 31, 35, 50, 58, 59, 60, 67-69, 74, 88, 176, 181, 183, 200, 206-207, 215, 254, 255, 256, 259, 261, 264, 265, 277, 279, 294
Reich, Wilhelm 206, 247, 290
Repo, Marjaleena 113- 114, 158
Rhodes, Cecil 109, 178-179, 189
Rigby, Andrew 263
Robbe-Grillet, Alain 224
Rolling Stones 196
Roosevelt, Franklin D. 134, 135
Rosendal Neilsen, Aage 36, 88, 216-217, 221
Rosenstein, Joseph 157, 158
Roth, Philip 19
Rothenberg, Jerome 229-230
Rotherfield Hall 62, 66, 74
Rousseau, Jean-Jacques 70, 111
Rowan, John 261
Rowbotham, Sheila 114, 183, 195-196
Rowthorn, Bob 155
Royal Albert Hall 60, 233
Ruitenbeck, Hendrick H. 20
Russell Tribunal on War Crimes in Vietnam 116, 136
Sagay, Sam 166
Salkey, Andrew 166, 229, 287
Saltiel, Adam 120
Sanders, Ed 32, 39
Sandys, Duncan 267
Sargant, William 26
Sartre, Jean-Paul 26, 27, 41, 52-53, 60, 65-66, 82, 132, 187, 206, 224, 271
Sawh, Roy 88, 166, 180, 181, 182, 183, 185, 186, 190, 191-192, 193, 195, 251, 289
Schatzman, Morton 24, 30, 206, 255, 261, 262, 263, 264-266, 276, 281, 295, 297
Schatzman, Vivien 265, 295
Schelsky, Helmut 271
Schneemann, Carolee 11, 14, 45-46, 48, 51, 57, 61, 75, 78-79, 89-90, 141- 142, 174, 213, 229-231, 241, 242, 245-248, 272, 294, 297, 309, 310
Seeger, Pete 24, 71
Sevlon, Samuel 166
Sexual Offences Act 1967 227
Sharff, Adam 271
Sharkey, John 57, 245
Sharpeville massacre 186
Sherman, Susan 12, 229- 230, 292
Showler, Brian 72

Sigal, Clancy 26, 34, 41, 45, 47-48
Sillitoe, Alan 46, 68
Sinclair, Iain 70, 77-78, 91, 161, 165, 169, 231
Singer, Aubrey 128
Singh, Ajit 155
Skolimowski, Jerzy 69, 279
Small, Martin 207
Smith, Adam 215
Smith, Jack 32
Snyder, Gary 63
Social Deviants 11, 75, 242, 248, 272
Soft Machine 61
Soll, Jerome 40
Sommerville, Ian 167
South Africa 57, 104, 111, 175, 178, 186, 189, 229, 267
South America *see under* Latin America
Special Branch 88, 166, 182, 192, 198, 287
Speck, Ross 98, 174, 200-203, 205, 206, 254, 262, 272
Stansill, Peter 262
Stephens, James 95
Sterilisation 188, 189, 194, 197
Stern gang 146
Stetler, Russell 256
Stewart, Kilton 222, 279
Straus, Erwin 98
Student Nonviolent Coordinating Committee (SNCC) 68, 88, 104, 110, 115, 117, 118, 178, 186, 192, 212, 214-215
Summerhill school 28, 62
Supola, Moses 229-230
Sweezy, Paul 71, 74, 133, 138, 140-141, 143, 151-156, 170, 180, 208, 271- 272, 291
Szabo 32
Szasz, Thomas 24, 31, 60, 271

Tavel, Ronnie 32
Thompson, John 22-23, 24, 25, 30, 35-36, 39, 265
Tomorrow's World 127
Tonks, Rosemary 33
Topolski, Feliks 56, 63
Totten, Malcolm 108, 115
Toynbee, Arnold 150
Travers, P.L. 258
Trevor, Harry 63, 257
Trocchi, Alexander 10, 14, 33-35, 38-41, 46, 48, 91, 165, 167, 217, 256, 257
Tshombe, Moïse 190
Tulloch, Courtney 112, 166, 182
Turner, J.M.W. 258
Tynan, Kenneth 199
Tzabar, Shimon 261
Union of Czech Writers 226
Universal Coloured People's Association (UCPA) 181, 190, 198, 251, 267
University of California, Berkeley 30
Vanderbilt University 104, 187
Veblen, Thorstein 11
Verwoerd, Hendrik 178
Vesper, Bernward 183, 262, 292
Vietnam War 12, 39, 57, 58-59, 66, 68, 77, 78, 81, 95, 101-102, 113, 116, 120, 124, 137, 139, 157, 186, 189, 193, 196, 202, 211, 218, 230, 237, 239, 242-243, 248, 249, 250, 267
Villa 21 26, 28, 37, 45, 46, 47, 72, 90, 206, 290
Vincent, Sally 75
Vinkenoog, Simon 14, 229, 231, 233
Wadja, Andrzej 69
Wakoski, Diane 32
Walker, William 134
Walter, Nicolas 207
Ward, Colin 207

Ware, George 88, 167, 181, 183, 187, 191, 192-193, 196-197, 280
Watkins, Jesse 26
Watts, CA 57, 68, 116, 218
Weber, Max 155
Weequahic High School 18-19, 20
Weese, Winston 190-191
Weil, Simone 169
Weiner, Harry 130
Weiner, Norbert 92
Weizsäcker, Carl Friedrich von 271, 280
Wells, John 127
Werner, Jutta 46, 62, 63, 142, 167, 218, 253, 271, 279
Wesker, Arnold 60-61, 240, 250
West Indian Register 182
Wevill, Assia 27-28
White liberals 78, 108, 119, 148, 173, 177, 184, 189, 212, 214-215, 242, 249, 251, 267

Whitehead, Peter 233
Whitmore, Richard 257, 258
Wilson, Colin 33
Winnicott, Donald 84-85
Wittuck, Andrew 180
Wollen, Peter 69
Women's liberation 12, 13, 114, 195-196, 252, 267, 268
Woodcock, George 151
Woods, Allen 75
Wordsworth, William 130
Worsthorne, Peregrine 196
Worthy, William 68
Wylie, Philip 129
Young, Nigel 71
Yugoslav Philosophical Society 224
Zeal, Paul 56, 63, 159, 183, 264, 265, 279, 282
Zeiger, Susan 13
Zionism 144-145

ibidem.eu